D0850110

RESOURCES AND STRATEGY

Resources and Strategy

Ian O. Lesser
Senior Fellow, The Center for Strategic and International Studies, Washington, DC

St. Martin's Press
New York

First published in the United States of America in 1989

Printed in Hong Kong

Library of Congress Cataloging-in-Publication Data

Lesser, Ian O., 1957–
Resources and strategy/Ian O. Lesser.
  p.   cm.
Bibliography: p.
Includes index.
ISBN 0–312–02372–3 : $45.00 (est.)
1. Strategic materials – United States.   2. Strategic materials.
3. War – Economic aspects – United States.   4. War – Economic aspects.
I. Title.
HC110.S8L47   1989
333.7′0973 – dc19   88–33331
                                                                          CIP

To my parents and SRB

Contents

Contents

Preface

Much has been said and written over the past decade on the relationship between access to resources and Western security. This concern, thrust to the forefront by the decade of the oil crisis, was given additional impetus by the invasion of Afghanistan, the war in the Persian Gulf, events in Southern Africa, and the growth of the Soviet navy. Resource questions are, however, in no sense new to the strategic scene. Indeed, considerations of resource access and denial have long played an essential role in the formation and conduct of military strategy.

One of the primary objectives of this book is to bridge the gap between past experience and current concerns, that is, to place contemporary issues in historical perspective. In so doing, it will be shown that current thinking about the role of resources in war, and as a component of military potential in peacetime, relies to a significant extent on notions derived from historical experience. The perception of resource vulnerability (including the perceived vulnerability of adversaries) constitutes a remarkably enduring element in strategic thought and practice—one which has been shaped, but not eliminated, by changes in the nature of warfare, not least the advent of nuclear weapons.

The analysis of both historical and contemporary issues necessarily proceeds along three broad fronts. First, one must consider what is asserted by theorists, both civilian and military, with regard to the nature of war and the place of resource factors in it. Second, it is important to trace the less formalized, less precisely articulated, but nonetheless crucial prevailing perceptions or 'mind sets' with regard to resource questions. Finally, there is the reality of the role resource issues have actually played in the formation of military strategy, and their influence on the outcome of individual campaigns and conflicts. One aspect of this is that contemporary issues (for instance, the recent attacks on shipping in the Gulf) cannot be judged with anything like the detachment and benefit of hindsight with which the two world wars, or even the events of the 1970s and early 1980s can be viewed.

Throughout, this study is concerned primarily with *perceptions* of resource vulnerability and their influence on strategy, rather than the measurement of actual vulnerability, although the latter is explored where appropriate. Given the very broad span of time covered, and the conceptual nature of the effort, the discussion is necessarily selective rather than comprehensive, with a corresponding emphasis on the critical examination of existing literature. Part II of this book, in which contemporary issues are discussed, and in which the focus is primarily on American policy, also relies heavily on interviews with individuals active in the current debate.

I am indebted to many individuals in England and the United States who through their generosity, knowledge and wise counsel have helped enormously in the completion of this study. In particular, I wish to thank all those who agreed to be interviewed—often more than once—and who provided invaluable insight into both historical and contemporary questions. Their contributions are cited in the text. Others who were of great assistance in a variety of ways include Ambassador Winston Lord, Dr Geoffrey Kemp, Joseph W. Harned of the Atlantic Council of the United States, Dr Harlan K. Ullman and Jean Newsom of the Center for Strategic and International Studies, Ambassador Robert Komer and, not least, the Warden, Fellows and staff of St Antony's College, Oxford. My greatest debt is to Sir Michael Howard for his overall advice and encouragement and his invaluable comments on draft chapters of the Oxford thesis on which this book is based. Finally, I wish to extend my thanks to Kevin Coleman and Guillaume Hensel of the Center for Strategic and International Studies for their very great assistance in preparing the manuscript.

Washington
September 1988

Part I
Developments to 1945

1 Introduction

Quincy Wright has divided the history of modern warfare into distinctive periods on the following pattern: the adaptation of firearms (1450–1648); the period of professional armies and dynastic wars (1648–1789); the capitalization of war (1789–1914); and the totalitarianization of war (1914–42). The last two periods cited are characterized by the increasing size of armies, the militarization of populations, the mechanization of warfare, the nationalization of the war effort, the intensification of military operations and, not least, the increasing importance of resource factors.[1] One may also propose a fifth, nuclear period, the resource implications of which will be discussed.

The aim of this study is to arrive at an understanding of the role of vital resources in military strategy, from the 'capitalization' or industrialization of warfare to the present. Resources will be discussed, both as 'motivating factors' (that is, the stakes of rivalries, causes of conflict, or objectives of belligerents) and as 'means of force' (that is, as components of military power and potential in peace and war, and as determinants of what is strategically possible).[2]

In sum, the evolution of resource access and denial into an increasingly comprehensive exercise has paralleled the expanding scope and intensity of warfare generally, and has been closely tied in theory and application to both maritime and continental strategic traditions. Under the influence of mercantilist doctrine, European conflicts from the 15th century onwards focussed increasingly on the access to and denial of sources of wealth, and principally the supply of precious metals which contributed to the maintenance of military establishments and the financing of campaigns. Only with the emergence of naval timber supply from the Baltic and elsewhere as an important factor in warfare from the mid-17th century onwards does the attack and defence of raw materials of direct military significance emerge as a distinctive component of strategic planning (which finds its modern expression in concerns over access to oil and 'strategic' minerals).

The rejection of mercantilist doctrines with regard to the promotion of autarky, and the relationship between wealth and military potential, first by the Physiocrats in France, and more importantly by Adam Smith and his intellectual heirs in England, put in place the

1

foundations of an alternative liberal tradition, in which the system of maritime trade in resources was viewed as a source of economic strength, the defence of which emerges as a strategic imperative.

Thus, by the time of the Napoleonic conflict one may discern two evolving traditions with regard to resource access and denial as a dimension of strategy. These found expression in, on the one hand, Napoleon's Continental System for the exclusion of British trade and the encouragement of continental self-sufficiency, and on the other, the British counter-blockade and efforts to protect her system of maritime trade. Despite the increasing importance of naval timber and other raw materials in strategy, the mutual blockade of the Napoleonic period was still shaped largely by the mercantilist desire to ruin the trade of the adversary, rather than the objective of denying materials or foodstuffs vital to the enemy's war effort.

With the progress of industrialization and the increasing dependence of European economies on raw material imports, the 19th century saw a general growth of concern about resource vulnerability, its implications for economics and military power, and its potential effect on the conduct of war. In Britain this concern took a traditional maritime form, centring on the protection of the sea lines of communication for vital resources against a potential *guerre de course*.

At the same time, the notion of a 'continental system' for the promotion of economic autarky was vigorously reasserted by theorists of the neo-mercantilist or 'national' school such as Fichte, List and others who would provide the groundwork for pre-World War I (and interwar) German notions of greater-space economy, autarky and continental access to resource-rich regions in the East.

These two opposing traditions with regard to vital resources—continental and maritime—would find extreme expression in the two world wars, in which considerations of resource access played a key role in shaping objectives, and developments in military technology suggested the possibility of the denial of resources vital not only to war production and operations, but to the survival of societies as a whole, that is, a true counter-value strategy. Yet even as resource denial rose to prominence in World War II, the belligerents would demonstrate extraordinary adaptability and resistance in the face of blockade, strategic bombing and other threats to raw material supply.

Despite the profound changes in the nature of warfare which have taken place since 1945, not least the advent of nuclear weapons and intercontinental delivery systems, considerations of resource access and denial have proven remarkably enduring as an important dimension of strategy. The variables which have shaped and continue to shape the role of resource issues in the nuclear age are many, and include the changing importance of individual resources, evolving technologies for the attack and defence of resource-related targets, and most importantly, evolving perceptions with regard to the balance between nuclear and conventional defence. To the extent that strategists and planners continue to think about conventional wars of substantial duration, as well as regional threats to oil and mineral supplies, the continued relevance of resource factors is assured. Moreover, in thinking about contemporary issues it is clear that perceptions continue to be shaped by strategic traditions which have evolved from centuries of resource access and denial in war.

Following a brief review of the earlier history concerning resources and warfare, Part I of this book will trace the development of resource issues in strategic planning through the two world wars, with particular emphasis on resource 'access and denial'. Part II will discuss resources and strategy in the nuclear age, from early post-war doctrine and planning, through contemporary concerns with regard to oil, strategic minerals, and the role of resource factors in the East-West strategic relationship. The focus of this second part will be primarily, although not exclusively, on American perceptions and strategy. This is justified not only as a means of keeping the discussion to manageable limits, but also because it is in the US that the resurgence of interest in resources and strategy has been most pronounced.

The concluding discussion will endeavour to place contemporary issues in historical perspective, drawing together observations which are offered throughout on the following questions: (1) what elements of continuity and change may be identified with regard to resource issues in strategy?; (2) what role have perceptions of resource vulnerability (as opposed to actual vulnerability) had in the formation of strategic plans and policies?; (3) what has been the role of technological change in shaping the relationship between resource issues and strategy?; (4) to what extent have varying strategic traditions shaped, and been shaped by, resource considerations?; and (5) to what extent have resource factors been decisive in wartime— are they likely to be decisive or even relevant in the nuclear age? Finally, some overall conclusions are offered on resource issues as a cause of wars, and the linkage between resource factors and geostrategic ideas.

Many topics of potential interest must, of necessity, be excluded. Certain resources have been ignored in this discussion, either because of their relative unimportance in the strategic plans of the great powers (for example, water, which is of undeniable importance to the policies of some states) or because they are so unique and specialized (for instance, uranium) that a full treatment of their role would require a far more detailed assessment than is possible within the scope of this study.

This book is concerned solely with resource access and denial as a dimension of *strategy*, by which I mean, as Liddell Hart defined it 'the art of distributing and applying *military* means to fulfill the ends of policy'; or, as Aron has termed it, 'the conduct of military operations as a whole'.[3] Thus, I do not systematically explore resource issues in the conduct of diplomacy, nor do I consider general theories of international relations or international economics, except as they bear directly on questions of strategy. Similarly, the question of peacetime economic sanctions and embargoes is largely beyond the purview of this study; the exception being those cases in which the relationship between the imposition of sanctions and military planning is evident (for example, Italy and Japan in the 1930s, or the OAPEC embargo of 1973).

Finally, this discussion of resources and strategy deals primarily with great powers and major military conflicts and rivalries. The strategic plans and policies of regional powers and small states, while of interest in many respects, are beyond the scope of this analysis. The resource requirements and strategic priorities of smaller states will arguably be very different from those of large, powerful countries, and this narrower focus also lends itself more readily to drawing comparisons over time.

SOME KEY TERMS AND CONCEPTS

Resources
Resources may be defined as 'the sum of material means' which states have at their disposal to assure their continued existence and prosperity.[4] For the purpose of this study, resources will be understood as raw materials, including agricultural products where appropriate. More specifically, this study will be concerned with the supply, and the interruption of the supply, of 'vital' raw material

resources such as petroleum and petroleum products, minerals, and other materials important to military production and operations, or essential to the functioning of the civilian economy in wartime. To the extent that particular resources (for instance, oil) have been considered so essential to security and prosperity in *peacetime* that their continued supply has been an objective of strategic planning, these too are considered. Changing military and civilian technologies, for instance, the shift from coal to oil as a naval fuel, the development of synthetic rubber, and more recently the widespread use of composite and ceramic materials as replacements for metal alloys, have shaped perceptions of what is 'vital' and what is not. This is a process of continual evolution, in which, however, certain resources have proven exceptionally durable as sources of strategic concern. The obvious example is oil, unique in terms of its pervasiveness of use, as well as its continuing importance to military operations almost 80 years after Churchill's famous conversion decision at the Admiralty. So, too, developments in military technology (the advent of submarine warfare and strategic bombing provide good examples) have altered perceptions regarding those resources which might be profitably attacked or effectively defended. Often, the differing pace of technological and strategic change has led to considerable misperceptions about the potential for resource access and denial.

Dependence and Vulnerability

Resource 'dependence' implies a significant degree of reliance on external sources of a raw material. This reliance may be a result of the absence or limited availability of a particular raw material, or because the use of external sources offers economic, technical or political advantages. Resource 'vulnerability' implies that an interruption of existing arrangements for resource supply will have direct or indirect effects on security, and that these effects cannot be avoided through the adoption of countervailing policies (for example, substitution or the development of indigenous resources). It should be clear that dependence does not necessarily imply vulnerability. Of course, one may also speak of the 'vulnerability' of a specific source of supply to interruption and, indeed, overseas sources are often perceived to be vulnerable as a consequence of their distance, proximity to hostile powers, the presence of an unstable or unfriendly regime in the producer country, or the ability of an adversary to interfere with supplies *en route* or at source.

Economic Warfare

This is a broad term encompassing a range of potential measures (for example, legislative and administrative actions, control of neutrals, blockade, strategic bombing, or other military operations) aimed at the defeat of an adversary, and with the specific object of depriving an enemy of the material means to fight. As a strategic 'term of art', economic warfare emerged out of the experience of blockade in World War I, and rose to prominence in strategic planning in the interwar period and during World War II. A variant, of lesser relevance here, concerns the use of 'economic warfare' in peacetime as a substitute for, or alternative to, the use of force.

Blockade

This is generally the interdiction of an adversary's lines of communications, and especially sea lines of communications (SLOC). Included here are both the 'close-cordon' blockade of ports as well as blockade conducted through operations at some distance from the shore. As in the two world wars, a blockade may also be carried out largely by diplomatic or market-related measures aimed at the control of resources, ultimately supported by naval power.

Guerre de course

This relates to commerce raiding, or the attack on an adversary's seaborn trade, including the transport of vital resources. As developed by continental naval strategists, the concept of the *guerre de course* might not necessarily imply an attempt to sever sea lines of communication over a prolonged period (although this might be the case, as in the German submarine campaign in the two world wars). Brief, selective attacks on commerce, with the objective of wreaking economic havoc, were also envisioned, particularly by French strategists of the *jeune école* in the two decades prior to World War I. As a term of art in naval stragegy, the *guerre de course* has been supplanted in contemporary parlance by SLOC or trade 'interdiction' or similar terms.

Autarky

The pursuit of autarky is understood as the quest for self-sufficiency with regard to vital resources. Measures aimed at reducing or eliminating the need for imports to supply the raw material and agricultural requirements of the state, particularly during wartime, might include conservation, substitution, the development of synthetics, or the acquisition of secure sources of supply through conquest. Self-sufficiency in the literal sense has generally been recognized as an impractical concept, even for states with a substantial resource endowment. The goal, therefore, even for regimes with a strong commitment to 'autarky' (for example, Fascist Italy and Nazi Germany) has in reality been 'autarky', that is, the power to control one's own destiny. In practical terms, this has meant the desire for relative self-sufficiency in war essentials.

2 Resources and Strategy to 1914

EARLY HISTORY

There is a very significant body of history related to resources and strategy which pre-dates the industrial era, and a very extensive study could be made of this. However, the development of industrial economies and the rise of production-intensive 'mobilization warfare' brought about significant qualitative changes in the relationship between resources and strategy.[1] For this reason, the pre-industrial experience is less promising as a historical basis for exploring contemporary resource security issues. By way of prelude, however, it would be useful briefly to review some of the more prominent examples from this earlier history.

One very early example of the importance of resource considerations to the formation of strategic policy has been cited by Arnold Toynbee: Sesostris III (1878–43 BC) built a series of fortresses south of the second cataract of the Nile, the purpose of which was to protect Egyptian access to the vital gold mines of Nubia.[2] Access to adequate supplies of grain played a key role in shaping the grand strategy of the Athenian, Roman and Byzantine Empires. The maritime strategy of the Venetian Empire was concerned, above all, with the protection of vital trade routes. The capture of Constantinople in 1453 and Alexandria in 1517 by the Turks effectively closed the land routes from Europe to the resource-rich areas of the East; giving impetus to the exploration of the Cape Route and the development of long-range navigational techniques. These, in turn, had a marked effect on European access to raw materials, as well as on the ability and the need to project military power.

The Attack of Trade in the Mercantilist Age
The exploitation of the silver and gold resources of Latin America by Spain helped to support the Hapsburg dominions in the 16th and 17th centuries, and the interdiction or protection of these resources played a significant part in the conflicts of the period.[3] On several occasions Spanish military campaigns were disrupted by the loss of bullion shipments to English and Dutch attacks, leading the Spanish govern-

8

ment to declare bankruptcy in the face of loans contracted to support expeditions abroad. Without exaggerating the importance of such attacks on Spanish commerce, it is clear that Spain's adversaries repeatedly sought to deal a blow to Spanish power in Europe by interfering with the supply of bullion.[4]

The attempt to restrict or deny an adversary's access to valuable goods, especially precious metals, as a component of strategy, flowed directly from the prevailing doctrine of mercantilism which asserted that 'money is the sinew of war', and that the will to power necessarily involves amassing precious resources by either of two methods, commerce or war—there being little difference between the two in the mercantilist conception. Here, commerce becomes nothing less than 'the continuation of war by other means'.[5]

In the view of John Evelyn, the links between resources, trade and military power were clear: 'Whoever commands the ocean commands the trade of the world, and whoever commands the trade of the world commands the riches of the world, and whoever is master of that commands the world itself'.[6] Thus, the mercantilist idea, by clearly linking the balance of trade with the balance of power, led naturally to a quest for economic autarky.

The close relationship between economics and strategy was reflected in the two fundamental objectives of economic theory of the period: 'the political and commercial unification of the state', and 'the maximization of external state power'.[7] E. F. Heckscher, in his study of mercantilism, placed particular emphasis on the role of power in mercantilist theory. While this interpretation has been criticized as paying too little attention to economic advancement as a motivating factor, it seems clear that in the broadest terms mercantilist countries regarded the accretion of resources and wealth as an intermediate objective; a means to the end of state power.[8]

As Heckscher has pointed out, the pursuit of self-sufficiency with regard to vital resources was, in fact 'self-contradictory', in the context of the prevailing mercantilist doctrine. 'The old idea of blockade, the cutting-off of the enemy's supplies, is inconsistent with the conception that a country's gain lies in export, and that import constitutes a loss.'[9] The consequence of this is a form of 'self-blockade', the most striking example of which would ultimately be provided by Napoleon's Continental system.

The employment of commerce raiding was a central feature of strategy at sea in the first Anglo-Dutch War. The principal actions of this conflict were, in essence, 'convoy battles' arising from repeated

Dutch attempts to shield important convoys from attack. Ultimately, the English fleet managed to attain a position of superiority which allowed for the severe restriction of Dutch trade with resource-rich areas such as the East Indies. The economic hardship produced by this interference with vital commerce, including inshore fishing, contributed substantially to the Dutch decision to seek an end to hostilities.[10]

In the series of wars between France and England spanning the period 1688–1815, the French navy repeatedly fell back upon the strategy of commerce raiding as a means of reducing her adversary's ability and will to wage war. Sébastien Vauban, the French military engineer, was an early advocate of the *guerre de course*, arguing that this would be the only feasible strategy after the collapse of French sea power which had been built up by Colbert.[11] Thus, during the War of Spanish Succession, Vauban asserted:

> If we were to be quit of the vanity of great fleets which can never suit our needs and to employ the ships of the navy partly on commerce warfare and partly in squadrons to support it, we should bring about the downfall of the English and Dutch within about two or three years, in consequence of their great trade to all parts of the world.[12]

Contrary to the experience of the First Anglo-Dutch War, however, French naval forces were never able to inflict the consistently severe losses on English shipping which might have forced England to sue for peace in the face of economic disaster. Indeed, English overseas trade, and the revenues flowing from it, continued to expand throughout this period despite the *guerre de course* threat. The failure of the French strategy in this regard suggested a lesson, later to be taken up by Mahan and others, that inferior naval forces could not hope to bring a superior power to its knees through commerce raiding; the *guerre de course* threat could not in itself prove decisive.[13]

In North America, too, the influence of mercantilist notions of economic self-sufficiency and the inherent vulnerability of overseas sources of supply for materials of strategic importance, as well as sources of revenue, was apparent. Washington, in his first annual address to Congress in 1790, declared that 'the safety and interest of a free people require that they should promote such manufactures as tend to render them independent of others for essential, particularly military supplies'.[14] Similarly, Alexander Hamilton, in his *Report on*

Manufactures of 1791, declared his aim to be the promotion of such manufactures 'as will tend to render the United States independent of foreign nations for military and other essential supplies'.[15] Indeed, Hamilton went further, declaring that the lack of an adequate navy for the protection of American commerce heightened the vulnerability of the nation to interruptions in the supply of 'essential articles', and therefore strengthened the argument in favour of increased autarky through 'manufactures'.[16]

The Problem of Naval Timber Supply

The issue of the supply of naval timber which concerned England, as well as her principal maritime rivals France, Spain and Holland, provides a notable early example of the role of resource factors in war. Since the question with regard to timber was not simply the well-established practice of the general attack and protection of trade, but rather access to and denial of a specific material of military importance, it marks an important development in the evolution of resource-related strategy. From the First Dutch War (1652), naval planners in the key maritime countries were constantly concerned about the shortage of naval stores such as pitch, tar, flax and hemp, shipbuilding timber—particularly oak, as well as the supply of fir, pine and spruce masts from the Baltic (and later from North America).[17] For England, especially, the timber supply was 'inseparably connected' with sea power. As long as England could maintain control of the sea, distant regions could be searched for timber; yet the very ability to maintain this control was dependent upon the availability of adequate supplies.[18]

Overall, the Royal Navy's timber supply policy must be judged a success, since throughout the period 1652–1862 (the Battle of Hampton Roads) enough naval timber was gathered to build the ships which won and maintained control of the sea. The policy was conspicuous 'only in the instances where it miscarried'. While the shortage of timber never produced the extreme results some feared, the failure of the timber supply did affect the condition and operation of the navy on at least three notable occasions—the Dutch Wars, the American Revolution and the Napoleonic Wars.[19] The relationship between the supply of ship timber and sea power gave access and denial of this resource importance far beyond that associated with ordinary articles of commerce. England's Baltic policy, dictated by timber requirements, emphasized the importance of keeping the sea open 'at all costs', and led to armed intervention on several occasions. The Baltic policy, with its emphasis on blockade and counter-blockade, also influenced the development of 'neutral rights' regimes.[20]

Writing in 1926, Robert Albion observed that the naval timber problem bore a close resemblance to the oil situation of his day:

> Oak, like oil today, was a natural product very abundant at the outset, but liable to ultimate exhaustion. The intensive commercial demands for the object encroached on the smaller but more vitally imperative demands of the Navy. For want of an adequate domestic supply, nations sought colonies and exerted diplomatic pressure in those days as they do now for oil. Finally, there seems to be evidence of faulty policy in regard to the domestic and international oil situation which closely resembles policies which produced serious results in the supply of masts and oak.[21]

THE RISE OF THE LIBERAL-MARITIME TRADITION

With Turgot, Quesnay and the physiocrats in 18th-century France, and more importantly, Adam Smith and his followers in England, there emerged an alternative 'liberal' school which rejected the mercantilist concentration on precious metals and the finite volume of vital resources. For Adam Smith, the objectives of defence and prosperity need not be in conflict. 'In modern war, the great expense of firearms gives an evident advantage to the nation which can best afford this expense and consequently to an opulent and civilized over a poor and barbarous state.'[22] Free trade rather than the pursuit of economic autarky was seen to provide the most secure basis for national security. Wealth was no longer, as in the mercantilist conception, a 'zero-sum game'. *In extremis*, liberal, theorists such as Bentham would assert that wars were economically counterproductive in that they always cost more than they achieve.[23]

Quite naturally, the liberal tradition would place little emphasis upon economic autarky and resource self-sufficiency, particularly in peacetime. The emergence of liberal economic ideas encouraged the view that the system of external trade, including the import of raw materials, represented a potential strategic asset in wartime, provided of course that access to raw materials could be secured at source, and that the sea lines of communication could be protected. Thus, the evolution of economic doctrine, particularly in Britain, supported the development of a strategic tradition which, unlike its continental counterpart, emphasized a maritime approach to resource access.

The Napoleonic Conflict

The experience of economic warfare in the Napoleonic conflict anticipated many of the developments which were to rise to prominence in the two world wars, and would make explicit the conflict between maritime and continental strategies of access to resources. With some notable exceptions such as naval timber and grain, however, the Napoleonic conflict was not simply one of resource access and denial, but rather of the attack and protection of trade generally. Manifest British naval superiority had the effect of forcing weaker navies to fall back yet again upon a strategy of *guerre de course*, an approach which would prove inadequate in the face of Britain's main battle-fleet strategy.[24] As Mahan noted, the French had hoped to bankrupt Britain through a *guerre de course*; 'what they obtained was the demoralization of their navy, the loss of the control of the sea and of their own external commerce, finally Napoleon's Continental System and the fall of the Empire'.[25]

> The idea of a comprehensive blockade of an entire country has its classical example in the Continental System as inaugurated by Napoleon in the Berlin decree of 1806. The apparent object of that system was to isolate Great Britain from commercial intercourse with other countries in the expectation that thereby an internal economic collapse would be precipitated. In itself, the Continental System was the culmination of a form of economic warfare which had already been developed, and had its routes in the assumptions and practices of mercantilism as commonly accepted by nations during the preceeding two centuries.[26]

While clearly not decisive in its own right, one cannot dismiss the effect of commerce raiding in the Napoleonic conflict. One writer has suggested that the attack upon British trade in this period was 'more successful than any since the War of the Spanish Succession'.[27] Following French naval attacks against British trade, including naval timber in the Baltic in 1810, shipping losses for that year totalled some 619 vessels, causing grave anxiety in the shipping and insurance markets. Together with the effects of the Continental System for the exclusion of British trade, Napoleon's campaign to disrupt the vital commerce of his adversary had significant though not overwhelming consequences.[28] Overall, less than three percent of Britain's shipping had been captured during the course of the conflict.[29]

The revolt in Spain, and later the defection of Russia from the Continental System—itself motivated largely by the refusal of the French to allow the export of Russian naval timber to Britain—contributed to the neutralization of the economic warfare threat. As E. F. Heckscher has concluded, 'the Continental System had little effect in its mission of destroying the economic organization of Great Britain'.[30] Even with regard to the 'narrower objectives' of wartime strategy, the policy fell far short of its goals, limited by inconsistency in its application and administrative ineffectiveness.[31] As an attempt to create a greater economic unit centred on France, the Continental System also fell far short of Napoleon's expectations. A Europe reduced to living on its own more limited resources was a less prosperous Europe overall.[32]

Notable measures were taken by the Admiralty to counter the *guerre de course* threat, in particular the innovation of a worldwide system of convoys.[33] Nelson himself highlighted the gravity of the task, noting: 'I consider the protection of our trade the most essential service that can be performed'.[34] The lessons of the Napoleonic period with regard to the protection of vital seaborn trade would be learned again in countering the submarine threat to sea lines of communication in the two world wars.

Britain's vigorous policy of blockade in the Napoleonic conflict, although not the centrepiece of her naval strategy, had a serious effect on French trade, including the supply of important war *matériel*. The most serious blow to France in this respect was the loss of her substantial colonial trade.[35] Indeed, the success of the British blockade gave impetus to the development of Napoleon's response in the form of attempted economic integration on the Continent, together with the exclusion of British trade.[36] The charge that the British blockade was a 'paper blockade' was outweighed by the application of a much more obvious paper blockade by France—the French fleet having been rendered essentially ineffective at Trafalgar in 1805. The inability of French forces to impose an effective blockade at sea meant that the policy of trade restriction was only truly enforceable on land.[37] In the circumstances of the conflict, economic warfare, including the denial of vital resources (although this was not a primary tactic) emerged as a potential means of forcing a decision. As Mahan has suggested: 'England had no army wherewith to meet Napoleon; Napoleon had no navy to cope with that of his enemy. As in the case of an impregnable fortress, the only alternative for either of these contestants was to reduce the other by starvation'.[38]

THEORISTS OF NATIONAL SELF-SUFFICIENCY AND IMPERIALISM

From the mid-19th century onwards one may observe the rise of a 'national' school which rejected much of both mercantilist and liberal theory, although it was in many respects no more than a rediscovery of certain mercantilist arguments, adapted to the circumstances of the industrial age. The central tenets of this school included the 'rounding out' of national sovereignty through conquest, the quest for strategic autarky and the protection of vital industries. The objective was, ultimately, the creation of larger economic and political units.[39] The 'national' school is of particular relevance to the analysis of the relationship between resources and strategy in the modern age, since elements of this doctrine had a profound influence on the policies of the totalitarian states in the 20th century, and complemented that tradition which stressed a continental strategy of access to vital resources.

A principal theorist of the national school was Friedrich List, whose notions of power, wealth and national welfare put forward an essentially mercantilist, or more properly, neo-mercantilist argument. List asserted that the principal goal of the nation must be to 'create the greatest quantity of common welfare in the interior, and the greatest quantity of security as regards other nations'. Thus, in the quest for autarky, 'power secures wealth and wealth increases power'. The greater the productive power of the state, the greater the strength of the nation in foreign policy, and the greater its independence in wartime. Economic principles cannot, therefore, be divorced from their political consequences.[40] These views followed closely in the tradition of neo-mercantilists such as Gottlieb Fichte, who had earlier argued that 'one must not only think of frontiers militarily well covered and solid, but far more still of a certain productive autonomy or self-sufficiency'.[41]

List observed that it was continued weakness in the sphere of economic self-sufficiency that had limited the growth of Prussian power.[42] It was in this context that List became an active proponent

of a unified 'Greater Germany', to include Denmark, the Netherlands, Switzerland and Belgium. Thus, List contributed to the
theoretical groundwork for a variety of Pan-German and later
National Socialist concepts such as *Lebensraum*, and the *Drang nach
Osten*, as well as the ideas advanced by the interwar Geopoliticians,
all of which embraced resource-related issues.[43]

Perhaps the most significant of List's contributions to strategic
thinking centred on the increasing influence of railways on the
balance of power, anticipating Mackinder in his recognition of the
threat posed by the expansion of rail (that is, continental) communications to maritime power. Improved rail transportation would,
he argued, facilitate the rapid concentration of forces and thus the
projection of continental power, as well as opening new vistas for the
extension of German influence and access to vital resources. In this
sense, he provided much of the conceptual impetus for the Berlin-
Baghdad Railway project, together with German aspirations for
increased influence in the resource-rich areas of Turkey and the
Middle East. List's thoughts on German economic expansion and
access to resources in the Balkans and the Near East, together with
the vital importance of the railways, would be echoed by many
others, including Naumann and von Moltke the Younger, in the
latter half of the 19th century and the early years of the 20th.[44]

Analysts of imperialism, including Hobson and Lenin, discussed at
length the economic causes of conflict, but had far less to say about
the role of resources in strategy *per se*. For Hobson, the central point
was the illusory role of colonies as markets for goods and outlets for
investment.[45] Similarly Lenin would later assert that imperialism,
and imperial conflict, is the natural consequence of the quest for
markets, outlets for both capital and goods, in highly developed
industrial economies—that is, 'the struggle for economic territory' in
the stage of 'monopoly' or 'finance' capital.[46] Access to raw materials
is noted as a factor, but only in connection with its importance to the
consolidation of monopolies. Here, resource access is viewed not so
much as a state strategy, but rather as a monopolist strategy.[47]

With regard to the growth of the British Empire, writers who are
less inclined to find a connection between capitalism and imperialism
have tended to focus on such factors as prestige, security, ethical
sentiments, the desire to construct ever larger social units, and 'the
striving towards national self-sufficiency' as the underlying motives
for imperial expansion.[48] Here again, the central concern is the
construction of larger, protected markets, and only secondarily, the

control over raw material supply itself. As Gerhard Ritter has noted:

> In the era of the new, overheated, and intensely aggressive colonialism that went by the name of imperialism, political thought took on a highly militant character throughout the world. Political Darwinism was not the only contributing factor. There was the so-called 'unmasking' of bourgeois idealism by the Marxist movement with its gospel of the class struggle. The *Lebensraum* theories of militant geopoliticians and economists also played a role, with their insistence on the need for secure markets and raw material sources.[49]

Thus, political ideologies at the turn of the century, in Germany and elsewhere, intermingled with concepts of economic vulnerability and opportunity (for instance, the expansion of economic and political influence under the banner of a 'Greater Germany' as expressed by the Pan-German League) in a manner which fuelled an already highly-charged and militant atmosphere.

RESOURCE ISSUES AND STRATEGIC PLANNING PRIOR TO WORLD WAR I

The growing concern over questions of resource access and denial, particularly in Britain and France, reached its zenith in the period leading up to World War I, and was to exert a powerful influence over strategic plans and practice. Yet, when one considers the profound changes which swept over the European continent in the years between 1871 and 1914—not least the enormous expansion of industrial production—it is apparent that the full extent of the demands imposed by modern industrial or 'mobilization' warfare was hardly anticipated by military planners. The American Civil War, which saw the employment of mass armies, railroads, telegraphs, gatling guns, repeating rifles, trenches and barbed wire, foreshadowed in many respects developments in World War I. It may also be regarded as the first modern war of materiel, in which the industrial capacity of the North more than offset the military tradition and initiative of the South. Few observers realized, however, that the failure to reach prompt military decisions in the early stages of a conflict would result in a long and exhausting war of attrition; additional evidence for which was to be provided by the experience of the Boer and Franco-Prussian wars.

It was in the context of developments such as those seen in the Civil War that the Polish financier Jean de Bloch (Ivan Bliokh) published his remarkable book speculating on the nature of a future European conflict.

> The . . . war will become a kind of stalemate in which neither army being able to get at the other, both armies will be maintained in opposition to each other, threatening each other, but never being able to deliver a final and decisive attack. It will be simply the natural evolution of the armed peace. . . .
> . . . Accompanied by [the] entire dislocation of all industry and the severing of all [the] sources of supply by which alone the community is enabled to bear the crushing burden of that armed peace. It will be a multiplication of expenditure simultaneously accompanied by a diminution of the sources by which that expenditure can be met.[50]

Bloch further asserted that the war of the future would not be terminated by fighting, but rather by famine. Nations were no longer 'self-contained units', and with the exceptions of Russia and Austria, all European countries were dependent upon imported beef and grain. Britain, in particular, was observed to be absolutely dependent upon such supplies.[51] Furthermore, neither the machinery of supply and distribution for vital imports, nor the capacity to pay for such supplies would remain unaffected by war. Thus, even alternative sources of supply would be open to disruption. In the case of Britain, Bloch believed that the fleet might perhaps be able to safeguard trade routes, but the price if not the absolute supply of vital commodities would become a problem due to commerce raiding. Bloch dismisses the German proposal that in time of war the loss of Russian wheat be replaced through the import of Indian wheat through the Suez Canal as 'not very easy of execution' in the face of the threat posed by French and Russian cruisers.[52]

In sum, Bloch can be regarded as a seminal writer on the question of the relationship between resources and strategy in modern warfare, particularly with regard to the potential effects of a *guerre de course*. Most importantly, he predicted that any interference with raw material shipments would be more threatening than the loss of a pitched battle, and that it would be the economic consequences of a future war which would be decisive.[53]

While Bloch's vision of a prolonged and costly war of attrition was aimed at demonstrating the futility of war in the industrial age, his vision could also serve to support the concept of the 'battle of anihilation', as propounded by Schlieffen and others. Although Bloch's critics agreed that such wars of attrition might indeed be unthinkable, they also asserted that a strategy geared toward a rapid decision could provide an alternative to such an outcome.[54] Here one begins to recognize the basis of the *Blitzkrieg* strategy which would later be advanced as an alternative to the debilitating resource-intensive war of attrition for which the German economy was perceived to be ill-suited (that is, assuming *Blitzkrieg* by design rather than improvisation). At the heart of the issue was the essential question of whether the new military technology necessarily favoured the defensive, as Bloch asserted. The professional military, to the extent that they took notice of Bloch at all, for the most part held that the new technology favoured 'the attack no less than the defense'.[55]

In the period leading up to World War I perceptions of resource vulnerability played an increasingly important role in shaping the strategic plans and policies of the major European powers, especially those of Britain and Germany. It is possible to identify the links between the fear of resource vulnerability and evolving naval policies, as well as to distinguish distinctive approaches to the issue of securing access to vital resources (that is, maritime versus continental strategies of access).

The increasing British concern with regard to the maintenance of naval supremacy in the face of active French, Russian and German naval programmes flowed, in large measure, from a desire to safeguard essential commerce in the event of conflict. Indicative of this is the manner in which the Navy League, formed in 1894, relied to a great extent on such arguments as the 'starvation theory' in stirring public support for a general increase in naval expenditure. Indeed, it has been suggested that public opinion, mobilized around such issues as the supply and price of food in wartime, lent great weight to the Admiralty's advocacy of an expanded navy in the second half of the 1890s.[56]

As early as 1858 Alexander Milne, as Junior Lord of the Admiralty, had warned the Prime Minister that the French threat to shipments of industrial raw materials nearing home waters was 'almost as serious as the danger of invasion'.[57] The preoccupation with the vulnerability of trade which was to characterize British naval planning through 1914 had been launched in earnest with the *Report of the Royal Commission on the Defence of the United Kingdom* published in 1860. The report stressed that the primary task of the navy would no longer be defence against invasion, but rather the protection of Britain's worldwide maritime trade, 'which becomes of more vital importance with every successive step of national progress'.[58]

Naval supremacy advocates in Britain drew as a matter of course on the argument that in the event of war an enemy, having defeated the British fleet, would then be in a position to quickly reduce the nation to submission by intercepting vital commerce. In this sense, both the actual importation of foodstuffs and strategic raw materials, and the export of manufactured goods to pay for them, were viewed as critical and inseparable elements. The widespread professional and popular belief was that national starvation would be the inevitable outcome if Britain were unable to maintain sea control in time of conflict.[59] In 1905 Britain imported roughly half of its meat supplies and four-fifths of its wheat, while total stocks of the latter ranged from only two to eight weeks supply.[60] As First Sea Lord in 1908, Admiral Fisher summed up the situation thus: 'The Navy is the first, second, third, fourth, fifth . . . *ad infinitum* line of defence. If the Navy is not supreme, no Army however large is of the slightest use. It's not invasion we have to fear if the Navy is beaten, its starvation'.[61]

In addition, British dependence upon imported raw materials apart from foodstuffs was equally marked, with seven-eighths of these materials coming from abroad by 1913. This figure included all of the cotton, four-fifths of the wool, and the bulk of the phosphoric iron ore and non-ferrous metals used by British industry.[62] It is illustrative that the British iron industry depended upon imports for 40 per cent of its raw materials, with only four weeks stockpiled reserves. Similarly, without foreign manganese, steel production would be severely impaired, if not halted.[63] Overall stocks of imported vital ores in Britain rarely exceeded one to two months supply.[64] The interdiction of such commodities would not only hamper the production of war *matériel* but also, it was argued, lead to widespread unemployment and the consequent inability of workers to pay for scarce foodstuffs. This vision of economic disaster represented the companion argument to the 'starvation theory'.

The element of resource vulnerability always implicit in the British position was made more explicit as a result of the extension, at least, in theory, of belligerent practice on the Continent, especially in France in the 1880s and 1890s. In this context, the doctrine of commerce raiding or *guerre de course* was developed extensively by

Theophile Aube, a founder of the French *jeune école* of naval strategy. Aube and others argued that France should concentrate on the development and deployment of fast torpedo boats and other vessels suitable for commerce raiding, rather than attempting to match the British production of capital ships. It was hoped that France might thus be in a position to interdict British shipping in the Channel in brief forays which would shake the financial markets, and thus the economy of the Empire, before the Admiralty fully realized what was happening. (The threat of financial panic rather than the absolute long-term denial of vital resources inherent in this doctrine, is similar in many respects to Iranian threats with regard to the closure of the Straits of Hormuz during the Gulf War.)

Thus, in the first major work of the *jeune école, De la Guerre Maritime* by Baron Richard Grivel, published in 1869, it was asserted that the strategy of 'commerce warfare, the most economical for the poorest fleet, is at the same time the one most proper to restore peace, since it strikes directly . . . at the very source of the prosperity of the enemy'.[65] The *jeune école* could cite the Confederacy's resort to commerce raiding as a counter to the Union blockade in the American Civil War, as well as the success of the Confederate raiders in compelling American merchant ships to adopt foreign registries. A similar strategy applied against Britain was perceived to have far greater potential for success as British reliance on the national merchant marine was so much greater than that of the United States.[66] Despite the poor results achieved through commerce raiding alone in earlier conflicts, the leaders of the *jeune école* maintained, as would Bloch, that Britain's vulnerability to this sort of attack had increased with the progress of industrialization. 'A century of developing industrialization had abolished any possibility of Britain attaining self-sufficiency, not only in food, but in most primary products.'[67]

The doctrines of the *jeune école* had considerable influence on the direction of naval construction and planning of the continental powers. Between 1875 and 1885 the French navy acquired 70 torpedo boats capable of threatening shipping in the Channel and the Mediterranean. Russia, Germany and Italy followed, acquiring large numbers of fast torpedo boats. In addition, France and Russia began in the early 1870s to deploy large cruisers capable of threatening British trade far beyond European waters.[68]

With regard to the extent to which vital British trade could be protected from interference during a maritime war, The Royal

Commission on the Supply of Food and Raw Materials in Time of War (1905) not surprisingly concluded that this would depend ultimately on maintaining control of the sea. Although it might take some time for the Navy to assert its supremacy, the Royal Commission was confident that such supremacy could be asserted and maintained. Moreover, the existing dispersal of vital trade over many commodities and many ships, together with the flexibility of route available to steam transport, appeared to improve the prospects for successful commerce protection.[69]

Admiralty testimony incorporated in the Commission's report acknowledged that the policy of attacking the floating trade of a country has always played an important part in maritime warfare, and would be likely to do so in the future. The Admiralty stressed, however, that command of the sea has been, and would continue to be, the essential precondition for trade protection or attack, and this, in particular, was the overall principle guiding the deployment of British naval forces in defence of trade.[70] With regard to the lessons of the American Civil War, it was stressed that the number of captures made by Confederate raiders was actually quite small (for instance, the *Alabama* averaged only three prizes per month), whereas the concentration of the Northern fleet in the blockade of Confederate ports could be regarded as a more effective strategy of denial.[71]

Taking into account the greater concentration of trade and overall vulnerability implicit in the British situation of 1905, the Report concluded:

> The harassment and distress caused to a country by serious interference with its commerce will be conceded by all. It is doubtless a most important secondary operation of naval war, and is not likely to be abandoned till war itself shall cease; but regarded as a primary and fundamental measure, sufficient in itself to crush an enemy . . . it is probably a delusion.[72]

Ironically, as the Admiralty developed more systematic plans for commerce protection, the actual threat of a *guerre de course* declined, for by the end of 1905 the possibility of war with France or Russia began to appear remote. Furthermore, it was accepted that the general problem of vital commerce protection would be less complex in the event of a conflict with Germany. This perception was based on the German navy's lack of cruisers suited for commerce raiding, together with the fact that Germany's naval bases were not well situated for attacking important trade routes. Finally, in contrast to France, it had never been an avowed German policy to adopt the *guerre de course*.[73]

Admiral Fisher was among the first to pay critical attention to the possibility of an unrestricted *guerre de course*, and the key role to be played by submarines in such a campaign. Admiral Jellicoe also noted that the submarine menace 'is truly a terrible one for British commerce and Great Britain alike . . .'.[74] Given this, Jellicoe asserted that it would be well to consider the position of Britain with regard to food and oil, the latter being 'the life blood of our future warships of all sorts in time of war'.[75] In this, both Fisher and Jellicoe anticipated important developments in the approaching conflict.

The writings of A. T. Mahan had a very significant influence upon British naval thinking of the period, including opinion on questions relating to resource access, sea lines of communications, and the *guerre de course*. The publication of *The Influence of Sea Power Upon History* (1890) and *The Influence of Sea Power Upon the French Revolution and Empire* (1892) led to a general intellectual rediscovery of sea power worldwide, and especially in Britain. One of Mahan's principal conclusions was that commerce destruction has never been decisive in its own right, despite its relative prominence in naval thought of the period. Rather, Mahan suggested that the overriding factor must be the possession of that 'overbearing power' capable of defeating the enemy and driving him from the sea.[76] In this sense, Mahan may be said to have had a moderating influence upon British perceptions of resource vulnerability in the face of a potential *guerre de course*.

As Mahan was publishing *Sea Power in Relation to the War of 1812* (1905) another and very different interpretation of international politics and strategy was being elaborated by Halford Mackinder. In his paper entitled 'The Geographical Pivot of History' (1904), Mackinder stressed the evolving importance of the Eurasian 'heartland' and the coming ascendancy of continental over sea lines of communication. The implications of this for access to vital resources were also noted:

The spaces within the Russian Empire and Mongolia are so vast, and their potentialities in population, wheat, cotton, fuel and metals so incalculably great, that it is inevitable that a vast economic world, more or less apart, will there develop inaccessible to oceanic commerce.[77]

The clear message of Mackinder, in contrast to Mahan, was that sea power was in decline and would become progressively less relevant to the centres of world power and resources. The newer powers, particularly the United States and Germany, as well as France and Russia, having less of their national wealth dependent on overseas trade, would be much less vulnerable to the pressure of naval blockade than some of Britain's former adversaries (for example, Spain and Holland). The perceived decline in the effectiveness of the naval blockade instrument was furthered by the development of railways. Thus, by the turn of the century, it could be argued that the best targets for blockade were nearly all British.[78]

In sum, the increasing dependence of Britain on imported food and raw materials, and the continuing vulnerability of her sea-borne trade, shaped the thinking of Britain's naval planners during a period in which her potential adversaries were deploying naval forces designed to exploit these vulnerabilities. It is ironic that the threat of a French *guerre de course* which had given great impetus to systematic planning for naval war, as well as providing the principal political lever for influencing Parliament and public opinion on the question of increased naval spending, was lifted just as more comprehensive mechanisms for the protection of vital trade were being put in place. The threat which would later emerge from German commerce raiding in World War I was, however, of such a different nature, largely as a result of the technical revolution brought about by the use of the submarine, that most of the carefully developed British doctrine regarding trade protection (for instance, the patrol of sealanes) was to be rendered useless.[79]

In the case of Germany, a very significant degree of reliance on imported raw materials, many from British Empire territories, also led to a general concern about the adequacy of naval forces to safeguard access to vital resources. The provisions of the 'Tirpitz policy', accepted and put into final form in 1897, called for a minimum level of naval expansion which would be necessary, in the event of war with France or Russia or both, in order to prevent a blockade of German coasts and to keep open supply lanes for food and other essential commodities. With regard to Britain, it was accepted that there could be little hope of matching British naval strength, but it was hoped that the 'doctrine of risk' (that is, deterrence) central to the Tirpitz policy would make the destruction of the German fleet a costly enough undertaking to encourage Britain to resolve differences short of actual conflict.[80]

The policies pursued by Britain and Germany with regard to Middle Eastern oil in the period preceding World War I provide particularly clear examples of the changing perception of, and reaction to, resource vulnerability. Throughout the latter half of the 19th century Britain was, to use a modern analogy, the Saudi Arabia of coal. Indeed, Britain possessed a virtual monopoly of the hard smokeless coal which had become the preferred maritime fuel. As the world's largest producer of coal, providing roughly half of the coal in world trade in 1913, Britain exercised extensive control over the foreign bunkering of naval as well as merchant ships. For some states, notably Germany and Russia, dependence upon British coal in the pre-World War I era bore a remarkable similarity to the oil dependency which was to emerge later. The Royal Navy itself had established an elaborate network of coaling stations worldwide, particularly along the principal routes of Imperial communication, to keep its ships supplied with British coal.[81]

This commanding resource position was used by Britain to support or hinder the naval operations of other powers. Thus, prior to the outbreak of the Spanish-American War in 1898, Admiral Dewey was permitted to use the British bases and coaling facilities at Hong Kong to support the activities of his fleet. So too, the world voyage of the American 'White Fleet' of 1907–09 was dependent upon access to British bases and coal *en route*.[82] Most notably, Britain used her ability to deny Russia access to naval coal in order to hinder the concentration of Russian squadrons in the Russo-Japanese War, thus contributing to the Russian defeats at Port Arthur and the Battle of Tsushima.[83]

The critical development which catapulted oil into the position of a resource vital to national security was the decision by the Admiralty to convert its battle-fleet from coal to oil, a move followed by all the major naval powers. The strategic consequences of the principal conversion decision taken by Churchill at the Admiralty in 1911 were far-reaching indeed, since Britain had thus committed herself to the unilateral abandonment of the advantages of coal self-sufficiency. Oil did, however, possess numerous technical advantages over coal as a naval fuel. First, it had a higher thermal efficiency, so that for a given weight of fuel an oil-powered ship would have a higher speed and/or range of operation. Large ships might achieve a 40 per cent increase in range over those burning coal. Second, the use of oil allowed ships to be refuelled underway, further improving the mobility of naval forces. Finally, oil was far easier to store and move aboard ship, allowing a reduction in the large number of crew formerly needed to shovel coal from bunker to boiler.[84]

The conversion decision provoked a sharp controversy in Britain, despite the similar policy adopted by the United States in authorizing the construction of the oil-fired *Nevada* class battleships in 1911. Of course, the oil supply situation of the United States was in complete contrast to that of Britain. Furthermore, it was estimated at the time that the initial acquisition of the necessary tankers, oil stockpiles and associated infrastructure would cost Britain at least £10 million.[85] The tactical advantages which could be realized through the use of oil-fired engines appeared to be offset by the fact that Britain had little direct access to oil, the leading producers in this period being the United States, Mexico and Russia. Consequently, a widespread perception of vulnerability arose among British policy-makers. E. G. Pretyman, head of the Parliamentary 'Oil Committee', maintained that the Royal Navy had been placed in a position of grave vulnerability: 'Whereas we possess in the British Isles the best supply of the best steam coal in the world, a very small fraction of the oilfields of the world lay within the British Dominions, and even these are situated in very remote and distant regions'.[86]

While the resource vulnerability arguments of the 'anti-oil' school could hardly be denied, it could well be argued that if an enemy was in a position to cut off the supply of oil through attacks on sea lines of communication, he would surely be in a position to cut off other essential supplies of food, raw materials and munitions (indeed, the German submarine campaigns would very nearly accomplish this in two world wars).[87] Thus, the real problem was the increased vulnerability of Britain's industrial economy generally, rather than the additional risk introduced by the transition to oil.

Through subsequent diplomatic and financial efforts, Britain was able to bring the bulk of the existing Middle Eastern oil production under her control. These efforts reached their peak in 1914 when Fisher and Churchill, citing the danger of 'oil starvation' in the event of a war with Germany, managed to put through Parliament a bill giving the government the right—later exercised—to take over the Anglo-Persian Oil Company. Access to adequate supplies of oil in wartime now constituted a point of potential strategic vulnerability for all European naval powers, with the Middle East rapidly becoming the object of intense interest. For the British, in particular, given the size and role of the Royal Navy, the Middle East, still considered the bridge to India and Asia, acquired an additional strategic purpose: access to and protection of the oilfields of the Persian Gulf area. The British strategy of access was naturally a maritime one, based upon the maintenance of secure sea lines of communication.

The quest for secure access to resources to fuel industrial development and imperial expansion also played a key role in German policy in the period leading up to World War I. In the face of a rapidly expanding population and industrial base, Germany had become increasingly dependent on foreign sources of food and raw materials. Many essential commodities were not produced at all in Germany, and some industries were almost wholly dependent on foreign sources of supply. Textile manufacturing provided a striking example of this, with roughly nine-tenths of the needed supplies of raw cotton, jute, silk and other materials obtained from foreign sources.[88]

Germany, which had been virtually self-sufficient in 1871, had by 1900 become thoroughly interdependent, with worldwide economic interests. One measure of the pace of this economic transformation is provided by the 200 per cent increase in German industrial production (in terms of value) between 1871 and 1914. By contrast, Britain showed a 60 per cent increase in the same period.[89] The continued development and expansion of the German export trade was deemed essential in order to pay for growing imports of food and raw materials. Thus, 'the German industrial revolution of the late nineteenth century was at once the cause and effect of the growing dependence of German economic prosperity upon foreign markets'.[90] At the same time, German colonial trade and overseas commerce would be at the mercy of British sea power in the event of a general European war. It was perceived that the German war economy could be effectively crippled by the denial of critical resources such as cotton, copper and oil. This, combined with serious doubts about the ability of the German navy to keep open essential sea lanes, led naturally to the exploration of opportunities for economic alliances in Central Europe, as well as initiatives beyond the Bosporus.[91]

The desire to extend Germany's continental lines of communication to areas with great potential for the supply of resources in the East, combined with the romantic desire to participate in a 'revival of the ancient civilizations of Mesopotamia, Syria and Babylonia', led Wilhelm II into an active policy in the Middle East.[92] The most ambitious element of this policy was the proposal for a Berlin-Baghdad Railway which, if extended to the Persian Gulf, would place Germany 'at the doorstep' of India. The organizers of this project had secured a concession from the Turkish government for a thousand-mile strip of territory in Turkey and Mesopotamia, including the right to construct a railway and to exploit the oil and other mineral resources to be found on either side of the rail line. The railway scheme thus became the centrepiece of the German conception of a *Drang nach Osten* through the Balkan Peninsula, over the Bosporus, and into the resource-rich areas of Asia.[93]

It has been argued that the position of Germany in Central Europe, together with the German perception of 'economic encircle-ment' and susceptibility to sea blockade, 'made as inevitable a penetration into Turkey as the geographical position of England made inevitable the development of an overseas empire'.[94] Similarly, the theoretical impetus provided by List and others flowed, in large part, from the search for alternatives to the construction of a major deep-water navy.

The Berlin-Baghdad Railway raised the spectre of greatly in-creased German influence in Turkey, posed a potential threat to Britain's lines of communication to India, and promised more active German competition for oil in the Middle East. At the same time there were further German efforts to secure oil concessions in Iraq, and to establish bunkering and trading stations in the Persian Gulf.[95] Looking beyond the clear romantic attraction of the railway concept, this continental expression of the *Drang nach Osten* may be viewed as a strategy developed in response to the frustration of German desires for sea-based imperial expansion and economic autarky. In the context of the competition with Britain, the railway plan also presented a means of 'outflanking' the British maritime empire.[96]

DEVELOPMENTS TO 1914: OVERALL OBSERVATIONS

Reviewing developments in the relationship of resource factors to strategic thought and practice through 1914, several preliminary observations may be made. First, there exists a strong pre-industrial tradition relating to the access and denial of vital resources, com-merce raiding, and economic self-sufficiency, which naturally reflected the geographical or 'geostrategic' orientation of specific states (for example, maritime or continental), as well as prevailing doctrines with regard to trade and military potential (mercantilist, liberal and 'national'). In this sense, considerations of resource access and denial have long occupied a place in strategy. Second, the progress of industrialization and technological advances in warfare, particularly since the mid-19th century, led in turn to the increasing interdependence and complexity of national economies, and the perception of the increasing vulnerability of those economies to the restriction of resource supply in wartime. Thus, by 1914 the theoretical and physical elements for a conflict in which resource access and denial would play a crucial part were firmly in place, and mounting perceptions of resource vulnerability clearly influenced the formation of strategic plans and policies, both in Britain and on the Continent. Overall, the pattern of evolution with regard to the role of resource denial in war to 1914 may be characterized as one of increasing comprehensiveness and importance, in which not only trade in general, but the supply of raw materials of direct military significance, came to be threatened. Indeed, by 1900 strategists had begun to envision—and fear—broader campaigns aimed not only at disrupting the functioning of war economies, but at threatening the survival of an adversary's society as a whole.

3 Resource Access and Denial in World War I

World War I can be regarded as a watershed in the evolution of the relationship between resource issues and the planning and conduct of warfare. Indeed, it could be argued that strategy itself changed its meaning over the course of the war. Whereas strategy had previously been concerned largely with the operational conduct of war by naval and land forces, with the evolution of the war into a mass struggle between states, the notion of strategy expanded to embrace the active mobilization of entire economies. This transformation inevitably placed questions of resource access and denial into sharper focus. The role of resource issues in the conduct of the war will be discussed in this chapter, with particular reference to: (1) the resource positions of the belligerents, and the policies adopted in response; (2) strategies of blockade and counter-blockade; and (3) the increasing importance of oil, and the policies pursued to assure or restrict its supply.

THE RISE OF MOBILIZATION WARFARE

World War I witnessed the rise of 'mobilization warfare', that is, not simply the mobilization of manpower and armed forces, but also the commitment of a nation's entire social and economic infrastructure. This has been characterized as 'total war', although the term may convey other meanings as well.[1] The transformation of European economy and society brought about by the enormous expansion of industrial production between 1871 and 1914 did not, with the exception of a few visionaries such as Bloch, produce a commensurate adjustment in strategic thought. Nor did the actual conduct of war in this period appear to keep pace with the industrialization taking place elsewhere. The American Civil War and the Franco-Prussian War 'had not, once the railroads had been left behind, involved either a terribly sophisticated use of technology or very much of it'.[2] On the eve of World War I, officers continued to exist in rather profound ignorance of what modern warfare really implied.

30

The populations of Europe tended to regard war 'not as an extension of industrial society, but as a liberation from it, and ethusiastically welcomed it as such in 1914'.[3]

Three factors can be identified as leading to a war of attrition, and consequently the growth of mobilization warfare. First, developments such as the machine gun and barbed wire vastly increased the power of the defence and contributed to strategic stalemate. Second, between 1870 and 1914 the size and logistic requirements of armies outstripped their mobility, with the result that forces beyond the railhead could not move far or fast enough to force a strategic decision. Finally, the economic capacity of modern industrial states meant that even enormous losses in men and materiel did not necessarily spell defeat. Taken together, these factors created an environment in which the offensive power of armies was to lag behind the productive power of national economies.[4]

One outgrowth of mobilization warfare was the increasing emphasis placed on what was later to be termed 'economic warfare' and in particular the restriction of the supply of vital resources to adversaries. The experience of World War I would also demonstrate the potential for escaping or mitigating the consequences of the interruption of vital raw material supplies through substitution, the use of synthetics, stockpiling and conquest. Thus, the war would point to the manner in which modern industrial economies, interdependent and potentially vulnerable, could also be a source of defensive adaptability in the face of resource shortages.

Anticipated and unanticipated vulnerabilities with regard to various important wartime commodities had a pronounced effect on the pre-war planning and wartime policies of the belligerents. While specific vulnerabilities gave rise to specific problems and attempted solutions, it can be said that all of the principal combatants tended to underestimate the resource and production requirements of modern warfare—this, despite the arguments of visionaries such as Bloch. It is illustrative that German requirements for shells during a single intensive action on the western front often exceeded total German requirements during the Franco-Prussian War.[5] An important aspect of the conflict from the resource perspective was the manner in which access to energy supplies such as oil and coal became central to the war efforts of the belligerents. Although the latter stages of the war were characterized by the heavy use of energy supplies on the battlefield, both on the ground and in the air, the early stages of the war were far less energy-intensive.

The early stages of the war were the last battles of the nineteenth century. Railways brought men, horses and guns to the frontiers and from there onwards the men and horses were on their own. It is true that 70,000 motor vehicles followed the swing of the German armies through Belgium and northern France, but the French at that time still relied on the horse for all purposes of war. It was an ironic beginning. German fuel difficulties soon asserted themselves in the west, and it was the western allies who were eventually to 'float to victory on a sea of oil.'[6]

ECONOMIC MOBILIZATION AND THE RESOURCE POSITIONS OF THE BELLIGERENTS

The course of economic mobilization to satisfy the requirements of the war followed a similar pattern in all of the principal belligerent countries. Gradual expansion of critical industrial capacity, particularly in the chemical and metallurgical industries, was followed by a gradual expansion of controls over those commodities essential to the production of war materiel.[7] The realization that mobilizing the armaments industries alone would not be sufficient, led inevitably to the extension of centralized control over the national economy as a whole, including, of course, the supply, distribution and use of raw materials.

The extension of control, one of the most important if least understood revolutions of the twentieth century, was carried out in fits and starts in the various countries from the end of 1914 on; Walther Rathenau in Germany, Lloyd George in Britain, Clemenceau in France and Bernard Baruch in the United States were some of the men with whose names this revolution will be forever associated. Those countries, notably Russia, where the military industrial base and the civilian establishment were too weak to carry out this revolution paid the price in the form of national collapse. Where effectively carried out, however, economic mobilization made possible increases in production which would have appeared wholly preposterous before the war. . . . To prove that there are no real limits to the productive forces that it is within the power of modern industrialized economies to unleash— that was the most important single economic lesson of the First World War, as it was of the Second.[8]

From the strategic perspective, the most vulnerable component of such mobilized war economies was the continued supply of sufficient amounts of key raw materials. Prior to the advent of strategic bombing, a strategy based on the restriction of supply through blockade or a *guerre de course* appeared as the most direct and effective means of interfering with an adversary's war economy, and thus his ability to wage a war of attrition.

At the start of the war, Germany and Austria-Hungary possessed Europe's largest reserves of coal, and these were to be augmented by the occupation of important coalfields in Belgium and northern France. The Allied powers, with the important exception of Britain, had relatively insubstantial coal reserves, but had access to oil through sea-borne trade and, in the case of Russia, from domestic production. The relative absence of coal in the west was to be more than adequately offset by the availability of British and later American supplies.[9]

Principal French vulnerabilities included essential chemicals, and after the German advances in the initial phases of the war, iron and steel production. In the case of chemicals, essential supplies had largely been imported from Germany before the war. With regard to steel production, of 125 blast furnaces in France, 95 lay in areas directly affected by the war.[10] Similarly, German occupation of her main coalfields in the Pas-de-Calais and Nord *départments* deprived France of roughly three-quarters of her coal output. As a consequence of this France was compelled to rely on imported British coal.[11] The occupation of French territory also had a severe effect on metallurgy, glass works, textile industries, sugar and industrial alcohol production, and so on. In short, 'the industries that suffered most were precisely those most required for the carrying on of the war'.[12]

In the case of Britain, it was clear that the wartime economy would be dependent on overseas supplies for virtually all raw materials with the exception of coal and half of the anticipated iron ore requirements. Indeed, in the course of the war Britain experienced serious and sometimes critical shortages, particularly during the early stages of the unrestricted German submarine campaign.

Italy's resource problems centred on the provision of adequate energy supplies, particularly in the face of increased consumption by the railways. This problem was made more serious by the reduction in British coal exports as a result of the pressures of war. As in France, hydroelectric power was expanded to meet the demand for energy. These supply problems arose despite the fact that the Italian front remained relatively static and confined to highland areas, and thus was relatively undemanding of energy apart from that supplied by animals.[13]

Russian industry entered the war with a long-standing dependence on imported coal, with the result that the major munitions works around Petrograd were forced to rely on domestic supplies, often from inconvenient points of origin.[14] Russia did, of course, possess considerable oil resources, producing some nine million tons per annum on the eve of the war.[15] This advantage was, however, largely offset by the inability of the inadequately mechanized army to put such resources to use. Moreover, road and rail transport on the eastern front was quite poor, with both German and Russian forces relying largely on horses for mobility.[16] Finally, the transportation of oil from Baku to the distant front in the west 'would have been impossible for the Russian railway network of that time'.[17] Overall, it was not realized in Russia that the conflict would evolve into an 'economic war'. 'Little thought was given to this aspect of the struggle in the days when it was taking shape, and even the necessity for economic war under modern wartime conditions was not fully perceived until the whole structure of the state was affected by it.'[18]

Austria-Hungary, normally self-sufficient in essential raw materials during peacetime, soon encountered formidable shortages of both food and raw materials. The normal balance of production between industrial Austria and agricultural Hungary proved inadequate to wartime demands, largely as a result of inefficient management. Indeed, Austria-Hungary suffered material and agricultural shortages 'earlier and more acutely than her less evenly provisioned ally'.[19] Largely as a consequence of food shortages, the Austrian leadership overcame its initial reluctance to participate in the German occupation of the Ukraine in 1917. Indeed, the Austrians were even more ruthless than the Germans in pursuing the confiscation of food and raw material supplies from occupied areas.[20] For Austria-Hungary, as well as Russia, the possession of substantial raw material resources was more than offset by inefficiency, lack of infrastructure and the inability to exploit key commodities.

Turkey was similarly ill-equipped for the demands of a resource-intensive war. Her principal difficulty was a chronic shortage of fuel. Supplies from Germany were available only on an irregular basis, and the coalfields on the Black Sea coast could only be reached by sea, with the predictable and troublesome result that Russian ships often sank transports *en route*.[21]

German planners were well aware of Germany's weak resource position. Walter Rathenau, for example, highlighted the German dilemma shortly before the outbreak of war:

> ... With natural resources which in the north are moderate and in the south non-existent, with a soil of moderate fertility, and with its economic development destroyed every hundred years by war and invasion, Germany represents the absolute antithesis of America's fortunate physical condition.[22]

Overall, Germany resisted the first phases of the economic war, particularly in the area of wartime finance. It soon became apparent, however, that all the available credits would avail Germany nothing in the face of an effective blockade of vital commodities. This essential vulnerability remained, despite the fact that Germany's pre-war tariff policies specifically encouraged the expansion of domestic industry and agriculture. The German production of iron and steel actually exceeded that of Britain, France, Russia and Italy combined in the years before the war, and the German chemical industry was unquestionably the most advanced. Yet, despite these strengths, Germany was not prepared for prolonged economic war. In addition, Germany's allies represented very doubtful contributors to her national strength, so that Germany was compelled to rely almost exclusively on her own resources.[23]

The German war effort suffered from shortages of a number of important raw materials. Although domestic coal and iron supplies, coupled with those of the occupied and neutral areas, were adequate, a severe shortage of hardening agents such as molybdenum and manganese did exist. More serious were shortages of metals such as copper, nickel, tin and mercury. Aluminium, normally imported from Switzerland and incorporating French bauxite, was now cut off. Finally, tropical materials such as rubber, silk and cotton were unobtainable in Germany, as indeed were such 'essentials' as petroleum, saltpetre, nitrates, graphite and asbestos.[24] Most significantly, Germany was plagued by chronic food shortages due, in part, to a lack of fertilizers. Food shortages, in particular, appeared to have an effect on civilian morale in the later stages of the war.[25] With regard to the supply of resources as well as operational strategy, the loss of Germany's overseas possessions was largely irrelevant. The colonial empire provided few of the raw materials for Germany's industry, and contributed only 0.5 per cent to her foreign trade.[26]

German efforts to enhance her resource security included the establishment of the War Materials Department (*Kriegsrohstoffab-teilung*) of the War Office in 1914 as part of an attempt to rationalize wartime resource management. By the end of the war this department was larger than the rest of the War Office together.[27] Its Director, Walther Rathenau, anticipated the problem of a prolonged conflict and recognized the alarming fact that essentially no concrete measures had been taken to prepare the economy for likely resource interruptions. There was, however, a marked lack of enthusiasm for corrective measures among the general staff, who saw little need for longer-term resource planning in the face of what would most likely be a short war. Thus, in response to a memorandum from a prominent industrialist suggesting the establishment of an economic general staff, Moltke reportedly replied: 'Don't bother me with economics, I am busy conducting the war'.[28]

One of the key programmes encouraged under Rathenau's direction was the accelerated development of synthetic nitrate production for use in the manufacture of explosives and fertilizer (the 'Haber-Bosch' process). The ensuing competition between the agricultural and munitions sectors for the limited production of synthetic nitrates usually favoured the latter, a factor which contributed to the growing food shortage.[29] Another of the more notable achievements in the area of the *Ersatzwirtschaft* or the 'substitute economy' was the development of cellulose as a replacement for cotton in the manufacture of explosives and as a basis for distilled alcohol. Similarly, sulphur was obtained from gypsum, synthetic camphor from turpentine, and *ersatzwool* from wood.[30] The German pursuit of wartime substitutes built upon an existing tradition of strategic substitution dating from the Napoleonic conflict when, for example, beet sugar was widely employed on the Continent as a replacement for unobtainable supplies of cane sugar from the Caribbean.

With regard to energy supplies, the situation of Germany was very different from that of her opponents in Europe. Despite the extension of German control over the mines of occupied France and Belgium, a coal supply crisis emerged early on, with increased supply obligations to allies as a result of the blockade, and overwhelming transport problems. These difficulties were made even more acute by the need to supply two widely separated fronts penetrating a considerable distance into enemy territory.[31]

The withdrawal of Russia from the war opened up new opportunities for Germany to acquire access to badly needed resources, particularly cotton and oil from the Caucasus.[32] Yet, the occupation of vast areas in the east, and the consequent extension of German supply lines, further increased the already considerable burden on transportation. This suggests a partial explanation for the fact that the end of hostilities in the east did not lead to an improvement in Germany's economic situation.[33] From the autumn of 1918, the continued contraction of German fronts led to a most unfavourable situation with regard to vital resources—the continuation of the war without access to Romanian oil, Ukrainian wheat and horses, Serbian copper, and French and Belgian coal.[34]

BLOCKADE AND COUNTER-BLOCKADE

The nature of economic warfare in World War I—the struggle for resource access and denial—is best understood in the context of blockade and counter-blockade.

It was as much a war of competing blockades, the surface and the submarine, as of competing armies. Behind these two blockades, the economic systems of the two opposing groups of countries were engaged in a deadly struggle for existence, and at several periods of the war the pressure of starvation seemed likely to achieve an issue beyond the settlement of either the entrenched armies or the immobilized navies.[35]

As has been suggested, the deliberate restriction of supply to an enemy is a very old aspect of strategy, and a corollary of seeking out an enemy's forces in battle. World War I was to see this aspect of strategy raised to prominence. In the case of Britain, and later the United States, the strategy of blockade flowed naturally from the geographical position of these two countries, the historical absence of large standing armies for intervention on land, and the significant influence both wielded over international trade and resources. Thus, 'close cordon naval blockade, the control at source of raw materials and manufactured goods, preemptive purchasing, strategic embargoes, international economic blacklisting . . . have all been important tactical choices in both countries', loosely collected under the label 'economic warfare'.[36]

At the same time, the relative geographical immunity from attack which the United States and Britain enjoyed encouraged the use against them of similar tactics of economic warfare. Such tactics as counter-blockade (for instance, the 'continental system'), territorial extension to deny imports and exports, and intensive commerce raiding, particularly through submarine warfare, were to be employed as substitutes for the decisive engagement of land and naval forces.[37]

The extent of the Allied naval blockade took German planners by surprise, although, in the event, Germany lacked the sea power to challenge the blockade directly. Throughout the war the Allies added continuously to the list of contraband goods, including commodities which appeared to be entering neutral ports in excess of peacetime requirements. By the end of the war, the list of 'absolute contraband' embraced an enormous number of materials and products, to the point whereby there was virtually no article of commerce which was beyond the purview of the blockade.[38] Moreover, the Allied blockade was maintained at so much greater distance than had previously been imagined as not really to be a close or coastal blockade in the traditional sense at all.[39] Methods of blockade aimed at preventing the passage of materials to the Central Powers via neutrals were made possible, to a great degree, by the dependence of much of the world's commerce on British shipping, and the dependence of much neutral shipping on British coal. Thus, the control over this critical resource served to further the restriction of supply generally.[40]

The strategies of blockade and counter-blockade were logical developments of economic warfare as a component of total war, and were advanced by the use of then new technology including the submarine and the wireless telegraph. Overall, blockade in World War I, and later in World War II, exhibited a number of characteristics: it was (1) a major strategy of total war; (2) implemented over a long period of time; (3) general in nature, with many goods specifically blockaded as contraband; (4) carried out primarily with naval forces; and (5) maintained over long distances.[41]

The economic effectiveness of the blockade was enhanced by the parallel stoppage of German exports such as dyes and finished products with which Germany might pay for those few imports which could be obtained. Indeed, the Allied policy of blockade eventually drove German planners to develop innovative if doubtful approaches to the problem of blockade running. Perhaps the most unusual of these schemes was the development from 1916 of 'trading submarines' to carry small bulk, high value cargoes. Over the course of this short-lived venture one purpose-built submarine made a total of two complete voyages to the United States. By 1917 the six remaining trading submarines under construction were fitted with torpedo tubes for use in the offensive campaign in the Atlantic.[42]

The effectiveness of the economic blockade of the Central Powers was, however, seriously compromised by supplies arriving in Germany through neutral countries. This was particularly true until 1917, when Germany's adoption of an unrestricted *guerre de course* led to the cessation of British trade with Germany's neutral neighbours, as well as the entry of the United States into the war and the consequent cut-off of American sources of supply. The overseas supplies which reached the Central Powers came primarily through Holland, Norway, Sweden, Denmark and, to a lesser extent, the neutral Mediterranean countries.[43] The availability of important supplies such as iron ore from neighbouring neutrals contributed to the German war effort and, indeed, probably contributed to Germany's ability to wage her *guerre de course* in the Atlantic. Ludendorff, for example, speaks of the 'paramount importance' of Swedish iron ore, asserting that a decisive British naval victory 'would have made it almost impossible for us to import iron ore from Sweden and the submarine warfare could never have assumed proportions so dangerous to Britain'.[44]

The effect of the Allied blockade, while significant, was not as impressive as had been anticipated, or at least was not so until very late in the war. Even in the case of food, shortages of which became acute in the winter of 1916–17, the neglect and mismanagement of German agriculture may have been largely responsible.[45] The decline in German domestic food production during the war actually exceeded the loss of supplies from abroad as a consequence of the Allied blockade.[46] With regard to industrial materials, widespread import substitution lessened the potential effect of the blockade on the war economy. Given the 19th-century improvements in land communication, a naval blockade against a largely continental power could be only partially effective in the absence of a parallel land blockade, and this was only to be achieved in complete form *after the armistice*.[47] The wars of attrition on the western and eastern fronts surely had a much greater relative effect on the economy and morale of the Central Powers. Thus, the strategy of resource denial can justly be regarded as a contributing, rather than decisive, factor in the defeat of the Central Powers.

While the Allied blockade was not, in itself, capable of bringing about a decisive victory, the loss of the battle in the Atlantic to the

German submarine campaign could well have led to an Allied defeat in the war as a whole.[48] The German naval war against British shipping, culminating in the unrestricted submarine campaign of 1917, came very close indeed to its objective of crippling the British war economy before being defeated by increased anti-submarine activity, and specifically, the adoption of the convoy system. As early as 1914, German naval strategists were pointing to the possibility of a rapid victory and British willingness for a peace settlement. Pohl, the chief of the German naval staff, stated his conviction that the war was having an enormous effect on the British economy, producing grave shortages of food, raw materials and markets. He further emphasized that Britain could not withstand this pressure over an extended period and, therefore, Germany ought to force Britain to continue the war.[49]

Just as they had looked to the Schlieffen Plan for rapid victory in 1914, Germany's military leadership in 1917 looked forward to the defeat of their adversaries within six months as a consequence of the unrestricted submarine campaign. Thus, Vice Admiral Scheer noted that with the opening of the submarine campaign, 'we now enter a new stage of the war in which the submarine arm is to bring the decision by strangling British economic and sea communications'.[50]

The effectiveness of the German submarine campaign led Admiral Jellicoe to state that the losses in British and neutral merchant ships 'may, by the early summer of 1917, have such a serious effect upon the import of food and other necessaries into the Allied countries as to force us into accepting peace terms, which the military position on the continent would not justify'.[51] In the first three months of 1917 alone, 470 ships were lost, with the effect that neutral shipping began to abandon the North Sea altogether, and those already in British ports frequently refused to clear.[52]

Conventional techniques of commerce protection proved unequal to the task of defeating the submarine threat. Such measures as the arming of merchant ships, camouflage painting and the establishment of patrolled areas proved largely ineffective. As in the Napoleonic experience, only the widespread use of the convoy system, adopted after lengthy debate and delay, led to a significant reduction in losses. The adoption of the convoy system for outgoing as well as incoming voyages led to further immunity against submarine attack.[53] Indeed, it is clear that the convoy decision, together with the expansion of merchant shipbuilding in the United States and Britain, by ending the principal economic threat to the Allied war effort, turned the war of blockade and counter-blockade distinctly in favour of the Allies.

One of the most notable features of the Allied wartime supply situation was the manner in which the United States became the focus for access to vital resources without which the war could not have been continued. Because of its tremendous endowment of food and raw materials such as wheat, cotton, petroleum and copper, as well as its actual and potential manufacturing capacity, the United States emerged as the leading source of wartime supply, particularly for Britain. As early as 1915, the volume of British imports from America was 68 per cent greater than in 1913.[54] For a wide variety of resources, the United States was 'an absolutely irreplaceable source of supply', and with the progress of the war, the focus of decision-making and power with regard to questions of supply and finance inevitably shifted to the United States.[55]

THE INCREASING IMPORTANCE OF OIL IN STRATEGY

With the continuation of the war, oil supplies came to play an increasingly important role, both in the conduct of the war on the western front, and as an objective in the Middle East, Romania and the Caucasus. While the trench warfare in the west remained relatively static, the essential nature of oil supplies did not loom large, as the need for mechanized transport was limited to the supply of fixed lines, rather than mobility in battle.[56] From 1916 onwards, however, army staffs began to pay increasing attention to the expanding requirements for fuel, particularly in the wake of Verdun where the destruction of many railway lines led to a more widespread use of motorized transport.[57]

While possessing a highly developed rail network, Germany was ill-equipped to wage a war in which the increasing use of motorized transport led to ever-expanding demands for fuel oil and lubricants. Prior to the outbreak of war Germany imported some 1 263 000 tons of oil: 719 000 tons from United States; 220 000 tons from Galicia; 158 000 tons from Russia; 114 000 tons from Romania; and 52 000 tons from India. From the outset of the war, nearly all these sources were closed to her.[58] The conquest of Romania in 1916, which held out the promise of improved oil supply, did not significantly relieve the German oil situation due to the widespread destruction of oil facilities. Moreover, Romanian production was not in itself large enough to make a great contribution to German needs.[59] In this context, General Ludendorff is worth quoting in some detail:

> The constant demand for fuel in the army and navy in the World War caused me not a little concern, for its lack was noticeable everywhere, and to procure it, just as the supply of foodstuffs, was one of the goals pursued by the conquest of Wallachia. Though the oilfields in Romania had for the most part been destroyed, a considerable amount of power for light motors and for aircraft had been supplied by the conquered country. The need, however, progressively proved so great that in 1918 I was compelled to turn to Transcaucasia. In consequence of the progressive mechanization of the Army, of the introduction of oil as fuel on battleships, and of the manufacture of air weapons, the demand for motor fuel and lubricating oil had since risen enormously.[60]

Although the German General Staff found Romanian oil to be useful following the conquest of that country, other sources suggest that there was no real question of strategic cause and effect.[61] Thus, in a rather different tone, Ludendorff also commented in 1933:

> The subjugation of Romania was a military necessity for us, and we took economic advantage of the conquest *en passant*. We should never under any circumstances have attacked Romania to seize her economic resources . . . although, of course, orders were given to avoid unnecessary destruction, particularly in the oilfields.[62]

The increasing use of tanks and aircraft in the later stages of the war brought about a further dramatic increase in the importance of adequate oil supplies. The severe shortage of oil probably contributed to the German reluctance to adopt the tank, as well as the relatively slow expansion of her aircraft production in comparison to that of the Allies.[63] The substantial supplies available to the Allies from Western Hemisphere sources made a very important contribution to the outcome of the conflict. With the mechanization of armies, 'oil and its products began to rank as among the principal agents by which the Allies would conduct the war and by which they could win it'.[64] The role of these supplies is well illustrated by Lord Curzon's frequently quoted remark: 'Truly posterity will say that the Allies floated to victory on a wave of oil'.[65]

In 1917, however, the security of this wave of oil, of which the Allied land and naval forces consumed some eight million tons of petrol and eight million tons of heavy oil respectively per year, appeared highly uncertain.[66] Germany, deprived of adequate oil supplies by the Allied blockade, was engaged in a campaign to reduce her adversaries to a similar crippled condition through a *guerre de course* aimed at the vital Allied 'sea train' of tankers.[67] The Admiralty director of stores commented in September of that year that 'without the aid of oil from America our modern oil-burning fleet cannot keep the sea'.[68] Indeed, in May 1917, the Grand Fleet had to suspend its training cruises and battle exercises in an effort to conserve fuel.[69] The oil situation appeared critical enough at one point to lead to the suggestion that the Royal Navy should revert to the construction of coal-fired ships.[70] The oil supply crisis of 1917 also led to Clemenceau's pointed note to President Wilson in which he appealed for additional oil supplies from America, stating:

> A failure in the supply of petrol would compel the immediate paralysis of our armies, and might compel us to a peace unfavorable to the Allies. . . . The safety of the Allied nations is in the balance. If the Allies do not wish to lose the war, then, at the moment of the great German offensive, they must not let France lack the petrol which is as necessary as blood in the battles of tomorrow.[71]

In the event, the United States answered the appeal for oil, eventually providing over 80 per cent of the Allied requirements for petroleum products, together with the essential tanker capacity to bring these supplies to Europe.[72] Other expedients, such as the use of the ballast tanks of liners and cargo vessels as fuel-carrying 'double bottoms' also contributed to relieving the pressure on oil supplies.[73]

There can be little doubt that the control of oil played an important part in the outcome of the war, and it is clear that fuel shortages imposed significant constraints on German action. In particular, it is likely that the German offensive in the spring and summer of 1918 would have been pursued with more vigour and success had adequate fuel supplies been available.[74] At sea, the lack of adequate oil supplies appears to have reduced German operational effectiveness. In the North Sea the German fleet disposed of relatively few oil-burning cruisers, and thus suffered a considerable disadvantage in cruising range and flexibility due to the limited number of suitable bases for coaling. This undoubtedly contributed to the very limited number of operations conducted by the surface fleet during the war. Even the very important diesel-electric U-boat operations were ultimately, limited by the lack of oil in a protracted conflict.[75]

In the Middle East, Germany's pre-war policies with regard to oil, continental communications, and the role of Turkey as a terminal point in the Berlin-Baghdad line in a future *Mitteleuropa* system remained essentially unchanged throughout the war. As late as 1918, Von Lossow of the general staff was stressing the importance of seizing the Causasus as a bridge between Germany and the oil resources of the Middle East—an opportunity to further German economic autarky which 'might not recur for hundreds of years'.[76]

Britain's desire to safeguard and improve her access to Middle Eastern oil contributed to the formation of strategy, particularly in the later stages of the war. As early as 1914, however, both Britain and Russia were concerned about the security of their respective oil supplies from the Persian Gulf and Baku regions. Indeed, one of the first efforts of Turkish forces based in Basra and Baghdad at the outbreak of war was to attack the pipeline from the oilfields in the Zagros hills to the facilities at Abadan.[77] Allenby's campaign in the Middle East, leading to the defeat of the Turkish forces in Palestine, was motivated in part by the need to protect the route to India and Persian Gulf oil. The protection of the oil facilities at Abadan at the head of the Persian Gulf was an issue of some concern, particularly to the Admiralty. Here the threat was not only from Turkish forces, but from potential local unrest as well.[78] In parallel to the British efforts to safeguard the oil fields and facilities of the Persian Gulf region, Russian forces moved to occupy Azerbaijan to secure Baku against the threat of Turkish attack.[79] Overall, the Middle East was 'indeed the one area where Britain herself was on the offensive', frustrating potential threats to India, ultimately 'rounding-off' her control of the Indian Ocean and gaining the strategically valuable oilfields.[80]

While oil-related issues had been prominent in Admiralty thinking from the outset, it was not until 1918 that the British leadership as a whole became actively interested in Mesopotamian oil as a war aim. Outside the Admiralty, the economic arguments for the extension of British control in Mesopotamia were frequently linked to the potential development of the area as a vast granary under British supervision.[81] The comparative neglect of oil as a factor in British strategic calculations here until late in the war was due, in large measure, to the fact that Britain drew the bulk of her wartime supplies from the United States. The Middle Eastern supplies which Britain did draw on came from fields in southwest Iran which had been under protective occupation by British forces since the outbreak of hostilities with Turkey. The known or likely oil resources of Mesopotamia were as yet largely unexploited.[82]

The introduction of oil supply factors into the formation of British war aims in the Middle East was given considerable impetus by the arguments of Maurice Hankey, Secretary of the War Cabinet. These, in turn, were instrumental in shaping the attitudes of Lloyd George and Balfour, both of whom came to regard Mesopotamia as a vital territorial objective.[83] Shortly before the opening of the second Imperial War Cabinet, Hankey wrote to Balfour:

> As I understand the matter, oil in the next war will occupy the place of coal in the present war, or at least a parallel place to coal. The only big potential supply that we can get under British control is the Persian and Mesopotamian supply. The point where you come in is that the control of these supplies becomes a first class British war aim. . . . Admiral Slade tells me that there are important oil deposits in Mesopotamia north of our present line. I have asked him to let the War Cabinet have any evidence as to the real importance of these deposits as they might have an important influence on future military operations . . .[84]

CONCLUDING OBSERVATIONS ON RESOURCES AND STRATEGY IN WORLD WAR I

While there is little to suggest that resource issues were themselves a 'cause' of World War I, the period 1914–18 witnessed a great expansion in the role of resource factors in wartime strategy. First, the denial of vital resources, or the restriction of their supply, long an aspect of war, became a central component of strategy—not least because of the difficulty of forcing a decision on the western front or at sea. In this respect, one may note a similarity to the manner in which blockade and counter-blockade evolved in response to strategic stalemate in the Napoleonic conflict. Second, the progress of industrialization, and the advances in technology associated with it, led to the rise of mobilization warfare which at once increased the dependence of states on assured raw material and agricultural imports, and provided the means for a very much more efficient interdiction campaign through submarine warfare.

Third, in terms of overall vulnerability to supply disruptions, the increased dependence of war economies on imported resources was, in fact, offset to a considerable degree by the flexibility of industrial-ized economies in adjusting to supply restrictions. The responses to blockade, including conquest, substitution and stockpiling, were both very numerous and very successful, the German *Ersatzwirtschaft* providing a particularly striking example. In certain specific cases such as oil, however, the lack of supply was to prove a serious impediment—pointing to the lesson which would be demonstrated again in World War II, that the loss of a single particularly vital resource may have a disproportionate effect on the functioning of the war economy.

Fourth, as objectives of strategy, resources played a measurable role, especially in the case of oil supplies in Romania, the Caucasus and the Middle East. Indeed, the growing importance of mechanized transport and aviation in the later stages of the war raised the actual and perceived strategic value of oil resources enormously.

Fifth, the war experience pointed to yet another lesson which was to be reinforced in 1939–45, that a general conflict in Europe could no longer be resolved with reference to European resources alone. The progress of the war saw the focus of resource supply and decision-making shift decisively to the United States. In particular, the tremendous expansion of the US merchant marine as a conduit for Allied supply was to have significant implications for the future.

For Germany, as well, a key lesson, and one which was to give impetus to 'geopolitical' and autarkic thought in the interwar period, was that a policy of resource access through *continental* expansion and economic integration would be essential to offset the substantial and diverse sources of supply available to the great maritime powers. Finally, for the Allied powers, it was clear that access to essential sources of supply for food, energy and other raw materials still rested critically on the maintenance of command of the sea, or to be precise, control of vital sea lines of communication when and where neces-sary. Thus, particularly with regard to resource access, 'sea power in its elements was truly the foundation upon which the eventual Allied victory in World War I was built'.[85]

4 Resource Access and Denial in World War II

As the experience of World War I demonstrated, the motives for waging war by the denial of vital resources are very strong in the context of conflict between highly developed industrialized economies. It was also made clear that the range of defences available against such a strategy can be highly effective. At the same time, the increasing mechanization of military forces and the expansion of aviation, and the consequent increase in dependence on assured raw material supplies—especially oil—thrust resource questions to the forefront.[1]

Since Allied strategy in World War II was designed to exploit the weakness of the Axis resource position, and Axis strategy designed to hide it, and since German strategy was similarly designed to restrict supply to the British economy, the period 1939–45 provides an excellent example of the use of such strategies as well as a test of their effectiveness.[2] In addition, it is useful to review developments in the interwar period from the point of view of the evolution of theory and planning related to resource access and denial as a component of strategy. In doing so, it will be seen that the resource-related planning, especially in the totalitarian countries, was much more intensive than had been the case before the previous conflict, and its influence on wartime strategy considerably more explicit.

Broadly, the theory, planning and conduct of resource-related warfare in World War II can be viewed as a conflict of competing 'geopolitical' doctrines or world views; a clash between the revisionist aspirations and autarkic policies of the self-proclaimed 'have not' states—Germany, Italy and Japan—and the *status quo* orientation of the traditional global powers, resource-rich, although mostly dependent on maritime communications for access to adequate supplies. It was, in many ways, a continuation of and development from, the continental and maritime traditions of resource access and denial, as they had evolved since the 18th century. Standing somewhat outside this structure, but no less concerned with resource questions, was the Soviet Union, sharing many of the autarkic aspirations of the Axis powers, yet endowed with a tremendous if largely undeveloped resource base.

47

The influence of these varying orientations can be seen not only in relation to the planning of war economy, or 'defensive' economic warfare, but also in relation to blockade and other tactics of resource denial as a component of 'offensive' economic warfare.[3] In reviewing the wartime experience, particular attention will be paid in this chapter to the influence of resource issues on 'grand strategy', although the effect of resource factors on operations has been noted where appropriate.

Before turning to specific aspects of Axis and Allied planning and strategy, one should note the contrasting nature of the German and Anglo-American approaches to pre-war economic preparation.[4] The difference, in principle, was that between active centralized planning and 'business as usual'.[5] Prior to the outbreak of war, theory and planning in France and the smaller democracies was rather close to the Anglo-American approach, while Japanese and Italian concepts of preparation generally followed the German pattern. Whereas in Germany there arose a large body of theoretical writing on 'geopolitics' and *Wehrwirtschaft* during the 1930s, problems of economic preparedness, including access to resources, were much less intensively dealt with in English, French or American publications until as late as 1938 or 1939. It can be argued that this contrast 'was in itself a reflection of the difference in actual preparedness policies'.[6]

RESOURCE ISSUES IN GERMAN AND ITALIAN PLANNING

One of the principal lessons of the World War I experience for the professional military in Europe was the absolute importance of broadening the scope of strategic planning to include elements beyond operational strategy and logisitics. This broader approach centred on an assessment of the war potentials of the powers, including their relative strengths in terms of industrial capacity, access to vital raw materials and foodstuffs, and financial resources. The concept of *Wehrwirtschaft* as it developed in Germany in the inter-war years, incorporated these broader elements of strategy, and flowed from the reflections of the General Staff on the reasons for defeat in the 1914–18 conflict.[7] A widely perceived lesson of the previous war from the German perspective (at best, it is a partial explanation for the German defeat) may be expressed thus: 'Hohnzollern Germany entered the war militarily prepared and economically unprepared. She lost the war because of her defective economic potential. The Allied powers won the war because of their superiority in iron, steel and foodstuffs'.[8] One might add to this list the overwhelming Allied superiority in energy supplies, particularly oil.

Looking first at the theoretical underpinnings of the 'new' German concern for access to resources as a component of strategy, it is clear that the rise to prominence of 'geopolitics' and its theorists played an important role. Indeed, Germany's resource position itself provided fertile ground for the development of geopolitical thought. Its roots may be traced to such earlier 19th- and 20th-century theoreticians as Friedrich Ratzel (1844–1904) and Rudolf Kjellen (1864–1922). Ratzel concentrated on the relationship between space, land and the notion of the state as an 'organic' entity. In this conception of the state as an entity which can expand, contract, prosper, and decline in much the same way as a living organism, political geography emerges as the critical means of analysis.[9] Although Ratzel was not in strict terms a geopolitician, he nonetheless contributed a great deal to the development of geopolitics.[10] In particular, his concept of space (*Raum*) was adopted by Haushofer and others, reappearing as the notion of 'living space' (*Lebensraum*) in which the issue of food and raw material supply figures prominently.

Rudolf Kjellen, Swedish professor of history and government, built upon Ratzel's organic conception of the state, adding to it the complimentary notion of economic self-sufficiency or *Autarkie*. Thus, in Kjellen's conception, the quest for space is a natural outcome of the drive for economic autarky which cannot necessarily be achieved within the state's own borders.[11]

Another notable precursor of the interwar geopolitics was Friedrich Naumann, whose influential book *Mitteleuropa* argued for the consolidation of the resources of Central Europe under the control of the German-speaking peoples as a prerequisite for economic autarky.[12] Indeed, Naumann's *Mitteleuropa* corresponded very closely to the maximum extent of the territory held by Germany and her allies in World War I, and was therefore accepted 'by large sections of the German public as a reasonable blueprint of German war aims couched in the language of political geography'.[13]

The arguments for autarky provided by Kjellen, Naumann and the German geopoliticians were substantially reinforced by the experience of economic warfare since 1914. Thus, it is not surprising that the two European countries where the doctrine of autarky was preached with the most zeal in the 1930s, Germany and Italy, were the countries which had experienced on the one hand the effects of a far-reaching blockade in wartime (and, indeed, for a period following the armistice), and on the other, the less drastic but nonetheless significant efforts to apply international economic sanctions.[14] The strategic basis of autarkic objectives was explicitly stated by Hitler in his proclamation to the 1938 Party Congress. In outlining the success of efforts to make Germany 'capable of standing on her own feet', he declared that 'the idea of a blockade of Germany can now be buried as a completely ineffectual weapon'.[15]

The potential vulnerability of Italy to economic blockade was highlighted by Lord Balfour in a speech of 23 December 1921 during the Washington Naval Conference, in which he stated: 'Italy is not an island, but for the purposes of this debate she almost counts as an island. I remember the extreme difficulty we had in supplying her with the minimum of coal necessary to keep her arsenals and factories running during the war. I doubt whether she could feed herself or supply herself or continue as an efficient fighting unit if she were really blockaded and her sea commerce were cut-off'.[16] It is illustrative that in the mid-1930s Italy was completely dependent on imported sources of chrome, mica, nickel, platinum, rubber, tin and tungsten, and almost completely dependent for coal, copper, iron ore, lead, manganese, petroleum, wool and zinc.[17] The fact that Italy received roughly 85 per cent of her imports by sea gave impetus to the fascist conviction that Italy must either dominate or be the prisoner of the Mediterranean.[18]

Even prior to the imposition of economic sanctions by the League of Nations in response to the Italian invasion of Abyssinia in October 1935, the pursuit of increased food and raw material self-sufficiency had been evident in Italian policy. In this effort the Italian empire was expected to provide 'decisive support'.[19] The experience of economic sanctions in 1935 and 1936, though incomplete and of limited effectiveness, served to reinforce the desire for a greater measure of economic independence. As early as 18 November 1935, the date of the application of economic sanctions against Italy, Mussolini had declared that this would be a date which would 'mark the beginning of a new phase in Italian history, a phase dominated by the fundamental postulate of seeking to achieve in the least possible time the maximum possible amount of economic autarky'.[20] By 1938, the pursuit of autarky had become a fixed national policy.[21]

The League sanctions, while prohibiting the export of various strategic minerals to Italy, did not include an embargo on essential oil supplies, the denial of which might have had more significant economic and military consequences.[22] Oil was undoubtedly a commodity of the greatest strategic importance to the continuation of the Italian campaign in East Africa. A committee of experts of the League of Nations had, in fact, estimated that the imposition of a general embargo on oil shipments to Italy would result in the exhaustion of current stocks within three and a half months, a development which might well have halted the campaign in Ethiopia.[23] Overall, the denial of resources, together with a range of other financial and trade sanctions, failed to inhibit Italian aims in Abyssinia, while contributing to Italy's alienation and eventual withdrawal from the League.

In reality, neither German nor Italian planners believed in the feasibility of 'absolute and permanent' autarky. Rather, they aimed at relative self-sufficiency in war essentials.[24] Since *autarky*, that is, self-sufficiency in any literal sense, was impossible, *autarchy*, that is, the power to control one's own destiny, became the actual basis for policy.[25] Thus, pre-war German efforts to create trade relationships in the Balkans and with the Soviet Union, and later, to acquire resources through territorial expansion and trade with neutrals, can be viewed as a means of securing *autarchy*. Moreover, such freedom of action was seen as being impossible for Germany to secure under conditions of dependence on the traditional regime of international trade—a situation which was perceived to bear 'within itself the greatest danger to Germany of political encirclement, economic starvation, and attack from all sides'.[26] Under these conditions, German control of middle Europe was portrayed as a defensive necessity.[27]

The school of geopolitics which developed in Germany between the wars, led by Karl Haushofer, was built upon the foundations provided by Ratzel, Kjellen, Mackinder and others, with the admixture of National Socialist concepts of *Volk* and race. 'Geopolitics was groomed to bring geography to the service of a militarized Germany. Its functions were to collect geographic information, to reorient it to serve the purposes of the government, and to present some of it to the public in the form of propaganda.'[28] Haushofer and his followers adopted Mackinder's theory of the Heartland to demonstrate that Germany's path to power lay in the consolidation of the German and Russian 'greater areas'.[29] This heartland, reaching from the Elbe to the Amur, was the base for German military expansion. 'It is—with the riches of the Ukraine, the Caucasus and the Urals—the nearest thing to the ideal state of German economic self-sufficiency.'[30]

Hitler's policy was deeply rooted in the notion that it would be impossible for Germany to build a war economy commensurate with great power status within her historical boundaries, and this conviction was made increasingly explicit in his writings and speeches. Although *Mein Kampf* addressed this issue solely in the context of agriculture, the problem of raw materials was addressed in the *Zweites Buch* (1928) and by 1934, in conversations with Hermann Rauschning, Hitler was stressing the need to free Germany from her 'dependence on the outside world' which was fatal to world power aspiration. In the years to follow, Hitler's attention was repeatedly drawn to the question of resource vulnerability.[31]

The perceived benefits of access to the resources of the Heartland were clearly stated by Hitler in 1936: 'If we had at our disposal the Urals, with their incalculable wealth of raw materials, and the forests of Siberia, and if the unending wheat fields of the Ukraine lay within Germany, our country would swim in plenty'.[32] In 1939 Hitler declared: 'We want to participate in the distribution of raw materials. This is the demand of economic reason and common sense'.[33]

German geopolitical theorists, while acknowledging the benefits to be derived from substitution, stockpiling and other measures, did not expect that economic self-sufficiency, and thereby the power to control the destiny of the state, could be realized within Germany's borders. The raw material and agricultural short-fall could only be eliminated through expansion; not through the acquisition of far-flung colonies, but rather through the construction of a colonial empire in Europe itself.[34] In a similar manner, with a view towards the resources of the greater Mediterranean area, Mussolini asserted that fascist Italy 'must expand or suffocate'.[35]

An important follower of Haushofer in the field of 'military-geographical education' (he studiously avoided the use of the term 'geopolitics') was Ewald Banse, Professor of Military Science at the Brunswick Technical College and member of the Society for Military Sciences and Military Policies.[36] Banse's writings, to the extent that they were enthusiastically received by German policy-makers and the officer corps of the Third Reich, provide a useful insight into the role of resource issues in Nazi strategic thought. In *Germany Prepare for War!*, published in 1934, Banse argued that the foundation of all economic war is the blockade, which cuts one's enemy off from the outside world and starves him of food and raw materials. Here it was asserted that Britain was the one country to grasp the 'transcendent importance' of this fact from the earliest stages of the previous war—and 'she should not be surprised if it is turned against her in the future'.[37] The shortage or absence of a relatively minor material such as nickel was perceived by Banse as having the potential seriously to limit the German war effort. In the case of a more important commodity such as oil, shortages might well have a paralyzing effect:

> If Germany continues in the future to be cut-off from the oilfields of the world without finding an ally among the powers that control them, she will be unable to carry on a war; for her own supplies have so far proved utterly inadequate . . . the only thing that could restore our freedom of movement would be the liquefaction of coal.[38]

Banse goes on to provide an extensive list of materials without which the prosecution of a modern war, that is, one of huge scale and duration, would be impossible. With regard to the preparation necessary for such a war, a number of alternative approaches were suggested, including: (1) autarky; (2) command of the sea; (3) alliance with states possessing the first two characteristics; (4) conquest of resource-laden areas; (5) stockpiling for a short conflict or until productive areas are acquired; and (6) exclusive reliance on 'national will to survive'. Finally Banse stresses the importance of geographical factors and communications in modern war, especially the ability to carry on a war of movement which required means of transport and supporting resources such as coal and oil.[39]

General Ludendorff, in outlining his vision of 'totalitarian war' acknowledged the importance of economic self-sufficiency as part of the broader point that military power rests on an economic foundation.[40] Yet, Ludendorff failed to realize how little his description of the crippling effects of the Allied blockade on the German effort in World War I accorded with his contention that wars are decided only by the clash of armies.[41] In his definition of total war, Ludendorff emphasized the inevitability of the complete mobilization of the nation under conditions which might be described as a state of siege. In order to assure the availability of the needed military supplies and foodstuffs for the besieged nation, he advocated economic autarky. Overall, Ludendorff's ideas on wartime economics can be characterized as broad generalities dealing with 'the organizational aspect of wartime economics rather than with the strategic possibilities of improving the raw material, food and labor supply of the nation at war through conquest'.[42]

Wehrwirtschaft, the German concept of war economy, has been defined as 'a will and endeavor which aims at superiority over the enemy in a future war in the economic field and by economic methods'.[43] In one view, *Wehrwirtschaft* implied the long-term preparation of the economy so that the production of war material could start quickly enough to bring overwhelming pressure to bear at the decisive moment—that is, 'pressing the starter button'.[44] Others have characterized it as a similarly long-term preparation aimed, however, at the capacity to fight a protracted war.[45]

A leading figure in the development and implementation of *Wehrwirtschaft* was General Georg Thomas who entered the Armaments office in 1928, becoming its chief in 1933. In 1934 Thomas assumed control of the new office of *Wehrwirtschaft und Waffennesen*, remaining Germany's leading expert in the field of economic mobilization until Albert Speer's takeover of the Ministry for Armaments and Munitions in 1942.[46] Thomas defined the field as encompassing 'the measures for the technical economic preparation of the economy for war, and as a preparation for that, the exercise of influence upon the peacetime economy in terms of armaments by those responsible for national defense'.[47] Thomas stressed the relationship between economic factors, including access to resources, and the outcome of a prolonged conflict. Writing in 1936, he declared that 'the course of the world war demonstrated this connection very clearly ... It is sufficient to point out that Germany's economic situation greatly affected her position throughout the war, and in the last resort it was decisive'.[48] Thomas further stated:

> The wrong idea of a short war has already been our ruin once, and therefore we should not let ourselves be guided by the wish-idea of a short war even in this age of armoured aircraft squadrons. Coal, iron and oil will play as great a role in the next war as the magnitude of the operations and the heroism of the troops engaged in them.[49]

Thomas was at the centre of an ongoing controversy between those who favoured the 'armament in breadth' called for in Hitler's programme, and those who argued for a more thorough 'armament in depth'. In support of the latter, Thomas pointed to the grave potential deficiencies in the longer-term supply of essential raw materials. Specifically, he held that Germany could not hope to achieve autarky in strategic raw materials, and that 'if armaments absorbed the resources of Germany's industries, she would not have the foreign credits with which to buy them from abroad'.[50] In retrospect, this argument did not anticipate the opportunities which would be presented by the progressive looting of resources from occupied territories.[51]

A review of Germany's raw material position prior to 1939 suggests that the widespread perception of resource vulnerability, reinforced by the experience of the previous war, was well justified, even if the conclusions drawn from this were less reasonable. Indeed, it has been suggested that if Hitler deferred to the wishes of his General Staff with regard to making more thorough economic preparations for war, 'Germany's second attempt to conquer Europe would have been delayed for five or ten years'.[52]

With the exception of coal, and the basis for all explosives— nitrogen, obtained largely through the synthetic processes developed during World War I—Germany was heavily dependent on imported sources of strategic raw materials. The most serious deficiency was in the area of oil supply; however, iron ore, bauxite, chrome, and nearly all of the various minerals (for example, wolfram) needed for the production of special steels came almost exclusively from abroad, together with other important materials such as rubber and cotton.[53]

Although the raw material position of the country at the time of the Nazi rise to power was clearly unsatisfactory, rather little was done to increase German self-sufficiency before 1936. When, in 1936, Hitler transferred the direction of raw material planning to Goering as Plenipotentiary of the Second Four-Year Plan, he stressed the urgency of expanding the production of 'strategic materials'.[54] In his 1936 directive to Goering, Hitler suggested that raw material needs could not be met satisfactorily through imports due to a shortage of foreign exchange, the bulk of which was required for food imports. 'The only alternative was to increase the domestic production of raw materials. . . . Complete self-sufficiency in raw materials he recognized was out of the question; a permanent solution of the raw material problem could only come through conquest.'[55] In a similar tone, Hitler also asserted that 'a final solution of the food problem can only come through an expansion of living space'.[56]

The Four-Year Plan of 1936 was designed to put in place the basis for a wartime resource regime in its military, economic and political aspects. The Plan had as its objectives the reduction of Germany's dependence on foreign sources of raw materials, particularly rubber, iron ore and oil, as well as the consolidation of National Socialist control over industry (the political aspect). As part of the Plan, works were built on the Brunswick Plain to exploit concentrations of low-grade iron ore in the Hanover area. Special facilities were required to make use of these ores, in contrast to the higher grade Swiss and Swedish imports. Even during the war, Germany would continue to rely on Sweden for roughly ten million tons of iron ore per year.[57] The increased production of synthetic materials such as rubber, benzene and oils was also emphasized.[58]

Great efforts were made to expand oil supplies, both crude oil and that produced synthetically from coal. The latter consisted of the Bergius or hydrogenation process, important for the production of aviation fuel as well as diesel oil and motor spirit, and the relatively less important Fischer-Tropsch process which also contributed to the production of synthetic chemicals.[59] By 1939 seven Bergius, seven Fischer-Tropsch and a number of tar distillation and carbonization plants were in operation. The number of such facilities would be increased to 18 Bergius and nine Fischer-Tropsch plants by 1943. Thus, by the outbreak of war, Germany was the only country to be producing synthetic oil on a significant scale.

Nonetheless, Germany's total oil production and import level in 1939—roughly seven million tons—was still relatively small in comparison to Britain, with imports of 12 million tons in the same year. The United States and the Soviet Union, with large indigenous crude oil resources, produced 164 and 29 million tons respectively. The German economy had become accustomed to relatively low levels of supply, and its strategic planning acknowledged this by anticipating that oil requirements for successive short campaigns could be met in part by withdrawals from inventories.[60]

At the beginning of the war, with trade links severed by the imposition of the Allied blockade, German planners sought to increase oil supply security through a combination of the following measures: stockpiling; increased imports from Europe, principally from Romania and, for a time, from the Soviet Union; the expanded production of domestic crude oil and synthetics; and conservation in the civilian economy. These measures, which would be coupled later with the seizure and exploitation of resources in occupied areas, resulted in an oil supply for 1941–43 which was significantly greater than pre-war levels.[61] Shortages would appear, however, in specific products such as aviation fuel, the requirements for which increased dramatically with the outbreak of war. Throughout 1941 the *Luftwaffe* would be able to support itself by drawing on stocks in relatively short operations. From 1942, however, this would become increasingly less practical as the demands of the war on the eastern front and the air defence of the Reich become more pronounced.[62]

The experience of shortages in World War I led the Nazis to place a high priority on the expansion of domestic agricultural production. On the whole, efforts in this field were successful; between 1932 and 1939 agricultural production was increased by nearly 20 per cent without increasing the amount of land under cultivation. This effort enabled Germany to reduce imports of foodstuffs, so that with the serious exception of fats and oils, adequate food supplies were at hand at the outbreak of war.[63] German planners anticipated that expansion in the east would contribute very significantly to the food supply of the Reich. In the event, hopes of agricultural exploitation in Eastern Europe and the Ukraine (the latter, in particular, having an almost 'mystical significance' in German planning) were dispelled by the severe decline in productivity experienced in these areas. As a consequence of this, the economic reality of continued acceptable levels of agricultural productivity in France, Denmark and The Netherlands 'made Western Europe the substitute for dreams of agrarian empire in the east'. Food imports would, in fact, be sufficient to avoid serious supply problems within the Reich itself until 1944–45.[64]

Overall, the pre-war drive for economic autarky was most successful in the areas of agriculture, rubber and aluminium production. By contrast, the iron ore and oil programmes represented notable failures in the quest for strategic self-sufficiency.[65] By 1937 the announced goal of self-sufficiency in oil supply through synthetics was very far from being achieved.[66] Thus, continued access to foreign sources for raw materials would remain an important consideration through the outbreak of war and beyond. Shortfalls in domestic programmes aimed at increased autarky led to greater emphasis on securing Germany's access to strategic imports through trade agreements, particularly with the Balkan countries and the Soviet Union. With regard to the latter, it is clear that the main objective of the Nazi-Soviet Pact of 1939 was to reduce the likelihood of war on two fronts. It is also clear that the opportunity to establish access to Russian resources, including oil, foodstuffs, textiles, and non-fuel minerals played a role in the formation of German policy towards the Soviet Union. Prior to 1939, Germany had imported only minor amounts of such materials from the Soviet Union.[67]

The economic aspects of the *Vorfeldkaempfe* or 'preliminary fighting', including the annexation of Austria and Czechoslovakia, as well as the extension of German influence in Spain, should also be noted. The occupation of Austria and Czechoslovakia made an effective blockade of the Reich more difficult, and facilitated German access to the food, oil and ore resources of Southeastern Europe.[68] At the same time, a close relationship with Francoist Spain allowed greater access to Spanish iron ore, pyrites, wolfram and mercury. Hitler clearly suggested this in a speech of 26 June 1937, in which he admitted that the battle in northern Spain was being waged primarily to secure ore supplies to the Reich.[69]

RESOURCE ISSUES IN BRITISH AND AMERICAN PLANNING

The 1930s saw the rapid emergence of 'economic warfare' as a central pillar of strategy in Britain and also in the United States. The very high hopes placed on economic warfare as a component of strategy may be judged from the fact that the term itself had hardly entered into use before there appeared in Britain a Ministry of Economic Warfare (MEW).[70] For the purposes of British planning, economic warfare was interpreted as a 'military operation, comparable to the operations of the three services in that its object is the defeat of the enemy, and complimentary to them in that its function is to deprive the enemy of the material means of resistance'. Three broad categories of economic warfare were envisioned: first, legislative action designed to influence activities within the belligerents' own territories; and second, diplomatic action aimed at controlling the activities of neutral countries which serve as sources or conduits for the supply of raw materials to the enemy. Finally, military action 'in the broadest sense' would be used to interfere directly with the enemies' access to essential supplies from overseas, either by destroying them *en route* or by preventing their distribution and use after arrival.[71]

The concept of economic warfare, based on the experience of the Allied blockade of the Central Powers in World War I, began to appear more frequently in the papers of the Committee of Imperial Defence (CID) in the mid-1930s. It also received considerable impetus from the confluence of three organizational developments. First, an Advisory Committee on Trade Questions in Time of War was set up in 1919 as a successor to the wartime Ministry of Blockade in order to consider issues of economic sanctions and pressures in war. This committee was to become increasingly active from 1935 through the outbreak of war.

Second, the establishment by the CID of the Principal Supply Officers Committee in 1924 created a 'machinery and habit of constant and sympathetic' consideration of supply problems in wartime. The committee's responsibilities embraced both the monitoring and preparation of the domestic war economy, and arrangements for prohibiting the export of critical materials to the enemy.[72] The third development was a response to evidence of growing interest in the economic aspects of warfare abroad, and particularly in Germany. In the winter of 1929–30, a small staff was established to study these issues, leading to the establishment of the Industrial Intelligence Centre in 1931.[73] Taken together, these measures set the groundwork for what might be seen as a pragmatic version of *Wehrwirtschaft*.

At the same time bodies such as the Shipping Defence Advisory Committee (SDAC), formed by the Admiralty in 1937, began to outline the requirements for enhancing the security of sea-borne trade in wartime, through such measures as the arming of merchant ships and the formation of convoys.[74] German naval forces, it was perceived, would certainly attempt once again what they had come close to achieving in the previous war, the 'starvation and strangulation of Britain' by cutting-off her essential overseas resource supplies. Moreover, with the outbreak of war, the enemy would now be in possession of better bases and could command a greater variety of means for waging economic warfare. Germany could bring aircraft as well as submarines to bear on British shipping, and could also mine and bomb British ports.[75]

Britain's dependence on foreign sources of food and raw materials was not substantially different in the 1930s from what it had been prior to World War I. This position of vulnerability was obvious in any comparison of relative self-sufficiency among the major powers. Britain did, however, have the advantage of access to overseas sources of supply which were likely to remain available in time of war. In the case of Germany, by contrast, it appeared that continued access to many such sources would be doubtful. Thus, for Britain, the critical requirement remained, as it had long been, the ability to prevent the closure of vital sea lines of communication—together, of course, with the ability to pay for essential imports.[76]

The increasing emphasis on economic warfare, particularly the restriction of supply of vital resources, as a critical component if not the principal thrust of British strategy in the late 1930s was supported on the theoretical level by arguments such as those put forth by Liddell Hart in a series of articles appearing in October 1937. Here, he suggested that Britain accept the notion of 'limited liability' in her military strategy, with a renewed emphasis on her traditional policy of blockade and economic warfare, for which she was well suited by virtue of her naval strength.[77]

These developments did not pass without notice in the United States, where the period of neutrality saw the development of what was to become, with entry into the war, the Board of Economic Warfare (later the Foreign Economic Administration). The purpose and policies of this organization were roughly comparable to those of the British MEW.[78] It is not surprising that the two predominant naval powers were to focus on the strategy of blockade as a means of bringing their maritime superiority to bear on a strategic situation in which there would be little opportunity for the early engagement of enemy forces on land. Moreover, as has been discussed, the Allied strategy of blockade flowed from a long tradition of resource denial in war. Finally, the perceived weakness of the enemy raw material base, together with the development of strategic air power, was seen to present new opportunities for the application of economic warfare.[79]

Not only had Germany lost important resource-bearing areas which she had possessed in 1914, but it was also thought that the material demands of war would now be even greater than they had been in the previous conflict. The self-proclaimed German drive for resource self-sufficiency in the 1930s, together with the considerable literature devoted to *Wehrwirtschaft* and the many works appearing outside Germany which analyzed Nazi resource weaknesses, supported the belief that the German war economy could be thoroughly disrupted by a strategy of resource denial.[80] Japanese vulnerability in this sphere was even more evident and, indeed, the alarmed reaction in Japan to the threat of embargo 'only added strength to the conviction that here was a new and valuable dimension in which a modern war could be fought'.[81]

The Anglo-American approach to war economy placed in clear relief the problem of resource self-sufficiency versus world trade. Plans and policies directed at self-sufficiency, not to mention autarky, were perceived as running counter to the objective of economic efficiency. In this sense, the contrast with German, Italian and Japanese concepts of war economy could not be more complete. Whereas the totalitarian states viewed dependence on the international system of trade as a fundamental source of vulnerability and a limitation on national aspiration, British and American planners naturally saw access to food and raw materials through trade as a source of strategic advantage—provided, of course, that lines of communication for vital resources, as well as the ability to pay for imports, would remain relatively secure.[82]

Resource considerations, increasingly central to strategic thought in Europe, had been receiving attention in the United States as well.[83] Despite the abundance of food and other strategic resources in the United States, the Industrial Mobilization Plan of 1933 recognized the fact that significant amounts of important commodities, particularly tropical products, must be obtained from abroad. Thus, it was stated that 'plans for procurement of the raw materials necessary to meet the procurement program must be made on the basis that the U.S. has lost control of the sea. The consequence of this would be the development of shortages of certain raw materials which are known as strategic'. The raw material situation of the US in time of war would be relatively well defined; the principal planning concern being the proper execution of tenable solutions to any specific procurement problems which might arise. The resource-related aspects of coalition warfare also merited attention:

Although the raw material position of territorial Britain is most precarious, that of her Empire is not only comparable to ours in many ways, but largely complementary. . . . With two or three possible exceptions, the United States would have no problem of procurement in time of war so long as the British, possessed of their Empire, were either allied or neutral. For aside from the question of possible difficulties in transport, through a shortage of shipping facilities, those sections of the world normally under British naval control are the most important sources of our strategic raw materials.[84]

American pre-war raw material planning emphasized the encouragement of domestic production, with relatively little effort in the direction of stockpiling programmes. Prior to 1939 US policy was based largely on 'economic and political circumstances which did not view the possibility of a real shortage of raw materials'.[85] The economic nationalism of the era contributed to this orientation, since large-scale purchases of foreign raw materials necessary for the construction of a viable stockpile would certainly have proven politically unpopular. Only with the outbreak of war in Europe did growing awareness of the potential threat to national security implicit in the resource question lead to concrete policies designed to enhance the raw material position of the United States. The Strategic Minerals Act of 1939 provided the basis for the further development of domestic reserves of strategic minerals, authorized the stockpiling of essential materials, provided financing for the expansion of mineral-related facilities, and authorized the Export-Import Bank to make loans in Latin America for the development of natural resources.[86]

Among the materials deemed 'strategic' by American planners in 1939 (many more materials were rated as merely 'critical' or 'essential') were the ferro-alloy metals chromium, manganese, nickel and tungsten; the non-ferrous alloys antimony, tin and mercury; the non-metals mica and quartz crystal; and tropical products such as coconut shell, manila fibre, quinine, rubber and silk.[87] With regard to producing areas, the western Pacific occupied a unique position in the supply of raw materials to the United States. The vital importance of this area was clear given the fact that virtually all of the world's supply of seven of the 'strategic' materials listed above was produced there. Mineral supplies from Africa, and the Atlantic shipping lanes associated with these, were also of considerable importance. Finally, the resource contribution of South America, though growing, was still largely a potential one in 1939. Canada, Mexico, Cuba and the Soviet Union (which supplied the bulk of American manganese imports since 1929) also represented important sources of strategic, critical and essential materials.[88]

Following the American entry into the war, Nicholas Spykman would emphasize the point that even the vast resources of the North American continent, together with existing stockpiles, might not be sufficient for effective prosecution of the war without access to vital overseas sources of supply. Writing in 1942, Spykman asserted that access to these supplies would, in turn, depend on continued Allied control of principal sea lanes, and in particular on the continued survival of Britain.[89] Should the German-Japanese alliance be successful across the oceans, that is, in the event of 'hemisphere encirclement', the raw material situation of the US would become perilous. In this worst case of the encirclement and blockade of the Western Hemisphere, Spykman argued that it would be exceedingly difficult for the US to maintain a war economy adequate for defence. Moreover, the ability of the US to fall back on hemispheric sources of supply alone would depend very much on the prospects for the economic integration of North and South America—and there were obviously clear political and other obstacles to this.[90] Consistent with this view was a statement by Cordell Hull in 1942 that 'the difficulties which we now experience in securing some of our essential imports provide an added unanswerable refutation to those who indulge in reckless assertions that our country can isolate itself from the rest of the world and prosper'.[91]

With regard to pre-war sources of raw materials for the British economy, the most important source area, in quantitative terms, was that which included Africa, Asia and the Antipodes; the least important at that time was the American continent. With the outbreak of war, Europe briefly became the most attractive area for procurement given established trade relations and the dollar shortage. Wartime developments, however, rapidly compelled Britain to seek increasing amounts of vital raw materials from America. Thus, the American contribution to Britain's raw material supply rose significantly, from only 8 per cent in 1939 to 37 per cent by 1941. Also noteworthy is the fact that raw material imports from America in this early period of the war were, with some exceptions, such as steel and timber, of secondary importance to imports of food and munitions.[92] This growing dependence on North American sources coincided with increased demand for resources in both the US and Canada as defence production was expanded, and was a direct consequence of the loss of all of Britain's 'near' supplies with the exception of those from the Iberian peninsula.[93]

The threat of shortages arising from the competing demands of North American production, together with the Japanese advance in the Pacific which cut off valuable Far Eastern sources of supply (for example, rubber, hemp and tin), made active co-operation and co-ordination between Britain, the US and Canada a clear necessity. The supply problems flowing from the Japanese advances in Asia were of a fundamentally different sort than those which had been presented by the German conquest of Europe. The events of 1940 led to the loss of valuable sources of a large number of materials, the replacement of which was possible but posed severe foreign exchange difficulties. The Japanese offensive, by contrast, while leading to a dramatic cut-off of the principal Allied source of certain vital materials such as rubber, 'left the balance of supplies for the majority of materials unaltered'.[94]

The entry of the US into the war made possible, and even more imperative, the establishment of comprehensive machinery for co-ordinating the expansion and allocation of resource supply. A co-ordinated approach was equally necessary to assure continued

American access to British sources of supply. As suggested earlier, American dependence on the British Commonwealth extended to significant amounts of a number of resources, including chromium, industrial diamonds, mica, graphite, cobalt, manganese, lead, tungsten, nickel, tin, rubber, jute and sisal, asbestos and bauxite.[95] The effective allocation of Canadian resources was also of importance.[96]

Even prior to Pearl Harbor, there had been informal co-operation on resource supply involving such figures as Sir Arthur Salter, Jean Monnet and Bernard Baruch. In October 1939 Britain and France had agreed to establish five permanent executive committees for the co-ordination of the supply of food, armaments and raw materials, petroleum, aircraft and shipping, and 'to ensure the best use, in the common interest, of the two countries' resources of raw materials . . . and to share fairly between the two countries any cuts that may be imposed'. In this way, the Allies began in 1939 where they had left off in 1918.[97]

During 1941 the shifting of the emphasis of economic warfare from the control of resources at sea to control at source made necessary increased co-operation between Britain and the US, both to secure access to strategic materials and to deny them to the enemy.[98] Thus, from the outset, the control of resources as a component of coalition warfare had both offensive and defensive characteristics which frequently overlapped. This interaction was most evident in the co-ordinated pre-emptive purchasing which was carried out extensively, particularly with regard to minerals in Latin America and elsewhere.

The establishment of the Combined Raw Materials Board on 26 January 1942, formalized and expanded Anglo-American co-operation in the resource area.[99] 'The Board was given comprehensive responsibility for the planning of the raw materials effort of the two countries and for collaboration with the other United Nations to provide for the most effective utilization of all raw material resources at their disposal.'[100] From January 1942 to December 1945 the Board produced 457 series of recommendations covering the supply, purchase and distribution of some 50 important war materials.[101] Although the central activity of the Board was the allocation of materials in the face of shortages, the expansion and development of sources of supply was also dealt with successfully across a broad range of resources.

RESOURCE ISSUES IN SOVIET PLANNING

The enormous resource endowment within the continental expanse of the Soviet Union meant that it shared with the United States the potential of achieving virtual self-sufficiency in food and many raw materials. Moreover, the geographical position of the Soviet Union, while providing extensive strategic depth, precluded ready access to such imports as might be necessary in wartime. This had been clearly illustrated during World War I when the Allied Powers, shut off from the western approaches to Russia, found great difficulty in transporting material for her resupply (the Murmansk Railway had not been completed by the time of the Russian withdrawal from the war).[102] The principal problems of supply for Russia in World War I had been ones of internal organization, particularly with regard to industrial capacity and transport.[103] Much of the Soviet industrial capacity, and the bulk of her sources of supply would, however, enjoy the advantage of relative immunity to strategic air attack, a fact which was noted by German planners in the 1930s, together with the course of Soviet military and industrial policy which took considerable advantage of the opportunities for strategic dispersal.[104]

Soviet policy in the interwar period had achieved an enormous expansion of industrial capacity, with the equipment of the armed forces given first priority.[105] Parallel to the drive for industrialization was a concerted effort to further economic self-sufficiency in the face of perceived vulnerability to a coalition of 'hostile powers' and the requirements of 'building socialism in one country'. The quest for autarky, not unlike that pursued by Germany, Italy and Japan in the 1930s, was given additional impetus by the experience of blockade in the period of the Western intervention following World War I. Overall, the largest possible measure of resource self-sufficiency was sought during the interwar period.[106] By 1939, for example, the Soviets would claim, somewhat inaccurately, that the Soviet Union was the first country to solve the problem of the manufacture of synthetic rubber in actual practice.[107]

As V. D. Sokolovsky states in *Soviet Military Strategy* (and here one should not discount the possibility of a certain amount of *ex post facto* rationalization) the period between the Civil War and the 'Great Patriotic War' was of great importance in the development of Soviet military theory and forces, and this process 'was closely allied

with the economic and political strengthening of the Soviet State. . . .
The strengthening of our military-economic foundation was also
expressed in the increased amount of state reserves and mobilization
reserves of strategic raw materials, assuring the functioning of the
national economy for two or three months and up to four months for
certain types of raw materials'.[108]

The leading figures in the formation of Soviet strategic doctrine in
the 1920s and 1930s were clearly aware of the unique economic
circumstances of the Soviet Union and the need for strategy to reflect
resource considerations. H. V. Frunze, as Commissar for War, was
largely responsible for introducing the military reforms of 1924–25. In
his lectures, Frunze emphasized the need for economic mobilization;
technical backwardness and incomplete industrialization 'formed the
crucial issue around which the Soviet command had to adjust its point
of view'. Similarly in 1928 Tukhachevsky had outlined the emerging
consensus that 'total war' required the mobilization of all aspects of
the power of the state. It was asserted, for example, that diplomacy
could make a great contribution to war planning and effort by
managing the relations of the Soviet Union so that certain strategic
objectives could be achieved. Thus, a blockade could be rendered
'less than total' through diplomatic measures, 'so that a portion of the
capitalist world would be applying its strength toward assisting the
struggles of the Soviet Union'.[109] Although the frequently reiterated
Soviet notion of 'military science' embraced economic and other
factors beyond operational strategy ('military art'), it is curious that
resource and economic factors are not specifically mentioned among
Stalin's 'permanently operating factors' in war.[110]

It was acknowledged that fundamental problems remained in the
effort to further the 'forced development' of the Soviet defence
industrial base. These included the development of indigenous raw
materials and strategic items, the establishment of a metallurgical
base, the problems of strategic location and dispersal, and the role of
foreign purchasing commissions and non-Soviet technical aid. The
first stage of the 'military-industrial plan' did, in fact, draw on foreign
sources to a considerable degree, as in the German-Soviet negotiations for technical and financial assistance in 1929–30, culminating in
a major agreement with Rheinmetall.[111] Overall, however, the Soviet
leadership consistently placed great stress on drawing strategic
materials, to the extent possible, from sources over which there was
direct Soviet control.[112] The central issue was perceived to be the
development of 'that super-abundance of resources indigenous to the

Soviet Union into the autarky which was so essential' to waging a war of attrition. This need was reinforced by the fact that 'no article of Soviet military dogma envisioned a short or "lightning" war'.[113]

The expansion of Soviet military production in the interwar years, while in excess of what had been imagined in the West, was still short of production levels in Germany or the United States. Thus, while substantial reserves of material had been built up, the power to replenish these reserves remained insufficient to support a long war without the import of large amounts of material from abroad. It was, therefore, of vital importance from the resource security standpoint not to risk a two-front war which would close Russia's supply links to the West.[114]

With the outbreak of war, the Soviet command was faced with the enormous problem of the evacuation of industrial capacity to the east in the face of rapid German advances. Soviet planners realized that the withdrawal of industrial capacity from threatened areas would be 'a matter of life and death' in the event that German forces were to overrun large areas of European Russia. This transfer of industrial capacity in the second half of 1941 and the beginning of 1942 was a very significant achievement. In many instances raw material and food reserves were evacuated as well.[115] Despite the extensive pre-war planning for just such an eventuality (for example, the programme of 'shadow factories'), the economic withdrawal itself took place 'under conditions of very considerable disorganization'.[116]

The difficulties facing Soviet industries in the east included a very serious shortage of certain resources such as molybdenum and manganese. A large proportion of the latter had been mined in the Nikopol region, now under German control, necessitating the development of new mines in the Urals and Kazakhstan.[117] Similarly, molybdenum mines were opened in the difficult steppe terrain of Central Asia. Desperate efforts were also made to increase the production of aluminium, nickel, cobalt, zinc, chemicals and oil in the east.[118] With regard to oil, deposits which had been identified in the Volga-Ural region, removed from the zone of fighting, and the development of which had already been underway prior to the outbreak of war, were rapidly exploited in 1941 and 1942. In the pre-war years, however, the Caucasus fields yielded some 90 per cent of Soviet production, and a successful German offensive in the Caucasus would clearly have posed a threat to the continued mobility of Soviet forces.[119] This, despite the fact that the vast majority of Soviet infantry divisions relied on horse-drawn transport.[120] Increasing Soviet dependence on the mineral resources of the east was paralleled by a similar reliance on eastern agriculture.[121]

As the German advance cut into Soviet resources, particularly coal and electric power, industrial production inevitably declined. By November 1941 the Soviet war economy was experiencing its most critical period of strain. German occupation of the Donets Basin alone deprived the Soviet Union of some 57 per cent of pre-war coal supply. In addition, 68 per cent of pig iron, 58 per cent of steel, 60 per cent of aluminium and 38 per cent of grain production was lost in areas held by the enemy. 'Mass without power' was, therefore, the 'inevitable and inescapable form of the first coordinated offensive fought by the Red Army in 1941–42'.[122]

The Soviet war economy did benefit from those improvements to the transportation infrastructure, particularly in the east, undertaken before the war. Yet, in a country where resource abundance and the potential for relative self-sufficiency would prove the basis for the wartime survival of the Soviet state, transport and communications remained the Achilles' heel.[123]

In those cases where the evacuation of facilities and resources was impossible, a 'scorched earth' policy was brought to bear in accordance with Stalin's instructions of 3 July 1941:

> In case of a forced retreat of Red Army units, all rolling stock must be evacuated; to the enemy must not be left a single engine, a single railway car, not a single pound of grain or gallon of fuel. . . . Collective farmers must drive off their cattle and turn over their grain . . . for transportation to the rear. All valuable property, including non-ferrous metals, grain and fuel which cannot be withdrawn, must without fail be destroyed . . .[124]

It has been suggested that the 'scorched earth' policy was not a planned and well prepared strategy, but rather a policy of desperation.[125] As early as 1941, however, the Soviets did manage to carry out extensive demolitions and destruction of valuable resources, and their denial, coupled with guerrilla actions surely hindered the German economic exploitation of occupied areas. The general decline in productivity in these areas due to the ravages of war also played a major role in the frustration of German hopes with regard to the resources of the east. Yet, despite the considerable achievements of the policy of denial, 'it would be naive to assume that everything of economic importance was withdrawn or destroyed'.[126]

Finally, one may note the importance of Soviet resource exports to German-Soviet relations prior to the German attack. Estimates of such exports suggest that in the period immediately following the Nazi-Soviet Pact substantial supplies of Russian grain, cotton, oil, timber, and most importantly manganese and chromium were arriving in Germany at a time when the British blockade had cut off many pre-war sources of supply. In May and June of 1941, 'when Stalin dreaded more than ever a German attack', vital raw materials such as copper and rubber were being rushed to Germany from the east in an 'an effort of appeasement as frantic as it was futile'.[127]

RESOURCES AND THE EUROPEAN WAR

The heavy dependence of the German steel industry on imports of iron ore from neutral Sweden made the preservation and, if possible, the expansion of supplies from this source an important strategic interest of German planners.[128] At least one economic historian has argued that access to Swedish iron ore was a *sine qua non* for the continuation of the German armaments programme, and that the planned attack on Sweden as part of operation *Weserrubung* in 1940 was dropped for fear of the cessation of ore deliveries (for instance, as a result of strikes or sabotage).[129] Thus, it is argued that 'from the moment she took the field against Poland until her victory over France, Germany could not have done without Swedish iron ore. If the mines of Lapland had ceased working, the blast furnaces of the Ruhr would have shut down too'.[130]

More persuasively, it has been argued that while the supply of relatively cheap Swedish ore (in exchange for German coal) was of undoubted value to the German war economy, its denial would certainly not have 'stopped' the war.[131] As Alan Milward has stated, 'the level of resources of the German economy was such as to quite nullify the effect of any withdrawal of Swedish supply. We must therefore conclude that if the mines of Lapland had ceased working it would, in fact, have made no difference to the course of the war'.[132] Nonetheless, Swedish supplies were of sufficient importance to suggest that one motivation for the Norwegian campaign was to secure the annual ten million tons of ore from Sweden.[133] Hitler was also aware of the likelihood of a pre-emptive British landing in Norway, and the timing of his move against Norway was shaped by the imperative of arriving there first, not least to protect German imports of Swedish ore.[134] The unsuccessful British intervention in Norway in the early stages of the war was intimately connected with the question of the supply of Swedish iron ore. A principal aim of the campaign was to be the interruption of the shipment of Swedish ore to Germany through the port of Narvik, while opening the prospect of British access to these important supplies. Earlier, consideration had also been given to the mining of the sealanes around Narvik, as in 1917–18, to prevent the free transport of ore to Germany.[135]

THE THREAT OF BLOCKADE, CONTINENTAL RESOURCES AND GERMAN STRATEGY

The occupation of the greater part of continental Europe provided Germany with access to a vastly enlarged potential resource base. In principle, *Wehrwirtschaft* could now draw on the resources of the continent rather than those of the Reich alone.[136] Of course, the nations under German control were not, and never had been self-sufficient in resources—the creation of a 'New Order' in Europe could not alter this fundamental fact. With the exception of coal, iron ore, some foodstuffs and a few other basic materials, continental Europe was heavily dependent on access to extra-European sources of supply. The most serious resource liability would emerge in the area of oil supply.[137] Nonetheless, the mobilization of such important resources as Romanian oil meant that Germany's overall raw material situation showed few signs of deterioration in the early years of the war. 'It was, indeed, not until late in 1944 that the production of armaments was seriously threatened by the lack of raw materials, and by that time other factors were of much greater importance.'[138] In the case of Romanian oil, in particular, the very existence of this alternative source of supply would affect the formation of Allied strategy to a considerable extent.[139]

It appears that the German authorities did not perceive any immediate problems with regard to oil supplies until the end of 1941, as the fighting in 1939 and 1940 had been relatively inexpensive in terms of consumption, particularly if one takes into account the large stocks captured in Europe, especially in France. The French failure to destroy these stocks may have had significant consequences as captured supplies are thought to have made a major contribution to requirements for the attack on Russia in June 1941.[140]

In the case of occupied Russia, the tremendous potential accretion of resources posed by the conquests in the east did not fully materialize. As in the case of agriculture, the 'scorched earth' policy adopted by the Soviets, together with transport problems and the failure to establish a secure *Ostwall* behind which captured resources might be more fully exploited, combined to frustrate German hopes of substantial resource gains.[141] Notably, Germany gained rather little from the potentially valuable Russian oilfields, as the Caucasus offensive was halted, and demolitions and guerrilla attacks virtually eliminated the usefulness of the Maikop facilities. Developments in Russia might have led to a serious German fuel shortage if it had not been for the very rapid improvement in the production of synthetic fuels achieved in 1943. Continued expansion of the synthetic fuel industry allowed Germany to meet rising demand until the spring of 1944.[142]

German grand strategy clearly took account of the limited resource position of the Reich, as well as the likelihood of Allied attempts to restrict her access to supplies. In particular, it may be argued that the concept of *Blitzkrieg*, in the strategic rather than the tactical sense, implied a short-war economy and consequently less reliance on the maintenance of costly stockpiles. The sort of mobilization in depth required for a long war would have meant large investments in food and raw material stocks, thus reducing the funds available for military purposes more narrowly defined.[143]

On the other hand, the substantial stockpiles established in Germany prior to the outbreak of war argue against placing too great an emphasis on this interpretation of the *Blitzkrieg* strategy. In addition, it has been suggested that the role played by Goering in economic planning argues persuasively that *total war* rather than *Blitzkrieg* was the strategic objective of German war planning. In this conception, German preparations were directed to the requirements of a lengthy war, in which resource security would play a crucial role. Indeed, the construction of a large air force and navy could be seen as part of this strategy, both to defend against the threat of blockade, and to carry the economic war to the enemy through bombing and submarine campaigns. That German strategy from 1939 was based largely on rapid and continuing improvisation was, in this view, a reflection of incomplete prepration.[144]

While debate continues on how expressly the *Blitzkrieg* strategy was formulated, it is clear that German strategy, whether as deliberate choice or improvisation, led to a series of short offensives in which Germany's weak resource position did not seriously inhibit war economy or operational ability.[145] As an attempt to pre-empt a strategy of blockade, or as a long-term plan for total war, questions of resource access and denial were central to German strategy.

The threat of blockade also affected the organization and equipment of the *Wehrmacht*. The US Strategic Bombing Survey, for example, points out that because of the threat of fuel shortages means of warfare involving heavy oil consumption, such as a fully motorized army, or a great force of heavy bombers, had to be forgone—despite the potential value of such assets to German strategy.[146]

THE DRIVE FOR RESOURCES IN THE EAST

Considerations of economic warfare, including access to resources, most clearly influenced German strategic aims in Russia:

> The parallel with the Napoleonic wars is interesting in this respect as in so many others. Admiral Mahan contended that the British blockade forced Napoleon into decreeing the Continental System, and eventually—when Tsar Alexander refused to cooperate in that program—into his disastrous invasion of Russia. The Nazis also organized a continental system to combat the blockade, and they too found Russia an uncertain collaborator.[147]

One may suggest that the failure to secure anticipated supplies from Russia prior to 1941 (deliveries of oil were particularly disappointing) hardened the determination to seek these supplies through conquest.

> Russia offered a reservoir of food, labor and raw materials to make up for the increasing shortages in these resources in the greater German area. The iron ore was of great importance for it promised to free Germany once and for all from dependence on the rich Swedish ores. Most important of all it offered oil. . . . If war had been avoided in 1939 the synthetic oil program would have provided a very large part of the military oil requirements by the mid-1940's. By 1941 it clearly could not. The acquisition of oil supplies from the Caucasus had become for Goering by June 1941 'the chief economic goal of the invasion.'[148]

In a revealing study dated 13 February 1941, and entitled 'The Effects of An Operation in the East on the War Economy', General Thomas suggested that during the first few months, Germany's food and raw material position would be relieved if a rapid conquest succeeded in preventing the destruction of stocks, capturing the Caucasus oilfields intact, and solving the transport problem. In the event of a longer war, effective resource relief would require the solution of the transport problem; prevention of the destruction of Russian transport assets; prevention of the evacuation of population; the seizure of fuel supplies and power stations; and the securing of the delivery of resources not existing in European Russia. The restoration of adequate supplies of rubber, tungsten, copper, platinum, tin, asbestos and manilla hemp would depend on the re-establishment of communications with the Far East. Thomas also asserted that the area south of the mouth of the Volga and the Don must be encompassed in the operation, as the Caucasus oil supply would be essential for the exploitation of occupied Russia as a whole.[149] Even in the event that the oilfields of the Caucasus could be captured reasonably intact, German planners recognized that formidable transport problems would remain, and that 'the opening of the sea routes and the security of the tankers in the Black Sea' would be the prerequisite 'for the use of Russian supply sources in sufficient quantity to support the further continuation of the war'.[150]

It is noteworthy that two days before the opening of Operation Barbarossa, Hitler declared:

> The course of the war shows that we have gone too far in our efforts to set up an autarky. It is impossible . . . to try to produce by synthetic means all those things we lack. . . . We must follow another course and conquer that which we need. . . . So the aim must be to secure by conquest all areas which are of special importance to our war industry.[151]

Nonetheless, it was not until 1942 that German staff officers themselves began to accept, at Hitler's insistence, the need to concentrate on the resource-related objectives of the southern front.[152]

Another purpose of the second German offensive in Russia, opened on 28 June 1942, was to deny important remaining economic centres to the Soviet Union. Priority was to be given to operations in the southern sector 'with the aim of destroying the enemy before the Don, in order to secure the Caucasian oilfields, and the passes through the Caucasus mountains themselves'.[153]

The German failure to complete the Russian campaign successfully in 1941 does not seem to have been significantly influenced by a shortage of oil supplies, although the lavish use of oil in this campaign probably did make the capture of Russian oilfields in Maikop and Baku a major objective of the 1942 offensive.[154] German planners also appear to have been divided on the issue of whether the drive for the Caucasus was motivated mainly by the need to secure oil for German use, or to deny it to the Russian forces. Elaborate preparations were made, however, in order to restore and exploit captured oilfields as quickly as possible.[155] These preparations proved far from sufficient to overcome the substantial labour and transport obstacles to the exploitation of oil in occupied areas.[156] The Baku fields alone produced two and a half times as much as all of Axis Europe. With the failure of the German campaign in the Caucasus, the hope of obtaining access to substantial oil resources evaporated.[157]

The resource value of the Caucasus region also played an important part in the formation of Soviet strategy in the 'second phase' of the war in the east. As Sokolovsky reports, in selecting the direction of the 'main thrust', the Soviet High Command clearly took into account economic, and particularly resource factors. Thus, the High Command could not disregard two important conditions: first, a main thrust on the southern flank of the Soviet-German front 'would expel the enemy from such economically well developed areas as the Northern Caucasus, the Donbas, Krivoy Rog, Nikopol, and the Eastern Ukraine'; and second, their liberation 'would increase the economic potential' of the Soviet Union.[158]

With regard to Eastern Europe as well, Soviet strategy in the later stages of the war would aim at both the destruction of German forces in the field *and* the capture of territory with important sources of fuel and mineral supplies.[159]

German strategy towards the Balkans was similarly influenced by resource considerations. The advance through the Balkans to Greece would seal off the region, and especially the Romanian oilfields, from Russia and from the British in the Eastern Mediterranean. In addition, while the ferro-alloys of the Balkans were not the primary aim of the campaign, their value was recognized.[160]

In retreat, as well, the desire to obtain and defend resources perceived as vital strongly influenced German strategists, not least Hitler who was clearly obsessed with resources such as the coal of the Donets Basin, often with little practical justification. Thus, despite

the urging of his advisors, Hitler refused to adopt a flexible strategy
with regard to the establishment of a defensive line west of the Don,
especially as German forces were on the threshold of the 'vital
strategic objective of the Caucasus oilfields'.[161] Hitler insisted on the
defence of the Nikopol manganese mines in the Ukraine long after
the military situation had become untenable, and ordered an offensive in Hungary early in 1945 to safeguard the Hungarian oilfields.
Finally, large and well equipped forces were kept in Norway and Italy
to protect economic resources while inferior troops in Germany were
retreating in the face of attack on two fronts. 'Thus, the concern for
raw materials and supplies which had so influenced [Hitler's] war
strategy impelled him in the end to dissipate what military resources
remained to him'.[162]

THE OIL SHORTAGE AND GERMAN OPERATIONS

It is evident that shortages of fuel brought about by the Allied
blockade and, more significantly, the strategic bombing operations
against oilfields, synthetic fuel plants and stockpiles, imposed limitations on German aviation from 1942 onwards. The shortage of
aviation fuel would become critical by 1944, and indeed by the end of
January 1944 the operational ability of the *Luftwaffe* was very
substantially reduced.[163] The shortage of high-octane fuel, although
somewhat offset by technical modifications in the design of German
aircraft engines, reduced potential performance, and imposed limitations on pilot training time. In addition, difficulties in the transport of
the large amounts of petroleum products required by the *Luftwaffe*
almost certainly constrained bomber as well as fighter operations.[164]
It is illustrative that the total amount of fuel suitable for aviation
available to Germany in 1944 was liberally estimated at ten per cent,
or less, of the amount then being produced in the United States.[165]

There can also be little doubt that the mobility of German land
forces was impaired by the lack of fuel, and this is widely cited as
having contributed to the failure of the Ardennes offensive (a major
objective of which was the seizure of oil stocks at Antwerp), and the
inability to halt the Soviet advance into Silesia.[166] The effect of fuel
restrictions on German naval operations was also evident. As early as
November 1941, Admiral Raeder admitted that the *Tirpitz* could not
be sent into the Atlantic for the purpose of commerce raiding

'because of the general oil situation'.[167] So, too, the supply of Axis forces in North Africa in 1942 was severely hindered by a shipping crisis, coupled with a crippling fuel shortage affecting Italian maritime forces and the Italian economy generally.[168]

THE GERMAN *GUERRE DE COURSE*

The lessons of World War I with regard to the potential of the submarine as a weapon of resource denial were not lost on German planners. The massive submarine campaign against Allied shipping formed the basis of the German counter-blockade strategy. Thus, to an even greater extent than in the previous world war, the focus of German naval planning was on commerce raiding. This orientation was reflected in the 'pocket battleship' and E-boat construction programmes as well as the submarine effort.

Admiral Doenitz, as co-ordinator of the submarine programme, observed that the U-boat was 'an ideal weapon of offense' and the 'most suitable weapon for direct attacks on Britain's supply lines. . . . In this way the U-boat came very near to costing Britain the First World War'.[169] In his *Memoirs*, Doenitz states that it was upon these premises that he continued to press for the rapid expansion of the U-boat programme so as to be in a position to strike 'a decisive blow' against Britain's vital supply lines. Without such an expansion, Doenitz argued that Germany must be content with 'pin pricks' against the British merchant navy.[170] German planners also noted that in the previous war insufficient attention had been paid to the interdiction of Allied oil shipments in such areas as the Gulf of Mexico. By contrast, the attack of such shipments was given increased priority in the submarine campaign following the entry of the United States into the Second World War.[171]

As in World War I, German submarines inflicted heavy losses on Allied shipping—eight million tons in 1942 alone—but ultimately failed to sever the sea lines of communication for vital resources across the Atlantic despite the additional vulnerability of shipping and port facilities to German air attack. The very serious threat posed by the active German *guerre de course* persisted at least until September 1943, by which time the Allied naval and air forces had prevailed in the Battle of the Atlantic. In the attempt to bring about the defeat of the Allies through the imposition of a counter-blockade, the German submarine force paid a 'suicidally high' price, losing almost 75 per cent of the total operational force over the course of the war. 'These losses make clear that commerce raiding was not a "cheap" way to victory.'[172]

OIL AND THE ALLIED WAR EFFORT

As in the later stages of World War I, access to American petroleum supplies was essential to the Allied war effort. The expansion of offensive activity through operations in North Africa in 1942, in particular, sharply increased demand for American oil. At the same time, German forces had seized the oil of Romania and two important Russian fields, with the oilfields of the Middle East a potential target for future German operations. These developments, coupled with the occupation of the Pacific oilfields by Japanese forces, raised the possibility that the Allies might shortly become entirely dependent on American sources of oil supply.[173]

The progress of the war had firmly established the overwhelming strategic importance of oil for the mobility of land, naval and air forces. By 1939 virtually all naval vessels and some 85 per cent of the world's merchant ships were fired with oil. To move 100 miles, a typical armoured battalion required some 17 000 gallons of fuel. Such were the oil and lubricant requirements of modern warfare that by 1943 petroleum products accounted for two out of every three tons of cargo shipped to American forces overseas. The US Fifth Fleet consumed 630 million gallons of fuel in two months of operations, and at the peak of the fighting on the western front, the US Army Air Force alone consumed 14 times the total of petroleum shipped to Europe for all purposes between 1914 and 1918.[174] In the face of such enormous demand there was a series of far-reaching American proposals which were aimed at securing (largely post-war) access to additional reserves in the Middle East through government vehicles such as the Petroleum Reserves Corporation established in June 1943 and later dismantled in favour of private sector ventures in the region.[175]

German submarine operations in the Caribbean and along the Gulf and East coasts of the United States, as well as along the Atlantic supply routes, posed the most formidable threat to Allied oil supply. The problem in relation to oil supply was not one of availability *per se*, as in the case of the German supply situation, but rather one of adequate and secure transport. The defeat of the German *guerre de course* in the Atlantic through more effective anti-submarine warfare, together with a tremendous expansion of tanker construction, ended the most serious threat to Allied oil supplies from the Western Hemisphere.[176]

THE DEFENCE OF ALLIED RESOURCES

The occupation of French North Africa by Allied forces in the autumn of 1942 marked the turning point in the reconquest of sources of raw material supply. 'For the first time since the fighting began in the spring of 1940 the Allies emerged from a campaign with augmented rather than depleted supplies of raw materials.' As a consequence, Britain regained a major source of supply for iron ore, pyrites, phosphates, zinc, lead and other resources. From this point onwards, 'growing mastery on land, sea and air was also to bring mastery over the world's resources of raw materials, though large amounts were not to come in time to alter the economic strategy of the struggle'.[177]

Considerations of continued access to resources clearly influenced Allied defensive strategy in the Eastern Mediterranean and the Middle East. The vital importance of these areas lay not only in their position with regard to communications with India and Asia, but also their value in terms of access to strategic resources such as the oil of the Persian Gulf region. Lord Selborn, Minister of Economic Warfare, issued a key memorandum in which he illustrated this point, stating that:

> Practically all the supplies for the Allied front which stretches from Libya to Afghanistan enter through two relatively narrow inlets— the Red Sea and the Persian Gulf—and almost all the oil on which that front, India and East Africa depend, comes out through the latter channel. Reverses which cut communications between Egypt and the Cape, or Egypt and the Persian Gulf, by endangering our position in the Middle East, would give the enemy the hope of opening the direct route from the Mediterranean and the Far East.[178]

Similarly, the maintenance of appropriate bases on the South American and African coasts was held to be of considerable importance as part of the strategy of control of sea lines of communication. Such bases were necessary to prevent significant Axis blockade running, as well as to safeguard Allied supply routes linking Britain and the US with Australia, Egypt and the Middle East.[179]

Prior to the containment of the German offensive in the Caucasus by the Red Army, the threat to Allied oil supplies in Iraq and the Persian Gulf was taken very seriously indeed by Allied planners. The British Chiefs of Staff went so far as to suggest that the vital Abadan area be held even if this meant risking the defence of Egypt. According to a 1942 Oil Control Board Report, the lack of the very large additional tanker capacity which would be needed to make good a loss of oil from Abadan and Bahrain through expanded imports from the United States meant that the loss of these areas 'would be calamitous inasmuch as it would force a drastic reduction in our total war capacity and probably the abandonment of some of our present fields of action'.[180] In the event, the tenacious Russian defence in the Caucasus, together with the decisive British victory at El Alamein which made the redeployment of forces to the north possible, if now largely unnecessary, eliminated the principal resource threat in the Middle East. 'Thanks to the stubbornness of the Red Army and the miscalculations of the German High Command the German threat to Allied oil supplies was banished for good.'[181]

In a very real sense, the key to victory in the Allied quest for resource access was the defeat of the German *guerre de course* in the Atlantic. This has already been suggested with regard to oil supplies; however, it is equally true with regard to virtually the whole range of materials vital to the Allied war economy, not least agricultural products. Thus, 1943 represented a turning point in the war of blockade and counter-blockade in much the same way as 1917 had marked a critical point in the previous war. The fears concerning resource access which were widespread in 1942–43 were gradually dispelled, and the Allies had little need to fear an interruption of vital overseas supplies in the period leading up to the great offensive operation of the war.[182]

THE RESTRICTION OF AXIS SUPPLY

The *denial* of resources to the Axis war economy through blockade and strategic bombing constituted an essential facet of Allied strategy in the European war. In the early stages of the conflict, when there was not as yet any possibility of a direct assault on occupied Europe, British and later American planners placed considerable emphasis on the importance of wearing down German economic strength and morale, although opinion with regard to the effectiveness of the blockade weapon varied. On the one hand it was acknowledged that Germany's control of occupied Europe, while no panacea for resource problems, had given her greater access to a variety of essential resources, thus reducing the potential effect of the blockade weapon. Nevertheless, it was hoped that a broadly based programme of economic warfare would have a significant cumulative effect on the German war economy. In short, it was perceived that things could still be made considerably more difficult for the German planners.[183] The enthusiasm for economic warfare, and the blockade weapon in particular, was supported in the British case by the work of the pre-war Industrial Intelligence Centre (IIC) and later by the MEW Intelligence Department, a principal mission of which was to establish the resource position and therefore the potential vulnerability of the enemy. It is noteworthy in this regard that in 1939 IIC analysts were influenced by the assumption, later revised, that Germany would enter the war with her economy already 'fully stretched'.[184]

The Allied blockade in World War II was ultimately as dependent on naval power for its effectiveness as previous blockades had been, but that power 'being potentially available, had actually to be brought to bear only to a very limited extent'. Increasingly, as the policy of blockade progressed, new techniques of control were developed which made thorough use of Anglo-American economic power as a substitute for the direct use of naval forces.[185] As had been the case from 1917 onwards in the previous conflict, by 1944 the movement of virtually every raw material in world trade was subject to British and American scrutiny and control, the principal instruments of which were the system of contraband and 'navicerts', the use of quotas in allocating supplies to neutrals, and various blacklists aimed at preventing trade with the enemy. These efforts were supported by measures in the areas of finance and insurance aimed at inhibiting deliveries to the Axis by neutral shipping.

Resource considerations played a substantial role in Allied relations with key neutrals and non-belligerents over the course of the war. Notable examples include Turkey, whose continued benevolent neutrality was essential to impede a potential German thrust towards the oil of the Middle East, and whose co-operation was sought in ending the export of chrome to Germany. Similarly, the Allies were anxious to assure continued access to Spanish iron ore, pyrites and wolfram, and to deny these resources, particularly wolfram, to the enemy. The Allies ability to supply badly needed oil and cereals to Spain, and the German inability to do so, provided an important means of influencing Spanish neutrality, essential to the preservation of the Allied position in the Mediterranean.[186]

While the Allied blockade was undoubtedly very successful in cutting off German access to a broad range of strategic materials, the effects of this on German production was less than had been anticipated. With regard to non-ferrous metals, for example, it is clear that a great part of the blockade effort went toward cutting off those metals thought indispensable to the manufacture of special steels, armour, and cutting tools, that is, chrome, nickel, tungsten and molybdenum. Of these, only tungsten prove impossible of substitution given sufficient metallurgical skill— of which Germany was a noted source—and a willingness to produce goods and armaments to less exacting specifications.[187] Beyond the question of the effect of the blockade on German war production and morale, an additional argument for the continuation of the blockade was couched in terms of grand strategy. In brief, it was asserted that German strategy was at least partly determined by the need for access to vital resources from Russia and the Middle East. Thus, termination of the blockade would have left Germany much freer to concentrate on a military decision against Britain.[188]

The Allied strategic air offensive against Germany, directed in large part towards the impairment of the enemy economy through the restriction of supply of certain perceived key materials, complemented Allied blockade measures aimed at resource denial. As in the case of the blockade, early misperceptions regarding the nature of the German war economy led to over-optimistic assumptions regarding the potential effect of strategic bombing on the German capacity for war. British planners at the MEW 'long thought that the German war effort was nearing its peak and that it would soon be reduced by lack of raw materials'. Post-war surveys were to reveal that only with regard to oil 'was there any substance in these prognostications'.[189] In terms of British planning, however, the attack on oil could not be given an established priority until the immediate threat of invasion had been removed.[190] It has been observed that of the many target systems (for example, aircraft production, ball bearings, synthetic rubber, and transportation) considered, surveyed and attacked by

Allied bomber forces, none was more carefully studied than oil.[191]

The end of Romanian neutrality in 1940 opened up new options for interfering with the supply of oil to Germany. Prior to this, Britain and France, and later Britain alone, planned to reduce the flow of oil to Germany through such measures as pre-emptive purchasing, the charter and removal of vessels required for the transport of oil on the Danube, and possibly the sabotage of facilities at Ploesti and the blocking of the Danube itself.[192] By May 1941, however, it was evident that the only means of effectively interfering with Romanian oil supplies to Germany would be the bombing of the refineries themselves. This task was later accomplished primarily by the US Army Air Forces. Following limited attacks on refineries in and around Ploesti in May 1942 and August 1943, The USAAF, assisted by the RAF, launched a concentrated offensive against Romanian oil from the beginning of April 1944.[193] The consideration given to Allied action in the Balkans following the Italian collapse included the prospect of gaining access to more convenient bases from which to attack Romanian oil.[194] By August of 1944, however, Romanian deliveries ceased entirely with the occupation of the oilfields by Soviet forces, freeing additional Allied bombers for attacks on synthetic oil plants in Germany, as well as refineries in Austria and Hungary.[195]

In addition to the attack on Romanian oil, two separate plans were formulated for the attack on facilities in the Caucasus. The first Anglo-French plan was considered as a means of stopping the increasing amounts of oil being delivered to Germany following the Nazi-Soviet Pact. This plan was abandoned after the start of the German offensive in the west.[196] The second Caucasus plan, formulated by British planners, and completed by August 1941, was essentially a contingency plan to attack the Russian oilfields in the event that German forces captured the principal oil centres.[197] The failure of the German offensive in the Caucasus made such an attack unnecessary.

The highly successful American assault on the German day fighter forces from February 1944 removed the principal obstacle to precision attacks on the vital synthetic oil plants within the Reich itself. The offensive against the synthetic oil plants, which began with a massive attack by the Eighth Air Force, quickly produced results. By the following September, German oil production had been substantially reduced, with the most dramatic and damaging fall occurring in the output of aviation fuel, which was reduced to 10 000 tons per month, as compared with the *Luftwaffe's* minimum requirement of some 180 000 tons per month.[198]

The combined result of the attacks on Romanian oil and synthetic production in Germany was very substantial. By drastically reducing the amount of oil available to German forces, particularly the *Luftwaffe*, at critical points in the conflict, the overall warfighting ability of these forces was severely hampered. Moreover, attacks on synthetic oil production had the indirect effect of creating a shortage of explosives (on account of which the production of hexogen had to be discontinued) and synthetic rubber, a development largely unforeseen by Allied planners.[199] In retrospect, it was also suggested that increased emphasis might have been placed on the destruction of the Bergius plants which were primarily responsible for the production of aviation fuel.[200] Overall, as the British official history of the strategic air offensive concludes:

> There can be no doubt that the attacks on oil had an immense effect on the course of the war. The defeat of Germany was due to a combination of pressures, but the attack on oil made a large contribution to the Allied victory. No doubt victory was certain once the Allied armies had established themselves in France. But the final stages would have been more difficult and more costly, if the attack on oil had not reduced the mobility and efficiency of the German air forces and the German armies.[201]

A range of other resources and supplies identified as 'essential' were made the targets of Allied strategic bombing (for example, aluminium and ball-bearing production), although none were attacked as heavily and with the same effect as oil. With regard to aluminium production, the large and dispersed nature of the target system, together with the lack of intelligence on critical bottlenecks, meant that attacks on transport and electric power probably had at least an equal effect on production. Other resource-related target systems proposed included coal, gas and electric power, and at one stage incendiary attacks on German crops and forests were considered.[202] The costly attack on precision bearings, 'listed everywhere as a strategic commodity of the highest importance', was largely neutralized in its effect by the extensive substitution of lower grade bearings in German armaments production. In retrospect, the failure of the reduction in supply of many 'strategic' materials to cause serious production problems for German war industries supports the often sceptical attitude of Allied air force commanders at the time towards 'panacea' targets.[203] Again, however, oil was the outstanding exception.

One clear lesson was the importance of accurate intelligence to pinpoint key production and supply bottlenecks against a wide background of potential economic targets. A generalized campaign of area bombing producing a low level of destruction across a broad range of industries, such as that carried out by Bomber Command, is widely viewed as having been less effective than the precision attack of a smaller number of selected targets (for instance, oil). The post-war interrogation of Albert Speer revealed his clear belief that it was 'the American attacks which followed a definite system of assault on industrial targets', and particularly the synthetic oil and chemical industries, 'which were by far the most dangerous. . . . It was in fact those attacks which caused the breakdown of the German armaments industry'.[204]

RESOURCE ISSUES IN THE PACIFIC WAR: JAPAN'S QUEST FOR RESOURCES

Japanese strategic planning after 1930 provides a striking example of the pervasive influence of resource-related issues. At the end of the first interwar decade, Japanese foreign, economic and defence policy was concerned primarily with the consolidation and expansion of her influence on the Asian mainland, and particularly in Manchuria. The concept of a movement southward to gain access to the valuable resources of Southeast Asia and Indonesia was not seriously envisaged until after the economic depression of 1929 and the ensuing drift towards active militarism.[205] Thereafter, the perception of resource vulnerability fuelled a drive for economic autarky through trade arrangements and conquest in Asia. The aim of establishing a Greater East Asian Co-Prosperity Sphere bore a fundamental resemblance to the German concepts of *Lebensraum* and the economic consolidation of *Mitteleuropa*, and indeed, was strongly influenced by them.

German geopolitical thought clearly had a wide following and a substantial degree of influence within the Japanese leadership in the 1930s. Throughout this period, the rather crude propanganda concerning relations with Manchuria and other areas borrowed heavily from the notion of *Lebensraum*. Moreover, the concern about

Japan's resource position, prevalent 'across the board' in key circles such as the army, navy and industry, turned to paranoia as the threat of embargoes loomed on the horizon.[206]

Haushofer, in particular, exercised very considerable influence on Japanese élites based, in large measure, on his earlier experience in and writings about Japan. In his *Geopolitics of the Pacific Ocean*, Haushofer had focussed on the emerging power of Japan, and her political, military and economic destiny in Asia.[207] The concept of the Co-Prosperity Sphere was, to a considerable degree, the outcome of the eager Japanese study of the German 'Great Space Economy'.[208] Only with the conclusion of the Nazi-Soviet Pact, itself consistent with Haushofer's argument for a reconciliation of the two powers, did Haushofer's reputation in Japan decline.[209]

The raw material and food situation of Japan in the late 1930s suggests that Japanese perceptions of resource vulnerability were grounded rather substantially in fact. With regard to virtually all the materials critical to a wartime economy, Japan's position was precarious. Notably, Japan was not in a position to supply herself with sufficient iron ore to satisfy anticipated wartime steel production requirements. In this respect, her reliance on imported ores in 1938 was clearly the greatest of any of the major powers.[210] Similarly, Japan relied almost entirely on imports for her lead, tin and nickel requirements.[211] Finally, all but complete reliance on imported oil, cotton, wool, timber, rubber and other important resources severely restricted the possibilities of supplying the country's needs in a major conflict. Most importantly, it was observed that 'in view of the risks to shipping in wartime the very possibility of obtaining these supplies is endangered'.[212] Relatively modest enemy air and submarine forces could block vital sea lines of communication as well as coastal transport, thus threatening the entire system of supply.

Japanese efforts to gain direct access to foreign oil had historically been blocked by the commanding position of American and British companies, a fact that hindered Japanese efforts towards expansion in Asia during the 1930s and was to play a role in the decision for war, as well as being a source of tremendous difficulty in the conduct of operations.[213] 'Oil, from the Japanese viewpoint was not just another basic commodity; it was the country's historic Achilles' heel. . . . From the time Japan seized Manchuria in 1931 until it attacked Pearl Harbor ten years later, the country was engaged in a continuous effort to gain some measure of control over the refineries and oil supplies on which its national economy so heavily depended.' Discussion in the West of the possibility of an oil embargo against Japan only served to confirm Japanese perceptions of vulnerability.[214]

On the problem of planning for wartime oil supply, it is noteworthy that a 'very high' German naval official reportedly visited Japan as early as 1935 to study the Japanese oil position and to brief the Japanese government on the direction of German planning in this area. The German report flowing from this study suggested that given the likelihood of a wartime cut-off of imported supplies, together with the fact that a war against the United States would be a long and costly one against an enemy possessing oil resources in abundance, Japan could not possibly rely on stocks alone. The possibilities presented for the acquisition of oil through conquest in the Pacific, however, were more favourable than those presented to Germany in 'the territories on the borders of the Atlantic Ocean'.[215]

The inadequacy of the domestic food base represented another source of concern to Japanese planners. Agricultural policy after 1932 aimed at self-sufficiency in wheat production, but with regard to other supplies, and particularly rice, a solution was sought in the establishment of a colonial empire, not unlike German hopes of securing vast food resources in the east. Thus, Korea and Formosa became the focus of Japanese efforts to develop additional sources of food supply in the 1930s. The inadequacy of even these sources suggests that the assurance of an adequate and predictable supply of rice from Southeast Asia was an important aspect of Japanese strategy.[216]

Because Japanese strategic planning rejected the notion of a prolonged conflict, stockpiles at the beginning of the war were considerably smaller than, for example, those in Britain. 'Everything depended on the success with which food imports could be obtained from the Co-Prosperity Sphere'; their denial as a consequence of the American submarine campaign in the Pacific would represent 'a mortal blow to Japanese strategic planning'.[217]

The extension of the partial American trade embargo to include all grades of iron and steel scrap, in response to the Japanese invasion of Indochina in September 1940, had serious effects on the Japanese supply situation. Moreover, Japan would henceforth be even more dependent on vulnerable imports from China, Korea and Manchuria.[218] As a deterrent, the scrap embargo had little effect on Japanese policy. Instead, it was viewed as a challenge to Japanese aspirations, as well as a likely omen of more serious measures such as a comprehensive embargo on oil.[219] The progressive denial of

American materials to Japan continued through 1940 and 1941, with a gradual expansion of the list of controlled items to include such important resources as copper, zinc, nickel, lead, phosphates, and notably uranium.[220]

As the pressures on Japanese resource supply increased as a result of the continuing war in China, together with the mounting economic sanctions, Japanese planners placed increasing emphasis on attempts to secure larger quantities of raw materials from the Dutch East Indies.[221] Pressure on the Dutch administration to export greater amounts of oil, rubber, tin and other resources naturally increased in the wake of the German occupation of The Netherlands. In the course of negotiations through the spring of 1941, agreement was reached on certain questions, including the right to drill for oil and export some additional commodities. Overall, however, Japanese negotiators were frustrated in their efforts to secure expanded access to materials 'most vital to the Japanese military program at the time'.[222]

The possibility of a complete embargo on oil supplies to Japan weighed heavily in the calculations of the United States and Britain. Throughout the period 1939–41 careful consideration was given to the question of whether a complete embargo on oil supplies would compel Japan to moderate her policies or push her decisively towards war. The War Plans Division of the US Navy, in a report of 19 July 1941 entitled 'Study of the Effect of an Embargo of Trade Between the US and Japan' suggested that a Japanese move beyond Indochina was unlikely in the near future *unless an oil embargo was instituted*. Such an embargo, it was predicted, 'would probably result in a fairly early attack by Japan on Malaya and the Netherlands East Indies and possibly would involve the U.S. in early war in the Pacific'. Thus, it was recommended that trade 'not be embargoed at this time'.[223]

In an effort to forestall a Japanese drive for the oil of the East Indies, the common strategy of the oil companies and the US government was to allow Japan sufficient supplies to prevent her perception of vulnerability from reaching the breaking point, but not so much as to allow the military to build substantial stockpiles.[224] 'Some sources attribute the timing of the Japanese attack on Pearl Harbor and the Dutch East Indies in 1941 to the failure of the U.S. government to faithfully execute its chosen strategy.'[225] In July 1941 the Japanese occupation of Indochina led to a joint retaliatory response by the US, Britain and The Netherlands, effectively completing the gradual tightening of the oil flow which had been pursued

with the co-operation of the major oil companies.[226] Thus, with
regard to the various efforts to restrict Japanese supply which
dominated the relationship between the US and Japan between 1937
and 1941:

> Their express purpose . . . was to achieve much the same result as a
> military campaign, to force Japan to retreat from her more
> ambitious ventures in the Pacific sphere. If they ultimately pro-
> voked the opposite result of an attack . . . that only demonstrates
> that armed combat and denial of supply were potentially substitut-
> able strategies . . .[227]

The imposition of the oil embargo brought to a head the question
of the timing of a major Japanese offensive in the Pacific. While
previous sanctions had been a matter of some concern to the
Japanese leadership, the oil embargo posed supply problems of a far
more serious nature. In 1940 the US provided 80 per cent, and The
Netherlands East Indies 10 per cent of Japan's oil imports, represent-
ing 90 per cent of her total needs.[228] As Admiral Shimada stated after
the war, 'if there were no supply of oil, battleships and any other
warships would be nothing more than scarecrows', not to mention the
effect on the land and air forces and industry.[229] Even with increased
synthetic production (still in its infancy in Japan), oil from Sakhalin,
and possible purchases from Peru, civilian and military needs could
not be met under the prevailing circumstances. Moreover, as the joint
embargo began to take effect, some 400 000 kilolitres of oil per
month would be lost from existing stocks. It was asserted that if
operations were not begun in very short order, the oil situation would
most certainly become untenable by the second year of a war.[230]

The Japanese Official History judges that 'the hopeless prospect
for oil supply was one of the main motives which forced Japan to
resolve for the Greater East Asia War'.[231] Admirals Oikawa and
Nagano have also suggested in retrospect that 'the question of oil was
one of the important reasons why Japan went to war'. Admiral
Shimada, more reservedly, called oil 'one of the factors, but it was
not the fundamental factor' leading to war.[232] At the Imperial
Conference of 6 September 1941 Nagano stated that 'the resource
situation meant that we would very much like to avert a prolonged
war. . . . However, if we get into a prolonged war, the most important
means of assuring that we will be able to bear this burden will be to
seize the enemy's important military areas and sources of materials
quickly, at the beginning of the war, making our operational position

tenable and at the same time obtaining vital materials from the areas now under hostile influence'.[233]

It is illustrative of the priority placed on the resource question that the 'Draft Proposal for Hastening the End of the War with the United States, Great Britain, the Netherlands and Chiang', approved at the 12 November 1941 Liaison Conference following the Imperial Conference of 5 November, noted the following as summary point one:

> Our Empire will engage in a quick war, and will destroy American and British bases in Eastern Asia and in the Southwest Pacific region. At the same time that it secures a strategically powerful position, it will control those areas producing vital materials, as well as important transportation routes, and thereby prepare for a protracted period of self-sufficiency.[234]

The oil embargo placed Japan in a position whereby her available supplies of fuel for military use would steadily decline. This, in turn, led to the perception that only a limited time remained in which to secure a diplomatic solution to the problem of oil supply. By November-December 1941 the Japanese leadership clearly felt that they could wait no longer.[235] In broad terms, Japan required the oilfields of Java, Borneo and Sumatra simply to satisfy the fuel requirements of the campaign in China.[236] Japanese planners did not anticipate serious obstacles to the take-over and operation of captured oilfields. Although a great deal had been written outside of Japan about plans to sabotage the oilfields in the East Indies in the event of an invasion, Japanese experts believed that large-scale destruction was unlikely. Even in the event of such sabotage, it was asserted that the shallowness of the Borneo fields, in particular, would allow new wells to be bored very quickly (that is, within a year). [237] Nevertheless, it was acknowledged that delay would increase the risk of the serious destruction of oil facilities.[238]

In the event, the Japanese experience after seizing the oilfields and refineries of the East Indies was not without serious setbacks. Many key installations were put out of action by carefully planned demolitions. Thus, Japan was a full year in restoring the Sumatran fields to only 60 per cent of pre-war production, and the refineries to only 40 per cent of their pre-war levels.[239] In this respect, the Japanese experience was not unlike that of Germany in the attempt to exploit oil resources in occupied areas.

Wartime developments in the Pacific would demonstrate that the Japanese inability to maintain control of the sea, and thus the security of communications for vital supplies such as oil, severely limited the usefulness of conquered resources. The heavy losses suffered by the Japanese merchant marine—some 80 per cent of total tonnage by 1945—effectively crippled the Japanese war effort. While the oilfields of the East Indies had been overrun with relative ease, the transport of this oil to refineries and on to the fleet proved a difficult task. By the summer of 1944 oil shortages seriously circumscribed Japanese naval movements. Even the use of anchorages in close proximity to the oilfields could not solve the problem of insufficient supplies of refined product. As a consequence of this, the Japanese fleet was compelled to burn unrefined Borneo oil which was far less efficient as a naval fuel. The Japanese fleet thus entered the crucial naval battles of 1944 hindered in its operations by severe fuel shortages.[240]

THE DENIAL OF JAPANESE RESOURCES

The blockade in the Pacific, as a component of Allied strategy against Japan, was of a radically different character from that conducted against the Axis in Europe. In the Pacific there were no neutrals through whom materials might pass to the enemy (although limited trade was conducted with unoccupied China), and thus the elaborate administrative controls which were a principal feature of the blockade in Europe had little place in the wartime restriction of supplies to Japan. The blockade in the Pacific War was, therefore, an exercise conducted mainly by naval and air forces with the object of severing Japanese sea lines of communication with Europe, and more importantly, between the home islands and the Japanese occupied areas in the Pacific and on the Asian mainland.[241] Allied efforts, and particularly the American submarine campaign, were highly successful in paralyzing Japanese shipping and severely restricting her access to food, oil and other essential supplies. While there was undoubtedly some leakage of strategic materials into Japan (for example, by cargo-carrying submarines), it is clear that such leaks were insignificant in terms of volume.[242]

With regard to the impact of the blockade on the Japanese ability to conduct the war, one should note that while there is evidence of complete stoppages of war production as a result of shortages at certain enterprises, specific effects on the Japanese war economy are difficult to measure with precision. The relatively small scale of the

Japanese war economy and levels of raw materials consumption compared to Britain or Germany, for example, renders attempts at measurement even more difficult beyond a generalized impression of significant impairment.[243] In the last months of the war, however, Japan was largely cut off even from the resources of Manchuria and Korea—a clear example of the successful application of a *guerre de course*. To the effect of the naval campaign against Japanese supply must be added the impact of the American strategic bombing campaign, including aerial mining.[244] Here, the destruction of coastal transportation links was a principal objective, not least because many key Japanese industries were located so as to utilize fuel and raw materials received by water.[245]

CONCLUDING OBSERVATIONS ON RESOURCES AND STRATEGY IN WORLD WAR II

Resource issues rose to prominence in the interwar period as a component of the revisionist aspirations of Germany, Italy and Japan. Perceptions of resource vulnerability, supported by German concepts of geopolitics and *Wehrwirtschaft* and their doctrinal counterparts in Italy and Japan, firmly established the quest for economic autarky as a component of strategy in the totalitarian states. The drive for resource self-sufficiency found its expression in elaborate domestic measures aimed at the stockpiling and substitution of key materials, the development of synthetics, and planned expansion to gain access to the food and material resources of 'greater areas'— notably an integrated European economy in the case of Germany, and a Greater East Asian Co-Prosperity Sphere in the case of Japan. Access to resources through conquest and measures aimed at the promotion of autarky also represented a response to the perceived threat of maritime blockade, the experience of which was clear in the minds of strategists.

Impending resource shortages loomed particularly large in Japanese perceptions, to the extent that a solution of the resource problem, and especially the oil problem, appeared as an absolute prerequisite for the fulfillment of Japanese imperial ambitions. As such, the acquisition of the oil, rubber and non-fuel mineral resources of the East Indies emerged as a primary strategic objective, together with the establishment of secure lines of inter-island communication for the transport of these supplies. The severing of Japanese maritime communications, and consequently the denial of captured resources to the home islands, played a key role in Allied strategy in the Pacific.

As in the previous world war, German offensive economic warfare involved the attempt to turn the weapon of blockade on Britain through a concentrated submarine campaign aimed at severing the Allied lines of communication for vital resources and war material. This most serious threat to the Allied war effort was defeated through the imposition of the convoy system and the development of improved anti-submarine warfare techniques, including the increased use of aircraft. Thus, as in the past, the *guerre de course* in the absence of overall sea control proved incapable of delivering a decisive blow.

Resource questions similarly rose to prominence in Allied strategic thought prior to the outbreak of war, based on the experience of blockade and counter-blockade in World War I, and in response to the evident preoccupation of German and Japanese planners with resource-related issues. Economic warfare generally, and the strategy of resource denial in particular, were seen to pose the possibility of achieving a decision with the minimum commitment of human and material resources. During the early stages of the war, such a strategy served as a means of taking the offensive in an environment in which the operational opportunities were limited and the vulnerability of the German war economy overestimated. So, too, the blockade and strategic bombing campaigns represented a means of bringing superior Allied naval, air and economic power to bear on the enemy.

Despite the clear success of the Allied blockades against Germany and Japan in cutting off large amounts of 'vital' raw materials and foodstuffs, the overall effect of the strategy of resource denial on the enemy war economies, *with the exception of oil*, is doubtful. 'The paradox presents itself that whereas virtually every raw material is, given full freedom of strategic and tactical choice, important for large-scale combatant warfare, practically no raw material, if denied, is indispensable, providing the possibility of substitution is allowed for when strategic and tactical choices are made.'[246] In addition to substitution, conquest, stockpiling and the development of synthetics would offset the potential effects of resource denial, again, with the principal exception of oil. Overall, both the Axis and Allied economies proved extraordinarily adaptable in the face of resource shortages.

The experience of the Allied strategic bombing campaigns pointed to the importance of the availability of adequate resource-related intelligence in order to establish with precision those target systems which are absolutely vital to the war economy. The number of such systems was in fact very small, while their attack could have substantial effects, as in the case of German oil supply from 1944. Even here, Allied planners did not fully appreciate the need to target the hydrogenation plants vital to the production of aviation fuel, or the fact that the attack on synthetic oil would cause substantial shortages in the supply of rubber and explosives. It would appear from the evidence of World War II that an effective strategy of resource denial calls for considerable discrimination in its application if it is to represent a successful balance of costs versus benefits.

The Allied strategy for access to resources, based on the maintenance of maritime communications for continued access to food and raw materials in world trade, made necessary the establishment of mechanisms for the close co-ordination of resource acquisition, allocation and use as a component of coalition warfare. In this sense one may suggest that Allied strategy involved the management of a third, Atlantic 'greater economic area', including the resources of the British Commonwealth, as a counter to the resources available to Germany and Japan as a result of territorial expansion. The Soviet problem of access consisted, moreover, of the mobilization of tremendous indigenous resource potential, together with the development of the transportation infrastructure for domestic and imported supplies.

Finally, the effect of resource denial, as one factor among a host of important logistical and operational factors, is clearly very difficult to measure in an exact fashion. That it made a substantial contribution to the ultimate collapse of Germany and Japan is certain. Also certain is the fact that this contribution, with some important exceptions, *was not nearly as great as had been anticipated*. It is clear, however, that from 1918 right through to 1945, resource considerations were everywhere in the minds of strategists, with perceptions of resource vulnerability playing an important role in the formation of offensive and defensive strategy.

Part II
Developments Since 1945: Resources and Strategy in the Nuclear Age

Part II

5 Resource Issues and Strategic Planning, 1945–73

The period from 1945 to the Middle East War and oil crisis of 1973 was one of transition from the wartime legacy of resource-related planning in the context of prolonged general war to the new requirements of strategic planning in the nuclear age. Despite the very substantial evolution in strategic thinking necessitated by the introduction of nuclear weapons, there would continue to be strong elements of continuity with traditional, pre-1945 approaches to resource questions. Events in this period will be discussed with particular reference to American policy, and a view towards answering a critical question: how did nuclear weapons affect the relevance of resource factors to military power, potential and planning? Key developments during this period which would influence the formation of strategy included the tremendous growth of civilian demand for raw materials relative to the potential military requirements in wartime, and most importantly, the very great expansion in the worldwide demand for oil. Finally, the increasing desire of newly-independent and developing countries for control over valuable indigenous resources would raise new questions with regard to the security of access to resources in peace and war.

MOBILIZATION CONCEPTS, POST-WAR RECOVERY, AND STRATEGIES OF CONTAINMENT

The experience of wartime resource shortages, and the realization, particularly in the American case, that the resources of the American continent alone might not suffice to meet defence requirements, led to a general increase in concern with regard to resource questions in the immediate post-war period. At the same time the very limited stocks of nuclear weapons possessed by the United States and the Soviet Union in the first few years after the war led to the realization on the part of many strategists, if not the public, that a third world

97

war might not be radically different in nature from the previous conflict. Although nuclear weapons might be employed, and would bring considerable destruction in their wake, their destructive power was not yet great enough to destroy the entire social and economic structure of the belligerents.[1] Thus, prior to the deployment of the first hydrogen weapons in 1953–54, Western defence planners continued to recognize, 'implicitly and explicitly' the 'relevance of economic mobilization and, as important, the command of the sea which would make it possible. . . . They also embarked on stockpiling strategic raw materials . . . a policy that speaks for itself'.[2]

Similarly, US Army planners in the 1950s advanced the idea that the industrial base would come into play after initial strikes by strategic nuclear forces, with active mobilization of the remaining economic capacity for the purpose of producing a large army capable of regaining territory in Europe. Whether or not this assumption was ever a valid one, the relatively small number of nuclear weapons extant at the time clearly encouraged the perception that the scenario was plausible.[3] The growth of nuclear arsenals would soon call into question such notions regarding mobilization, and would lead to a concentration on deterrence and a radical form of 'armament in width' (that is, single-shot, silo-based Intercontinental Ballistic Missiles—ICBMs).[4] Despite these new realities, however, resource-related planning would continue to focus on the alternative of conventional conflict, in the general and limited war contexts, with its attendant requirements for assured raw materials supply.

American concern with regard to resource supply was encouraged by the fact that the 1940s had seen the US move from the position of being a substantial exporter of such important materials as copper, lead and zinc, to being an importer of significant quantities of these resources. By the late 1940s the US had also become a net importer of iron ore and petroleum. While it is clear that these shifts were, to a great degree, a reflection of the existence of lower cost alternatives to indigenous supplies, they had the effect of contributing to the perception that a 'crucial turning point' had been reached in the long-range materials position of the United States. In addition, there emerged an increasing concern over the prospect of Soviet actions, directly or through proxies, aimed at cutting off Western access to the resources of former colonial areas, a form of pressure to which the US was 'moderately vulnerable' and the European allies 'distinctly vulnerable'.[5]

The increasing dependence of Western Europe on imported

sources of raw material supply in the immediate post-war period, particularly with regard to oil, was perceived to be a significant threat to security. This threat was seen to be all the more serious given the importance of sustained economic growth to European recovery, and by implication, political stability. Assured raw material supply, including adequate access to oil, was thus a virtual *sine qua non* for European recovery. Indeed, a 1952 US NSC report declared that 'Western Europe is not defensible, our investment in its rehabilitation will be dissipated, and it will be lost and become a liability to the free world, unless adequate petroleum products are available for its essential requirements'.[6]

By 1950 industrial output was growing at a rate of 9 per cent per year in Japan and 5 per cent in Western Europe (3 per cent in Britain), as compared with an increase of 3.6 per cent in the US.[7] This very considerable rate of expansion in Japan and Western Europe led to a sharply increased demand for raw materials, the greatest proportion of which could only be satisfied from foreign sources of supply. These countries, were, of course, dependent to a similarly high degree on overseas sources of supply for food and agricultural raw materials. The potential vulnerability of the European and Japanese economies was, however, somewhat offset by the diversified nature of the sources of supply for most commodities. The principal exception to this was oil, for which rapidly increasing emphasis was placed on Middle Eastern supply.[8]

The prospect of severe coal shortages in Western Europe led post-war planners to encourage the conversion from coal to oil, particularly in the industrial and transportation sectors. In 1951 total petroleum requirements for the Marshall Plan countries were estimated to be more than double the level of consumption in 1938. This rapidly growing demand, coupled with the desire to conserve Western Hemisphere reserves, meant that the Middle East would become a natural source of supply for the European Recovery Programme.[9] Indeed, by 1945 the focus of world oil production had already shifted from the Western Hemisphere to lower-cost sources in the Middle East.[10] In this context, the TAPLINE project which would create a direct pipeline from the Persian Gulf to the Eastern Mediterranean, was promoted in the late 1940s as a means of furthering the economic recovery of Europe through the provision of increased amounts of Persian Gulf oil without placing additional demands on tanker capacity. It is noteworthy that US Defense Department officials had argued at the time that the construction of additional tankers would represent a more flexible and secure approach given the potential for turmoil in the Middle East.[11]

The emergence and evolution of the 'strategy of containment' incorporated noteworthy references to the protection and attack of resource-rich areas. In George Kennan's formulation, not all parts of the world were of equal importance to Western security. There were, in fact, only five centres of industrial and military power—the US, the UK, Germany and Central Europe, the Soviet Union and Japan— from which sufficient amphibious power could be developed to threaten US national security. Of these, only one was in hostile hands, and the principal interest of the US in world affairs should therefore be to ensure that no further centres fell under such control. Also of significance, although of secondary importance to the above, would be those additional areas containing strategic raw materials.[12]

The extension of Soviet control over the resource-rich 'rimlands' could be checked through 'perimeter defence' or, alternatively, through 'strongpoint defence'. Kennan's 'X' article endorsed the former concept, asserting the need to 'confront the Russians with unalterable counter-force at every point where they show signs of encroaching upon the interests of a peaceful and stable world'.[13] By the time of this article's appearance, however, Kennan had already begun to embrace the concept of 'strongpoint defence', that is, 'the defense of particular regions and the means of access to them, rather than the defense of fixed lines'. The principal criteria for identifying these vital areas was the existence of substantial military and industrial capacity, together with the necessary raw materials and lines of communication. This approach was reflected in the US war plans of the period, which placed emphasis on the protection of Western Europe, the Mediterranean, Japan and, notably, the Middle East. In the case of the latter, it was recognized that the *denial* of the region's raw materials to the Soviet Union would also represent an important objective of wartime strategy. The adoption of NSC–68 in 1950 would see a return to the concept of perimeter defence, in which the safeguarding of resource-rich areas would remain a consideration in strategic planning.[14]

RESOURCES AND AMERICAN STRATEGIC PLANNING: EARLY CONCERNS

While dependence on Middle Eastern supply held advantages for economic growth in the Western economies, it also posed problems for military planners who were alert to the risks of reliance on such supplies in wartime planning. Soviet proximity to the oilfields of Iran and Iraq, together with the vulnerability of pipelines and the sea lines of communication for Middle Eastern oil, made uninterrupted access to these supplies in wartime an uncertain proposition at best. For some, Persian Gulf oil supplies might even be seen as a potential liability. In the event of a general war with the Soviet Union, for example, the US Army's *Intelligence Review* suggested that 'Middle East oil would be of negligible if not negative strategic value to the United States'.[15]

Early post-war concerns about the security of Middle Eastern oil supplies were reinforced when the Truman administration faced a potential crisis over the failure of the Soviet Union to withdraw from Iran by the scheduled deadline of 2 March 1946. One of the Soviet goals in the context of this delay was the acquisition of oil development rights in northern Iran.[16] Soviet forces, some of which had been deployed as far south as Karaj, 30 miles from Teheran, were eventually withdrawn in May 1946. Following the 1946 difficulty over Iran, a study approved by the US Joint Chiefs of Staff in February 1947 concluded that 'in a future major war, the total U.S. military and civilian [oil] requirements could not be met . . . by all the then current production in the U.S. and U.S. controlled sources, including that in the Near and Middle East'.[17] A report in the same year by the Joint Logistics Committee to the JCS emphasized that the potential production of petroleum in the Western Hemisphere would not be sufficient to meet essential civilian and military needs in the event of a major conflict.[18]

In a 1947 assessment of what a war between the US and the Soviet Union would be like, entitled 'Strategic Guidance for Industrial Mobilization Planning', JCS planners assumed that in addition to operations in Western Europe, Soviet strategy would include operations designed to overrun Turkey and the Middle East so as to obtain control of the Eastern Mediterranean and the oil supplies of the Middle East. The same study also suggested that the Soviet oil industry would represent the most profitable target system for attack by Allied strategic air power. The most effective approach to the attack of Soviet oil supplies would be the destruction of the roughly 84 per cent of Soviet refining capacity located in the Caucasus. Overall, some 80 per cent of the Soviet oil industry was thought to be within the operating radius of B-29s based in Britain and the Cairo-Suez area. Other important resource producing target areas would include the Donbas and Kuzbas mining areas, the Ploesti oilfields of Romania, and the 'Second Baku' area of the Urals.[19]

Overall, it was felt by JCS planners that the valuable oil reserves of the Mesopotamian and Persian Gulf regions were 'doubtless a tempting prize' to the Soviet Union, and that acquisition of these resources would eventually materially increase Soviet military capabilities and would immediately constrain those of the Allies; a situation similar to that which shaped Allied and German strategy towards the area in both world wars. The effects of such a development would be most immediate and severe in the case of Britain, dependent on imports from Iran and Iraq for roughly half of her total peacetime petroleum needs. In terms of Allied strategy, therefore, the retention of control over Turkey would be of great importance in severing Soviet overland communications to the oil resources of the Middle East.

In addition, the deployment of jet aircraft, heavier bombers and transports, and the generally increased use of air power, suggested that the requirements for petroleum, particularly aviation fuel, might be 'substantially greater than at the peak of World War II'. Given this, the US might not possess the necessary production capacity to meet this increased demand. Combined with the effect of the loss of Middle Eastern sources on wider Allied supply, this situation might well necessitate Allied operations 'in the Near East directed specifically towards obtaining POL [petroleum, oil and lubricants]'. The study therefore concluded that the Middle East represented a likely major theatre of operations against the USSR, and the retention of a base area in the region would facilitate attacks on key Soviet resource-producing areas, as well as contributing to the recovery of Middle Eastern oil resources should this prove 'essential to the Allied effort as the war progresses'.[20]

A JCS-mandated study of the strategic premises underlying American policy towards the stockpiling of raw materials, undertaken by the Joint Strategic Survey Committee in 1947–48, highlights a number of the assumptions then current with regard to resources and war. The premises cited for access to strategic raw materials suggest that, even given the American monopoly on nuclear weapons, a general war with the Soviet Union within 'the next few years' was thought likely to be a virtual repeat of the World War II experience in terms of its nature and duration.[21] The Committee's final evaluations, approved on 2 February 1948, included the following comments:

> Refinement of present, and development of new, weapons of war is progressing daily. The results which have been achieved when war occurs will have a major effect on our ability to maintain communications between the United States and the sources of essential strategic and critical materials. . . . The outcome of the present political and ideological struggle between the democracies of the West and the totalitarian states of the East will determine whether many sources of strategic and critical materials will be available to the United States at the beginning and during the war. . . . Hence, at present and until realignments have been stabilized, only rather vague assumptions can be made concerning access to many sources of important strategic and critical materials. . . . It seems probable that if the United States is involved in war, the war will be global and total and will last not less than five years.[22]

The JCS report assumed that for the purposes of stockpile planning, the resources of the Western Hemisphere would remain available in wartime, as would those from Australia, New Zealand, South Africa and Great Britain, with due allowance for losses in transit. It was considered 'unrealistic and dangerous' to assume that European sources of supply would remain available, with the possible exception of those of Spain. The accessibility of African sources of raw material supply would depend critically on the extent of potential internal unrest in those countries, and importantly, upon the status of France. Most significantly, the Committee report asserted that the Near and Middle East 'will most likely be inaccessible as a source of strategic and critical materials unless the United States moves adequate forces into the areas prior to the outbreak of war and unless the present ill will on the part of the Arab states toward the United States is eliminated'.[23] This assessment would not be irrelevant to the question of resource access in the Middle East in the 1980s.

The 'Short Range Emergency War Plan' (HALFMOON) approved by the JCS in the spring of 1948 lists the 'seizure of Middle East and its oil resources' as the first of a number of likely Soviet objectives in a general war. In addition, it was assumed that the Soviets would engage in an active *guerre de course* against Allied sea lines of communication by means of submarine, mining and air operations. With regard to Allied strategy, HALFMOON envisioned that it would be necessary for the Allies to regain access to Middle East oil resources by the end of the second year of war, and that an offensive to regain these resources could be aimed at Kirkuk and the Persian Gulf, or both. The former would require overland operations in unfavourable terrain, while the latter implied the prospect of difficult amphibious operations.[24]

The Joint Outline Emergency War Plan (OFFTACKLE), which succeeded HALFMOON, incoporated less exaggerated estimates of Soviet capabilities, and placed somewhat less emphasis on the importance of retaining or retaking the oil resources of the Middle East.[25] Plans developed in 1949, however, returned to the notion that the successful conduct of a general war would require Western control of the Middle Eastern oilfields. It was maintained that if these oilfields were not retained or retaken in the initial phases of the conflict, the oil position of the Allies would dictate subsequent actions to retake them.[26]

American perceptions of resource vulnerability also extended to the question of the security of supply in peacetime or periods of crisis short of war. The fear of possible interruptions in the supply of strategic raw materials, coupled with concern over the potential depletion of US reserves of key materials, led to a number of important resource-related initiatives beginning in the late 1940s. Of particular concern was the security of strategically important extractive industries located abroad. The prevailing Cold War rhetoric made frequent reference to the Soviet objective of global disruption, including the interference with the resource flows on which the West was perceived to be highly dependent.[27] In the case of Venezuelan oil production, which amounted to roughly one-fifth of the daily production in the US in 1948, planners in the NSC and elsewhere pointed to the potential vulnerability of facilities to sabotage and other communist-inspired actions. This problem was addressed in a 1948 report by the Department of the Army to the NSC, which concluded that national security required that 'all practicable and appropriate measures be taken to minimize the vulnerability of strategically important industrial operations in foreign countries'.[28]

It is noteworthy that at the time of the Berlin crisis of 1948, the United States was dependent on Soviet supplies for 31 per cent of its manganese consumption, 47 per cent of chromite consumption, and 57 per cent of platinum-group metals consumption. The denial of these supplies did not, however, seriously affect the ability of American defence industries to meet the requirements of mobilization for the Korean conflict in 1950.[29] Growing concern over resource questions, given impetus by the threat of resource shortages flowing from the Korean mobilization, led President Truman to establish the President's Materials Policy Commission (PMPC) in 1951, with William S. Paley, President of the Columbia Broadcasting System, as its Chairman. The task assigned to the PMPC was to explore the nature and dimensions of the 'materials problem' and to formulate long-term public and private sector responses. The report's major premise was that 'the overall objective of a national materials policy ... should be to insure an adequate and dependable flow of materials at the lowest cost consistent with national security and with the welfare of friendly nations'.[30] The PMPC noted that special problems were associated with ensuring the adequacy of resource supply in wartime or crisis. In particular, while considerations of cost may be subordinate to the imperative of access in war, in a period of 'preparation against the threat of war' costs are an important concern.[31]

Of the roughly 100 minerals used by American industry at the time of the PMPC report, one-third—for example, sulphur, coal and phosphates, but including only two metals—were supplied entirely from domestic sources. Another third of these mineral materials were obtained almost entirely from foreign sources, and this fraction had taken on added importance with the increasing demand for colombium, cobalt, high-grade quartz crystals, and other materials unobtainable (or uneconomic to produce) in the US. The last third, consisting of materials such as iron ore, petroleum, copper, lead, zinc and bauxite, was obtained partly from domestic sources and partly from abroad. Of the 72 'strategic and critical materials' cited by the US Munitions Board, the US relied entirely on imports for its supply of over 40 such materials, and for at least part of its supply in all the rest.[32]

The Paley Report asserted that the US must endeavour to maintain a strong and expanding economy with a diversified resource base capable of meeting the potential demands of war production, and importantly, the Cold War requirements of 'military strength-in-being'. The provision of such essentials as steel, electric power, oil and aluminium would be of particular value given the long lead time required for the expansion of their supply and their role in war production. The report called for the enhancement of 'efficiencies' on both the supply (for example, production and stockpiling) and demand (for example, recycling, weapons design, co-ordination with allies) sides. In this context, the report acknowledged the impetus given to resource-related planning by the mobilization requirements associated with the Korean conflict.[33] With regard to the probable pattern of demand for 'total war'—in which military requirements might claim up to 50 per cent of national materials production (as compared to roughly 40 per cent in World War II)—the report suggested that this would be shaped by a number of factors: first, the likely need to assemble a large, effectively armed force, as quickly as possible; second, the large and increasing supply requirements of modern American forces (a typical soldier in Korea required some 35 per cent more cargo landed per day than did a soldier in World War II); third, the increasing size and complexity of military assets; and fourth, the 'strategic situation' of the US and its allies with regard to resource supply and the logistics of mechanized warfare fought at some distance from bases of supply.[34]

The changing nature of the resource inputs for the production of aircraft, armoured vehicles, ships and other military assets, referred to by the PMPC, is noteworthy. It is illustrative that a jet aircraft manufactured in 1951 required twice as much copper and steel, and two and a half times as much aluminium, in comparison to its forerunner of 1944. In addition, the production of more sophisticated aircraft and other weapons introduced new and unprecedented demands for 'exotic' materials such as uranium, beryllium and zirconium for the manufacture of nuclear weapons, and columbium and other alloys for use in high-temperature and high-stress applications. The report speculated that with the passage of time, the application of new technology to weapons development would cause the demand for materials to grow in size and complexity.[35]

In retrospect, it is clear that these predictions were only partially correct. While the employment of exotic materials would grow in importance, the overall level of raw material demand for armaments production and for military purposes generally would become less significant in comparison to rapidly expanding civilian demand. In the early 1950s it was widely perceived that large-scale war, and the preparations for it, would require enormous increases in resource consumption. This view—elements of which may still be encountered today—derived in large measure from the experience of World War II, in which increases in overall raw material consumption were substantial in comparison to pre-war levels. It must be remembered, however, that the 1930s were a period of relatively low economic activity, with a consequently depressed demand for raw materials. Moreover, there has been a tendency to assume that war economy is 'peculiarly intensive' in its requirements for raw materials. While this is undoubtedly true for certain resources, for instance, uranium, hardening agents and special alloys, one author could suggest in 1958 that 'in general and in the aggregate, we find that demands for industrial raw materials per unit of national product for a wartime "product mix" are not markedly different from those of peacetime'.[36]

Another factor which the Paley report did not fully reflect was the likelihood of assured access to traditional industrial resources becoming less critical to military power and potential with the increase in importance of technological inputs. First, more expensive and complex, and theoretically more effective weapons, can be deployed in smaller numbers. Second, the nature of modern weaponry—including advanced conventional as well as nuclear systems—almost certainly lessens the likelihood of prolonged wars of attrition.[37] All of these mitigating considerations were beginning to take shape in the 1950s. The fact that they were not emphasized in the PMPC study and elsewhere points to the enduring nature of perceptions regarding resources and strategy. Advances in the use and substitution of 'strategic' materials since 1945 have complicated the process of determining precisely which resources will be most necessary. As Klaus Knorr has asserted with regard to resources and national security, 'it is dangerous to predict the next crisis from the last'. Thus, while the importance of natural rubber as a strategic good has declined since World War II, other commodities such as oil are likely to remain vital.[38]

While the PMPC report conceded that 'revolutionary weapons' might shorten a war, it was asserted that prudent strategic planning based on the experience of previous conflicts should assume that a war 'would continue with increasing violence for a number of years, and that the demand for materials would continue to be high and perhaps even rise as industrial capacity moved upward'. In such a conflict, the principal problem of resource supply would be the inadequacy of the US resource base. At the same time, the increasing resource demands of allies would further constrain the availability of overseas supplies. Finally, Allied strategy would have to contend with the likely interruption of resource supplies through the bombing of resource-related facilities, the invasion and denial of important resource-producing areas, and the attack on sea-borne trade. In this context, the report cited the fact that in the first seven months of World War II, the German *guerre de course* in the Atlantic led to the loss of 22 per cent of the shipping engaged in the transport of aluminium ore to the US, and tanker sinkings averaged 3.5 per cent per month of tonnage in use.[39]

With regard to the important foreign sources of raw materials for US supply in 1952, the PMPC study states:

> For three key commodities—tin, quartz crystal and industrial diamonds—the United States is 100 percent dependent on foreign sources. The Nation's position is worsening for 25 other key commodities; in fact in 1952 the United States had become virtually dependent on foreign sources for four of these. The United States produced (1951) only 55 percent of the lead, 38 percent of the bauxite, 26 percent of the antimony, 20 percent of the flake graphite, 10 percent of the cobalt, 9 percent of the mercury, and 8 percent of the manganese it used. Obviously, enemy action could reduce or stop the flow of many key materials.[40]

The Paley Commission emphasized that the US and other non-communist states must co-ordinate their resource strength, and specifically rejected the notion that resource security might be pursued through economic autarky. The guiding principal was, rather, to be the pursuit of access to indigenous and imported resources on the basis of the lowest cost. 'Self-sufficiency, when closely viewed', the study declared, 'amounts to a self-imposed blockade and nothing more'.[41]

The PMPC did, however, endorse the strengthening of the national materials stockpile programme, as an important contribution to military strength-in-being. Since the first legislative authorization for stockpiling, the Strategic Materials Act of 1939, the building of a national stockpile had been pursued with varying urgency and effectiveness. The wartime experience in the resource sphere had led to widespread recognition of the need for a stockpile of strategic materials. The actual acquisition of materials for the stockpile was, however, pursued in a generally less than vigorous manner until the outbreak of the Korean conflict and the consequent acknowledgement of the need to strengthen the programme.

Unfortunately, the expansion of the stockpile coincided with a period of sharply increased demand and higher prices for raw materials. In this respect, developments in 1950 bore a close resemblance to the resource scramble of 1939.[42] In assessing the benefits and potential drawbacks of stockpiling policies, the Commission noted that one of the possible dangers of over-reliance on stockpiling is that the possession of substantial stocks of strategic resources could lead to a 'Maginot Line kind of complacency', discouraging more active efforts to develop new sources of supply or substitutes. More convincingly, it was also asserted that the concept of stockpiling, although essentially well conceived, would need to be re-evaluated in light of the heightened vulnerability of resource production and storage facilities to enemy attack in the nuclear age.[43]

A similar concern with regard to the perceived resource vulnerability of the United States was evident in the Eisenhower Administration. This period saw the establishment of the President's Commission on Foreign Economic Policy (the 'Randall Commission'), which concluded that the 'transition of the U.S. from a position of relative self-sufficiency to one of increasing dependence upon foreign sources of supply constitutes one of the striking economic changes of our time'.[44] In a similar manner, the Committee on Interior and Insular Affairs of the Senate was directed to prepare a major report, published in 1954, entitled 'Accessibility of Strategic and Critical Materials to the United States in Time of War and for our Expanding Economy'. In contrast to the earlier findings of the Paley Commission, the 1954 Senate study concluded that the growing perception of the United States as a 'have-not' nation with regard to supplies of critical resources in wartime was essentially false, and policies based on such an assumption were bound to be misdirected. In addition, it was asserted that confusion over the terms 'proved commercial reserves' and 'potential and latent resources' contributed to the public acceptance of misleading notions of resource depletion and vulnerability.[45] Indeed, confusion on this point continues to influence the current debate on strategic minerals.

The 1954 report suggested that one of the most troubling consequences of the prevailing emphasis on securing access to foreign sources of supply, rather than encouraging the development of domestic resources, was that it had led the US to underwrite the security, prosperity and domestic and foreign policies of various resource-rich countries. Moreover, such an approach served to justify 'unprecedented global commitments, and the imposition of strategically unsound deployments'. There was, it was asserted, 'every possibility' that American dependence on overseas sources of supply represented that 'weak link' which might encourage the Soviet Union to embark on a war with the United States, on the grounds that such a war could be feasible and short.[46]

While the US had neglected the development of the potential for essential resource self-sufficiency in the Western Hemisphere, considerable effort had been expended to foster regional stability in resource-producing areas and to safeguard the sea lines of communication for vital materials in wartime. The Senate report asserted that, at the same time, the communist powers had developed the capability to deny the US access to these resources both at their sources and in transit, through the instruments of strategic bombing, submarine warfare, and economic and political subversion. Resource factors were thus certain to enter into the strategic calculus of Soviet planners in a future conflict. The Senate report concluded that one of the 'great goals' of Russian wartime strategy might well be the delivery of 'lightning blows at the sources of our raw materials':

> In the last war, the enemy had no alternative but to attempt to cut our supply lines. Today he need not bother with supply lines; he can strike directly at the sources of our strategic materials within his long-range airpower and neutralize them with conventional or with atomic and hydrogen bombs. . . . Our questionable ability to keep sealanes open is only one phase of the problem of the accessibility of critical materials in time of war. It will be fruitless to concentrate our forces on keeping the sealanes open. We will face strangulation of supply of strategic materials should the enemy choose to bomb and reduce our sources of these materials to rubble.[47]

This assertion bears considerable resemblance to arguments put forward in the 1930s with regard to the potential effects of strategic bombing on war economy.

In sum, testimony contained in the 1954 Senate report cast serious doubt on the ability of the United States to rely on access to resources outside the Western Hemisphere in wartime. Corrective measures, it was suggested, should concentrate on the development of resource self-sufficiency within North and South America, and the reduction, to the extent possible, of American dependence on overseas sources of supply. In many respects the report's conclusions represented a return to pre-1941 notions of Hemisphere encirclement and beleaguered isolation, together with some more noteworthy observations on the effect of the expansion of strategic air power, both nuclear and conventional. The emphasis on autarkic policies con-

trasts strongly with the economic efficiency arguments which formed
the basis of the Paley Commission report.

As has been discussed, the World War II experience provided the
basis for American thinking with regard to resources and strategic
planning through the 1950s and beyond (indeed, its influence may
still be seen today). The appearance of limited raw materials
shortages at the time of the Korean mobilization, referred to earlier,
led to renewed concern and activity with regard to resource
planning.[48] The Cuban revolution, and the loss of Cuban sources of
supply for a number of important materials kept alive the perception
of potential economic vulnerability. Prior to the revolution, Cuban
sources of supply figured prominently in American mobilization
planning. In the past, the island had provided the US with significant
amounts of manganese, nickel and chromite. The denial of these
materials suggested a 'fundamental reconsideration of America's
vulnerable economic position'.[49]

THREATS TO WESTERN OIL SUPPLIES: SUEZ AND ITS AFTERMATH

Writing in 1947, Bernard Brodie warned that the strategic rather than
the economic aspects of oil supply must dictate national planning.[50]
In the face of mounting Western dependence on Middle Eastern oil,
the series of supply crises spanning the period 1950–70 would provide
clear confirmation of this view. Whereas early post-war concerns with
regard to the security of Middle Eastern oil tended to focus on the
threat posed by the Soviet Union, events in Iran in 1951 led to
heightened Western concern over domestic and regional threats to
access. The Suez crisis, in particular, would also demonstrate the
manner in which oil supply questions could be the focus of intra- as
well as inter-alliance conflict.

The nationalization of the Anglo-Iranian Oil Company and its
facilities in Abadan by the Mossadegh regime in 1951 was perceived
as an unprecedented challenge to Western control of oil production.
The resulting international embargo on the purchase of Iranian oil,
production of which had in any event essentially ceased, together
with the threat of British military action to recover control over the
petroleum facilities, led to the prospect of a supply crisis in Europe
and elsewhere. Whereas the British view of the crisis concentrated

principally on the threat to control over oil supplies, for the US, Cold War politics rather than a direct concern for energy security provided the impetus for actions which led to the overthrow of the Mossadegh regime. The crisis did, however, mark the beginning of the transfer of responsibility from Britain to the United States with regard to the protection of Western access to Middle Eastern oil.[51]

The nationalization and rapid decline in the production and export of Iranian oil in 1951 was perceived as a potential threat to the war effort in Korea, as well as European economic recovery and Western rearmament programmes. With the departure of the last tanker from Abadan, the West was deprived of some 610 000 barrels per day of crude oil and petroleum products, at a time when supply was thought to be barely ahead of demand.[52] The efforts of the Foreign Petroleum Supply Committee, established by the US government with the participation of 19 American oil companies, effectively countered the anticipated threats to Western rearmament which might have resulted from the loss of Iranian supplies. Thus, it was surplus productive capacity, together with the establishment of a mechanism for the sharing of supplies, that allowed the importing countries to manage until the overthrow of the Mossadegh regime and the restoration of oil exports in 1953.[53]

In the view of oil experts and strategists in the mid-1950s the question of assuring adequate supplies of oil for the United States and its allies in the event of war had become increasingly complex and uncertain. While conventional measures aimed at increasing production and safeguarding supplies might be adequate in periods of crisis or limited war, the prospect of a general war with the Soviet Union in which nuclear weapons could be employed posed new problems of resource vulnerability. In such an event, the critical factor might not be the total available stocks or production potential in-being, as refineries, port facilities and storage depots would all represent vulnerable, high-value targets for strategic attack. Thus, the greatest advantage might well be derived from the existence of a large number of well-dispersed stockpiles, ready for immediate use, and located close to areas of need. It was suggested that more thorough study might lead to the conclusion that there is 'relatively less need as well as relatively greater military reason' for encouraging the development of the oil resources of the Caribbean and Far East than those in the Middle East. The resources of the Caribbean, it was argued, would be more likely to remain available in a general war, while those of the Far East would be needed to support operations in that area.[54]

In the period before Suez the importance of Middle Eastern oil and its vulnerability to Soviet attack were widely discussed. Indeed, the nature of the debate was similar in many ways to the concerns which were to emerge with regard to Soviet intentions towards the Persian Gulf in the wake of the invasion of Afghanistan in 1979. As in the contemporary debate, some analysts would argue that the oil resources of the Middle East were not as vulnerable to Soviet attack as they might appear at first glance. In this view, the geographical proximity of the Soviet Union was offset by the existence of difficult terrain in the path of an invading force—notably the Zagroz mountains of Iran.[55] For others this argument was weakened by the experience of the relatively easy entry of Soviet forces into Iran during the wartime Anglo-Soviet occupation of that country, although under circumstances in which Iranian resistance was slight.[56] The issue of access to oil played a critical role in the outbreak, conduct and outcome of the 1956 Suez crisis, and had a significant influence on the formation of strategy and the evolution of alliance relationships through the 1960s and beyond. Whereas the 1951 crisis had represented a threat to energy security only in the context of British perceptions, the events of 1956 would suggest a wider threat to European energy supplies. The crisis would also dramatically underscore the large vulnerability gap which existed between the United States and its European allies with regard to oil supplies.[57]

Oil represented the Suez Canal's most vital cargo. By 1956 Western Europe was receiving 75 per cent of its oil from the Middle East, with roughly half of this oil transiting the Canal, and the remaining amount arriving via Mediterranean pipelines. Moreover, the extent of European dependence on Canal-borne supplies was expanding rapidly. Approximately 15 per cent of total British energy supplies was based on access to the canal. In the case of France, this figure was roughly 25 per cent. By contrast only some 3 per cent of total US energy supplies passed through the canal. The US could also draw on a substantial amount of surplus productive capacity which could be brought to bear over a period of weeks or months.[58]

The Western perceptions of and response to the nationalization and seizure of the canal, leading to the joint Israeli, British and French intervention in late October 1956, were strongly influenced by the increasing European dependence on Middle Eastern oil, as well as the commanding US position in the international oil market. As one London newspaper asserted, 'The Canal is an oil pipeline, an economic lifeline'.[59] In addition to the immediate threat of an interruption of oil supplies through the closure of the canal, there was the longer-term threat of 'Nasserism' encouraging the further erosion of access to oil and other resources in colonial and former colonial areas.[60]

The blockage of the canal following the joint military operations in Egypt resulted in the normal flow of 1 350 000 barrels per day of Middle Eastern oil being cut off. When Syria blew up the pumping facilities of the Iraq Petroleum Company, a further 550 000 barrels of Iraqi oil was lost. Thus, the only remaining Middle Eastern supplies available to Europe were the 200 000 barrels per day imported from Saudi Arabia via Tapline. The inevitable result of this situation was a sudden increase in European oil imports from the Western Hemisphere. These supplies would form an important part of the American political 'leverage' throughout the crisis. The expansion of Western Hemisphere exports, together with the drawing-down of existing stocks, meant that Western European oil consumption was maintained at roughly 80 per cent of normal levels, although the financial consequences of the crisis were substantial.[61] The oil supply problem during the Suez crisis was never really one of an absolute shortage of product. The closure of the canal and the sabotage of pipelines had, however, led to a severe tanker crisis flowing from the suddenly increased distances and transit times.[62]

The decision to intervene militarily in Egypt was based on the perceived imperatives of removing Nasser, stemming the erosion of control over, and access to, oil-producing areas, and preventing oil-based 'economic strangulation' in the short-term. The strong American oil position, coupled with increasing European desperation with regard to oil supply, contributed to the US ability to press for the withdrawal of British and French forces from Egypt in December 1956. Finally, the experience of the Suez Crisis left political and military leaders in the NATO countries more actively aware that access to adequate supplies of oil was an essential prerequisite for economic prosperity and 'grand strategy'.[63] Moreover, it was clear that oil supply disruptions—Western vulnerability to which was steadily increasing—held within them the potential for serious strains in alliance relationships, as the events of 1956 had clearly demonstrated.

In the context of American strategy, however, the question of whether access to Middle Eastern oil represented a 'vital' interest continued to be a matter of debate. It was again asserted that Western Hemisphere sources were capable of supplying US needs, though perhaps at higher cost, and that even Western Europe could survive for limited periods without access to Middle Eastern sources. Indeed, this could be seen as one lesson of the 1956–57 supply crisis. The Suez Canal had been closed at times during World War II, and its use would very likely be denied to the West in a future major conflict. NATO strategy, it was argued, must take account of the fact that Middle Eastern supplies were unlikely to be available in a general war, and that Europe—with American support—could probably fight without such supplies.[64] Furthermore, while the oilfields and facilities, of the Middle East might appear to offer a tempting objective to the Soviet Union, with regard to both denial and access, the larger significance of such an attack in wartime could, in reality, prove less substantial. Whereas the Soviet Union could surely destroy or deny Middle Eastern oil facilities, the Soviet war economy could not readily make use of such resources due to the lack of suitable pipelines for the transport of the oil to Russia, and the parallel ability of the Western allies to deny the use of the oilfields through strategic bombing.[65]

Existing United States' policy did, in fact, emphasize the denial of Middle Eastern oil resources and facilities in the event that they were threatened by hostile forces. From 1957 this approach was modified in order to stress the 'conservation and protection' of Middle Eastern oil resources and facilities, with denial confined to direct military action in the event of confirmed seizure. The basis for this planning adjustment was the recognition that it would be difficult for the US to implement the existing plans for denial, as there were no US military forces available for denial actions in the area, and civilian oil company employees could not legally be used to carry out denial through sabotage. It was also recognized that the British were somewhat more favourably placed to carry out such operations, since there was no parallel legal bar to impressing British civilian personnel in the service of denial actions. Finally, it was clear that the American oil companies were particularly wary of denial plans, and any discussion of denial programmes with Middle Eastern countries could have serious diplomatic consequences. By contrast, discussions with Middle Eastern governments would be possible, and their co-operation in the event of a crisis more likely, if planning were directed towards 'conservation and protection' (for example, the plugging of wells) in the event of a crisis.[66]

One may identify a growing recognition in American strategic thinking that the oil supply problems of the United States could not be considered in isolation from those of Western Europe. Thus, one author would declare: 'Oil supplies for the rehabilitation and rearmament of free Europe are hardly less important for our security than oil for the armed services of the United States'. The economic reality of increasing European dependence on Middle Eastern oil supplies was seen to dictate that American strategy be tailored to the absolute requirement that these resources not be allowed to fall under Soviet control.[67] Nonetheless, it was asserted that the West must be prepared for the prospect of interruptions of this vital supply, including cut-offs originating in local or regional action, rather than direct Soviet intervention. This view is very much in the spirit of more recent writing on this subject, particularly the analyses which have come in the wake of the events of 1973 and 1979–80.

In his June 1958 remarks before the Council on Foreign Relations, Walter Levy examined the security dimensions of access to oil supplies. He warned that strategic planning should take adequate account of the fact that the threat of a loss of supply could transform a limited engagement into a general war. By contrast, the possession of secure sources of supply might be decisive in preventing escalation. In a statement which could well have been applied to contemporary developments in the Persian Gulf, Levy asserted: 'We must . . . avoid a situation where because of oil shortages that would vitally cripple our allies, we would be forced to redress the balance by the threat or even the use of force'.[68]

Levy further emphasized that in the event of a nuclear war, fought with forces in being, NATO's oil position would 'hardly be relevant to the outcome'. The only necessity with regard to oil supply in such a contingency would be the availability of adequate stocks to support the operation of deterrent and retaliatory strategic forces. Neither the US nor its allies, it was asserted, was preparing to fight a massive and prolonged conventional war. Since the cost of preparing for such a war would be unacceptable, it would make little sense to undertake the task of preparing for such a contingency in a specific aspect of war economy such as oil supply. Nevertheless, there remained the possibility of limited war in such areas as the Middle East, and in this context the nature of the Western oil position could be significant for the reasons set out above. In the final analysis, the continued accessibility of adequate quantities of oil 'may be decisive not so much for victory or defeat as for the ability to limit a war'. Thus, Levy went on to argue for the expanded development of Western Hemisphere sources, the maintenance of surplus production, refining and tanker capacity, strategic oil stocks, and the diversification of sources.[69] Then, as now, the alternative to such measures to reduce vulnerability in the event of a crisis involving the Soviet Union, would be the creation of a 'trip-wire' policy in the Gulf, with its associated problems of credibility and escalation.

The international oil position through the 1960s, at least until 1967, gave little apparent cause for concern. The fear over energy shortages which accompanied, and to an extent caused the Suez crisis, had been replaced by general confidence with regard to the energy situation in Europe and elsewhere as the international petroleum market experienced a prolonged period of expanding capacity and surplus production (OPEC was formed in 1960, largely in response to the oil companies' reduction in the price of oil, and thus producing state royalties).[70] US military planners produced optimistic estimates of the amounts of petroleum products which would be available to support major operations such as the reinforcement of Europe. Also, by 1961 the number of US flag tankers in operation had virtually doubled since 1955, improving the prospects for the movement of bulk petroleum in a crisis.[71] In 1960 six of the present 13 members of OPEC were colonies or protectorates, and the important resource-related straits of Hormuz, Aden and Malacca were all under European control.[72]

WAR IN SOUTHEAST ASIA

The denial of resources to the enemy had played a limited role in the formation of American and allied strategy in Korea, notably in terms of the argument for interdicting transport across the Amur. The concept of controlling resource flows in the countryside to cut off supplies to guerrilla forces also played a role in Korea. This aspect of resource denial was, however, pursued with considerably more vigour and determination throughout the Vietnam War. In the early 1960s a programme of some magnitude (and doubtful effect) was initiated with the aim of establishing resource control points on routes leading into and out of cities. Of more immediate concern to American planners was the wider logistic support, including the supply of raw materials, being provided to the Vietcong and the

North Vietnamese Army. In this context, the blockade of the South Vietnamese coast by US and Vietnamese naval forces was highly successful, and led to the North placing increasing emphasis on the Ho Chi Minh Trail. The fact that Cambodia was thought to be acting as an entrepôt for trade with North Vietnam has been cited as contributing to the eventual American involvement in that country.[73] One may suggest that the American experience in Vietnam also influenced the policy of relying on regional power (for instance, Iran) rather than the presence of American forces to safeguard the oil-bearing regions of the Middle East following the British withdrawal from the Persian Gulf in 1971.[74]

THE EVENTS OF 1967 AND 1970

The Middle East War of 1967 did not, on the whole, give rise to significant concern in the West with regard to the security of oil supplies.[75] Shortfalls in deliveries to Western Europe were adequately offset by increased American production and the diversion of supplies intended for US domestic consumption.[76] The effect of the closure of the Suez Canal was not substantial since the supertankers engaged in the transport of large quantities of oil from the Persian Gulf could not, in any event, make use of the canal with its limited controlling depth. The attempt by Arab OPEC members (OAPEC) to organize an embargo at the time of the 1967 war led to some degree of concern, particularly in Europe, 'but its abject failure suggested that producer efforts to manipulate or control the supply for political purposes were bound to fail'. The limited perception of vulnerability did little to discourage the continued expansion of oil use in the Western industrialized countries (and elsewhere), and the consequent increasing dependence on Middle Eastern oil supplies.[77]

The year 1970, however, saw a seminal development in the international oil position, one which in retrospect may be seen as the first step in a continuum of price and supply crises. In that year the new Qadafi regime in Libya took advantage of a temporary interruption in the flow of oil through a major Persian Gulf-Mediterranean pipeline to stage a confrontation with American oil companies operating in Libya, leading ultimately to the Teheran agreement of 1971 and 'price leapfrogging' that continued for over a decade. In the opinion of a noted commentator on energy security issues, 'after the

Libyan crisis, access to energy [again] became crucial to U.S. national security'.[78]

Estimates by the President's Task Force on Oil Import Control (1970) suggested that in the event of a large-scale conventional war, direct US military requirements would expand only to levels that could be met through Western Hemisphere supplies, together with appropriate emergency measures and civilian rationing.[79] No doubt, America's European and Japanese allies would be severely affected by the denial of supplies from the Middle East, even if imports from North Africa, Nigeria and Indonesia could be maintained. As one writer would suggest, however, 'on a cold, hard view . . . it is very difficult to imagine an extended conventional war with the Soviets during which virtually all of industrial Europe remained under NATO control'.[80] The more relevant security problem was perceived to arise from the possibility of a producer embargo under conditions of political tension short of war.

> From the national security standpoint it is essential that the United States avoid the temptation to adopt some sort of interventionist military policy as a means of dealing with the problem. An Indian Ocean navy, taking up the British colonial role 'East of Suez,' and similar approaches are likely to accomplish nothing but mischief. . . . In the case of all-out conventional war with the Soviets, continuing interventionism prior to that conflict will be equally likely to decrease as to increase the probability of maintaining wartime supplies. Against the contingency of a short-term political embargo, prior interventionist policies would be even more irrelevant. . . . *Oil provides no exception to the basic proposition . . . that U.S. national security interests and the rationale for the size and structure of U.S. military forces cannot be defined in terms of protecting access to markets or raw material sources abroad* [emphasis added].[81]

It is a mark of the profound effect which events from 1973 onwards would have on Western thinking on resources and strategy that the above quotation seems to be the very antithesis of the 'vital interests' approach embodied in the Carter Doctrine and subsequently reaffirmed. The view reflected above would, however, emerge again in reaction to the notion of 'resource wars', and form part of the continuing debate on the proper relations between resources and strategy.

OVERALL OBSERVATIONS ON RESOURCES AND STRATEGY, 1945–73

In sum, the period from the end of World War II to that immediately preceding the Middle East War and oil crisis of 1973 was a formative one with regard to Western strategic thought and planning in the resource sphere. The wartime legacy of planning for access to raw materials provided the basis for early post-war thinking on the nature of resource requirements in a general war. While such early planning was based essentially on a re-enactment of the previous war, the new realities posed by the deployment of nuclear weapons in increasing numbers began to assert themselves in the context of resource planning as in other aspects of strategy. The access and denial of vital resources might well be largely irrelevant in the event of strategic nuclear war, apart from the existence of high-value targets in the industrial base (although even here there were dissenters from the orthodoxy), yet the availability of adequate raw materials to wage conventional warfare of varying scale would remain a concern.

Resource considerations clearly played an active role in Western, and particularly American, strategic perceptions throughout the Cold War. The notion of containment, in both its 'strong point' and 'perimeter defence' incarnations made reference to centres of raw material and industrial production in an effort to define those areas vital to Western security. At the same time, perceived Soviet threats to the oil fields of the Middle East provided the principal basis for Western strategic planning in relation to the region at least until the time of the Suez crisis—itself closely related to considerations of oil supply security. From 1956, one may suggest that Western political and military leaders began to take increasing account of the regional and domestic threats to access to oil and other resources. With the increasing sophistication of thought regarding the relationship between nuclear weapons, conventional warfare and deterrence, analysts began to consider the implications of secure access to resources such as oil for the limitation of conflict, and the danger of escalation should access be severely threatened.

The rapidly expanding worldwide demand for fuel and non-fuel raw materials, stimulated by European and Japanese recovery and relatively high levels of economic growth, coupled with the experience of mobilization during the Korean War, led to several extensive studies of the US and broader, Western resource positions. The most important of these was the President's Materials Policy Commission which made a number of significant observations with regard to the direction of military technology, strategy and resource requirements. Most notably, the report acknowledged the increasing degree of dependence on foreign sources of raw materials as a fact which could not, and should not, be averted through autarkic policies. Thus, it was asserted that the protection of important overseas resources, and the means of communication with them, would remain a vital Western interest, and would necessarily shape American strategy and military deployments.

Finally, developments in the international oil market, principally the increasing power of producing states, culminating in the 1970 Libyan crisis, set the stage for the events of 1973–74 which would bring issues of oil and strategy, as well as the question of strategic minerals, to the fore. Developments in the 1970s and 1980s would intensify the debate, which had its origins in the early post-war years, with regard to likely threats, the prospects for intra-alliance conflict over resource questions, and the implications of resource vulnerability for the East-West strategic relationship.

6 Oil and Strategic Planning Since 1973

There is a long-standing Anglo-American, and to a lesser extent, a continental European tradition of defending, at the very least, critical portions of the international trade structure (including lines of communication) for resources. In a sense, the reliance on overseas trade has been treated as a historically accepted vulnerability. The period 1973 to the present has seen a series of crises posing actual or potential threats to Western access to oil supplies. The 'oil shocks' of 1973–74 and 1979–80, coupled with the Soviet invasion of Afghanistan and the recent war in the Persian Gulf, have given rise to a very substantial amount of comment concerning oil and security, often giving the impression that oil vulnerability is something new on the strategic scene. Clearly, this is far from being the case. Nevertheless, while resource vulnerabilities have been an enduring concern of political and military leaders, the events in the Middle East and Southwest Asia over the past two decades have caused such perceptions of vulnerability to reassert themselves strongly in Western, and particularly American, strategy.

Considerations of oil supply can exert a fourfold influence on 'national strategies' in peacetime. Elements of such influence include the definition of vital regional and other interests, the formation of alliance and arms transfer policies, the composition of force structures, and the decision to deploy military forces or initiate or enter a conflict.[1] As preceding chapters have discussed, a second general category of influence springs from the role of oil in the establishment and pursuit of strategy in periods of crisis and war.[2] In the nuclear age it is clear that oil has maintained its importance for strategic planning in peace and war. This has been so, in large measure, because of the tremendous expansion of demand for oil in civilian economies worldwide, together with the fact that conventional warfare of all sorts remains heavily dependent on adequate supplies of petroleum and petroleum products.

Whereas a substantial gulf exists between perceived and actual vulnerability in the case of many 'strategic' or 'critical' materials, Western vulnerability with regard to oil is far more tangible and problematic for defence planners. Oil continues to be different, 'not because it is a "noble" product as the Shah was fond of saying, but rather because it is so commonly used in such enormous quantities even while its supply is greatly concentrated'.[3] Oil remains, as Henry Kissinger has stated, 'the world's most strategic commodity'.[4] A number of questions may be raised in this context: first, how have Western, and particularly American, strategic plans and policies evolved in the face of a succession of oil supply and related regional crises? Subsidiary questions to be explored include the role of conventional and nuclear deterrence and defence in safeguarding access to oil, and, importantly, who constitutes the 'enemy' with regard to oil supply? Finally, what observations may be made concerning current issues in historical perspective?

One of the principal problems for strategic planning in the area of oil security has been the progression from a generalized assumption of vulnerability to specific policies tailored to identifiable threats. The very high degree of uncertainty with regard to the future demand for oil and its price, together with the diverse and unpredictable nature of the potential threats to oil supply, demands considerable flexibility in strategic planning. As Thomas Schelling has suggested, and events in the Gulf region have shown, the key principle underlying any planning for energy security must be the principle of uncertainty; 'the one certainty is uncertainty'.[5]

THE 1973 MIDDLE EAST WAR AND ITS AFTERMATH

As has been noted, the first phase of the 'energy crisis' had its origins in the events of 1971 and, indirectly, in the process of increasing assertiveness on the part of resource-producing countries set in motion by the Suez crisis. Even prior to the outbreak of the October War and the embargo and oil supply crises which followed, it had become evident that the economic and political conditions for a supply crisis already existed.[6] In 1970 the US Cabinet Task Force on Oil Imports had asserted that dependence on imports of as little as 10 per cent of American oil supply would threaten national security. By 1973 American imports amounted to roughly 35–36 per cent of total requirements, with some 11 per cent arriving from Arab producers.[7] More significantly, on the eve of the October War, Britiain, France, Germany, Italy and Japan were reliant on imports for virtually all of their oil, with the bulk of these imports coming from the Middle

East.[8] In March 1973 Air Vice-Marshall S. W. B. Menaul remarked: 'The strategic importance of oil . . . still does not receive the attention of military strategists that it merits.[9]

In response to the American resupply of Israeli forces during the October War, the Arab members of OPEC (OAPEC) cut oil production by 25 per cent and, on 20 October, imposed an embargo on oil shipments to the US, The Netherlands and Canada. Other countries, exempted from the embargo, also experienced supply shortages since the embargo affected shipments through Rotterdam, Europe's principal refining and trans-shipment centre.[10] The embargo and cut in production produced price increases far in excess of the 70 per cent envisaged by OPEC planners. The ensuing panic in the world oil market led to a rapid 400 per cent increase over pre-war oil prices.[11]

Despite the fact that the overall shortfall in supply was only some 7 per cent, the crisis sparked European fears of a substantial threat to the continued functioning of industry and transport, and led to 'anxiety-ridden diplomatic behaviour as each country sought to insure itself against the worst'.[12] One immediate response on the part of several key NATO countries was to deny landing and overflight rights to US aircraft engaged in the resupply airlift to Israel, at least in part to forestall any further OAPEC measures. More generally, the crisis gave impetus to European and Japanese efforts to construct bilateral agreements with oil-producing states as a hedge against future supply disruptions.

The developments in 1973–74 gave rise to the most acute fears in Japan, where dependence on oil imports was the most extreme of all the industrialized countries—roughly 99 per cent at the time of the crisis.[13] There can be little doubt that the ominous oil supply situation served to reawaken long-standing Japanese concerns with regard to the country's historic Achilles' heel. Finally, the anticipated massive transfer of funds from the oil-consuming to the oil-producing states led to exaggerated, but at the time very real, fears about the stability of the international financial system. Given the vastly increased perception of vulnerability to politically motivated uses of the 'oil weapon' it is not surprising that the question of Western intervention to secure access to oil at tolerable prices, and in adequate quantity, began to emerge in discussion of possible responses to the oil crisis.

During the 1973–74 shortages the US Navy was compelled to reduce ship time at sea by 20 per cent, and the Air Force to reduce flying time by some 33 per cent. By December 1973 fuel shortages were beginning to impose similar constraints on NATO operations. Dutch air and ground forces were compelled to refuel at US facilities in Britain and Germany, while training exercises involving the large-scale transportation of men and equipment were seriously affected.[14] In November 1973 the Danish government reportedly asked that NATO forces bring their own petroleum supplies to the NATO exercise ABSALOM EXPRESS as Denmark would be unable to meet the anticipated fuel requirements. Such measures were necessary despite the fact that NATO peacetime petroleum consumption for military activities represented an average of only 5 per cent of total national consumption. Finally, in November 1973, it was reported that the Philippines, Japan and Singapore had restricted oil supplies to US forces in the Pacific, forcing the US to employ wartime reserves in order to meet its petroleum requirements in the region.[15]

The principal point is that despite the short-lived nature of the shortage, the effect on defence capabilities was immediate and visible.[16] A US Department of Defense memorandum of November 1973 concluded that 'there can be no avoidance of the unpleasant fact that the ability of the United States to conduct its military operations with complete flexibility ... is now for the first time temporarily inhibited' by petroleum supply considerations.[17]

The spectre of 'economic strangulation' in the event that price or supply levels threatened the financial stability and economic survival of the West, led some strategists to suggest the use of force to seize key centres of oil production in the Middle East. The essential argument here was that continued acquiescence in cartel price rises brought with it costs in terms of national and global well-being and security so high as to justify military intervention or the 'internationalization' of major petroleum resources.[18] According to one 1974 estimate, in order to meet OECD oil needs it would be necessary, at a minimum, to secure and operate the oilfields of the Western Persian Gulf coast, and perhaps those in North Africa as well.[19] The 400-mile strip of coast from Kuwait to Qatar was cited as one of the most suitable targets for military intervention.[20]

Robert Tucker, in an important and controversial article in 1975, decried the unwillingness of the West to consider seriously the use of force in the face of such a substantial threat to its long-term welfare and security. Indeed, it was argued that 'until quite recently' the oil crisis would never have arisen 'because of the prevailing expectation that it would have led to armed intervention'. It was asserted that there was no evidence that the alternative of military intervention was being given 'serious' consideration by American strategists and planners, apart from probable contingency planning of a general sort.[21] Tucker further asserted that discussion with regard to the feasibility of intervention was frequently preceded by a series of 'worst case' assumptions. The rapid seizure and retention of a relatively restricted area, under conditions in which the possibility of a Soviet response was minimized, would, it was argued, stand a good chance of success.[22]

Since the late 1960s, when France raised the issue of the declining ability of the US to act as an emergency supplier to its Western allies, as it had in previous crises, international arrangements for sharing available oil supplies have been the focus of considerable attention. In the wake of the 1973–74 crisis, arrangements regarding stockpiling commitments and rationing plans were formulated through the newly established International Energy Agency (IEA). IEA emergency plans commit member countries (ironically, France elected not to join) to the maintenance of a 90-day reserve, a programme of conservation, and an international plan for the allocation of available volume in an 'emergency'—defined as a 7 per cent shortfall in supply. The IEA mechanisms are extremely complex, and there have been continuing concerns over the level of 'reserves' actually available for IEA-wide allocation within member countries.[23] To date, the emergency allocation system has not been 'triggered'. Yet there is widespread agreement that the existence of institutional mechanisms for coping with oil supply crises are of value in lessening the likelihood of a precipitate military response to the restriction of supply as a result of producer actions or regional turmoil. Despite persistent criticism, the IEA has been seen as both a potential deterrent to hostile action on the part of suppliers, and a basis for market intervention as an alternative to military intervention in support of Western energy security.

Another dimension of the Western reaction to the developments of 1973–74 can be found in the rise and decline of 'arms-for-oil' policies. From 1973 to 1978 the US, France and other arms exporters engaged in a policy of arms sales to Middle Eastern oil producers in an effort to enhance the security of oil supply in its political and strategic elements. Not surprisingly, the efforts of the Carter administration to limit such transfers elicited a generally unfavourable response in Europe where the greater perception of vulnerability to oil supply disruptions and the proliferation of bilateral oil agreements encouraged an arms-for-oil approach. By 1979, however, the arms-for-oil strategy began to decline in utility as a consequence of the crisis in Iran, absorption problems flowing from the earlier rounds of arms transfer, and the doubtful ability or desirability of Saudi Arabia evolving into a viable regional power.[24]

The upheavals in Iran, and the withdrawal of some five million barrels of oil per day of Iranian oil from the world market between 27 December 1978 and 4 March 1979, heralded the start of the 'second phase' of the oil crisis. Virtually overnight surplus production was eliminated, and world oil reserves began to be reduced by some two million barrels per day, with prices rising by 140 per cent as a result of the crisis. These developments posed a particular threat to Western Europe and Japan (and Eastern Europe) as substantial importers of Iranian crude oil. In addition, the Iranian revolution brought to the fore fears about the security and stability of other oil-producing states of the Gulf.[25]

The Soviet invasion of Afghanistan in 1979 was widely perceived as having radically altered the strategic environment surrounding Western access to oil. The eruption of the Iran-Iraq War in September 1980, and the breakdown of exports from these countries, removed an additional four million barrels of oil per day from the world market (some 10 per cent of non-communist crude oil production).[26] Taken together, these developments, occurring over a very short span of time, would transform the place of Middle Eastern oil in Western and, in particular, American strategic planning.

MIDDLE EASTERN OIL AND AMERICAN STRATEGY SINCE 1979

The primary security interests of the United States in the Persian Gulf may be defined as continued Western access to oil and the denial of the region to preponderant Soviet influence.[27] Early in the energy crisis the critical question was deemed to be 'how can the world pay for OPEC oil?' Although this problem has abated—at least for the moment—the issue of price has in any event been overshadowed in the wake of Iran, Afghanistan and the Iran-Iraq War by the more serious question of continued physical access to Middle Eastern oil apart from price.[28]

It is true that as other producing regions are developed (for instance, in Mexico or Venezuela's Orinoco Belt) the relative importance of Middle Eastern oil will continue to decline. However, since roughly two-thirds of the world's total proven oil reserves are in the Middle East, there is little prospect that the diversification of production can seriously reduce Western dependence on the area in the near future.[29] Indeed, additional discoveries of great magnitude in the North African or Middle Eastern regions might well worsen the 'geopolitics' of oil, as would the widespread use of enhanced recovery techniques in the region.[30]

In 1983 oil represented roughly 45 per cent of the energy in world trade. Of this amount, approximately 23 per cent was produced in the states of the Persian Gulf littoral. In the first half of 1983, oil from the Persian Gulf accounted for roughly 6 per cent of American oil imports, 40 per cent of West European imports, and 62 per cent of Japanese imports. The vast bulk of these supplies came by tanker through the Strait of Hormuz.[31] Despite the fact that the degree of American dependence on Persian Gulf oil was considerably higher in 1973–74, the West as a whole does not enjoy a marked reduction in dependence, and the oil-importing countries of the Third World are now even more dependent on such supplies. An often overlooked security dimension of the current oil situation is the fact that a serious supply disruption would have a severe effect on the cost of oil at a time when key debtor countries are trying to recover. Default would be a disaster, and the implications for political stability are evident.[32]

The perceived increased vulnerability of the US and its allies in the wake of the events of 1979–80 and the recent Gulf War, particularly in terms of the military uses of oil, has had a marked effect on defence planning. In past conflicts the US has been able to 'muddle through', with a long mobilization period following the commencement of hostilities. Today, 'the decline in Western control over energy supplies makes readiness in advance of conflict absolutely essential'.[33]

It is even asserted that a major war in the Persian Gulf would make full Western mobilization difficult if not impossible, particularly with regard to conflicts lasting longer than six months to one year. Such a situation, although clearly a worst-case example, would quite likely increase the prospects for escalation to nuclear war.[34]

Crude oil and petroleum products are considerably more important to the military services than to the civilian economy (although not, of course, in terms of volume). The largest percentage of this military consumption (85 per cent in the US case) goes toward ship and aircraft operations. In addition, the two-thirds of US defence consumption used for aircraft requires high-grade products and refining equipment—the rough conversion is two barrels of crude oil per barrel of military product.[35] In sum, the US Department of Defense is not only highly dependent on adequate oil supplies, but such supplies go to support the most vital elements of its mission—the operational readiness of strategic and tactical forces.[36] As suggested earlier, during the relatively minor oil supply crises of 1973–74, and again in 1979, the US Department of Defense 'was hard pressed to maintain even normal operational capabilities due to fuel shortages'.[37]

While oil consumption may increase dramatically in a full-scale conventional war (in World War II direct military consumption increased from one to 33 per cent of all US petroleum production), the scale of civilian use has also increased enormously by comparison since 1945. It is illustrative that the total oil consumption *worldwide* throughout World War II was less than current *daily* US consumption. Thus, the scope for transfer to the military sector is now very much greater than in the past.[38] In 1973 the US Department of Defense estimated a maximum total military demand of 10 per cent of then current consumption, declining to 7 per cent in 1980.[39] Of course, the technical problem of shifting stocks from civilian to military use might limit the timely provision of supplies for mobilization. In addition, considerable allowance must be made for probable losses along sea lines of communication and the vulnerability of pre-positioned stocks in Europe and elsewhere.[40]

Overall, even in a large-scale conventional war, the US would probably experience little difficulty in supplying the necessary volume of petroleum for military requirements from domestic production. In a nuclear war petroleum requirements would almost certainly be more modest due to the likely brevity of such a conflict, and reduced transport requirements.[41] One must also add that a full-scale nuclear exchange would result in the collapse of civilian demand.

The US Department of Defense divides the petroleum supply planning and stockpiling functions into two separate categories: peacetime requirements and war reserves. The latter are pre-positioned to support forward-deployed and reinforcing units in specific theatres, and are designed to meet requirements between the outbreak of conflict and re-supply (roughly 30–60 days—closer to the lower level in Europe). Following this period, re-supply is assumed to be undertaken from 'secure' sources such as the US Gulf Coast and Caribbean refineries.[42]

THREATS TO PERSIAN GULF OIL

Threats to the security of Persian Gulf oil may be divided broadly into domestic threats, regional threats and external (that is, Soviet) threats. One might also add the special category of threats to the vital sea lines of communication for oil, which may come from several quarters. It has been asserted that the nature of threats to stability in the Gulf has changed radically with recent developments in the area. The Iranian revolution, although largely the result of internal strains, represented a severe set-back to American credibility in the region. It served to underline the potential for domestic unrest, while raising questions about the wisdom of alignment with the West. The invasion of Afghanistan, which brought Soviet tactical airpower within range of the Gulf, also served to raise questions about the efficacy of the 'Western connection' for states in the region, and posed—at least by implication—'the option of accomodation with the Soviet Union as a hedge against further interventions'.[43]

The crises in Iran and Afghanistan were murky and interactive. Both started as domestic events and had major international consequences, and each event reinforced the other. The invasion of Afghanistan would have been less likely had Iran remained stable. The politico-military consequences for the Gulf would also have been considerably reduced if Iran had remained a dependable pro-Western state. These two events illustrate the point that threats to stability in the Gulf are multiple (domestic, regional and external), murky (they are ambiguous in their origins and not clearly delineated as such), and interactive (they tend to be reinforcing rather than discrete, autonomous or isolated events).[44]

With regard to domestic sources of instability, it is difficult to predict the manner in which political and social institutions in the oil producing countries will change in order to manage the problems which confront them. These problems include the potentially destructive forces of rapid development (and its sudden halt in the face of falling oil prices), of foreign education, of immense wealth and equally immense corruption, and of a massive influx (and more recent exodus) of foreign labour. One might add to these the pressures of Islamic fundamentalism and Marxist ideology.[45]

Threats to the region's security which originate in domestic politics are perhaps the most resistant to outside influence. Again, few of these domestic sources of instability which can threaten oil supply are without international ramifications. Separatist forces, which exist in many areas of the Middle East, including major oil-producing countries, are of particular concern. Saudi Arabia is not immune to similar pressures.[46] The West must be sensitive to the potential domestic sources of instability in the oil-producing countries of the Gulf. Yet it has been suggested that an excessive preoccupation with such threats may in fact jeopardize the stability of states such as Saudi Arabia. The constant American questioning of Saudi stability and the capacity of the royal family to rule effectively is perceived by some to threaten that very rule. A source familiar with the problem has commented that 'although it may not be appreciated in Washington, the US obsession with the possibility that Saudi Arabia may become another Iran is watched with keen interest by virtually every embassy in the city', and is recognized by other states in the Gulf.[47]

A second threat to Gulf stability may be seen in the prospect of aggression against an oil-producing state by another state in the region. The war between Iraq and Iran, now apparently on the verge of a settlement, provided the clearest example of the threat posed by this sort of conflict. Air attacks by both countries on oil tankers and freighters in the Persian Gulf, together with persistent Iranian threats to block the Strait of Hormuz, raised the spectre of a major interruption of oil supplies and a consequent increase in the price of oil worldwide. So, too, there has been a continuing risk of escalation which might involve other states in the Persian Gulf.

From 1984, and with increasing persistence after 1985, Iraq attempted to force Iran to curtail hostilities by interrupting that country's vital oil exports, income from which contributed substantially to the Iranian war effort.[48] These attacks took the form of air strikes against tanker traffic to and from Iranian ports on the Gulf, along with attacks on the Kharg Island terminal and other key facilities. This 'indirect' strategy, initially directed principally at Kharg Island, 'which Iraq has constantly and misleadingly called Iran's jugular' (between August and December 1985 there were 77 attacks on this facility alone) fell far short of expectations.[49] Observers have suggested that the failure of the Iraqi offensive against Kharg Island (which handles 85 per cent of Iran's oil exports) can be attributed to a general inability of Iraqi forces to mount a sustained and intensive, rather than sporadic, campaign against the facility. Thus, the nature of the Iraqi attacks allowed Iran to repair installations and redirect oil to less vulnerable facilities, with only a tolerable loss of the oil revenues on which its war economy has been dependent.[50] Iraqi attacks on the important and vulnerable Gha-naveh pumping facility in January 1986, however, did result in an immediate and significant reduction in Iranian oil exports.[51]

Iranian attacks on Gulf shipping, while of a continuing nature were not of a scale which might have been conducted in response to Iraqi air attacks on resource-related targets.[52] In this sense, Iran was reluctant to be drawn into a 'deliberate escalatory strategy' on the part of Iraq, aimed, at least in part, at provoking an extreme Iranian response, such as an attempt to seriously impede passage through the Strait of Hormuz, which might in turn have provoked a major Western intervention favourable to Iraq. Despite repeated threats with regard to Hormuz, Iran stopped well short of such extreme measures.[53]

There can be little doubt that a serious Iranian attempt to block passage through the Strait of Hormuz would provoke a Western military response beyond the current naval presence. It is unclear, however, that the effects of such an Iranian action would be crippling given the prevailing world oil surplus.[54] It is also quite unlikely that Iran has the capability to block passage through the Strait for more than a very limited period. An attempt by Iran, or perhaps even a terrorist group, to close the Strait could, however, have the effect of inducing a self-perpetuating panic in the oil and marine insurance markets, causing havoc out of all proportion to the scale and duration of the interruption. In this respect the consequences could be similar to those envisioned by the *jeune école* in the late 19th century in proposing sudden attacks of limited duration on British shipping with the aim of provoking a financial panic. To date, however, the oil and shipping structure in the Gulf region has proven to be remarkably resilient in the face of significant potential and actual threats. In the wake of a Gulf War settlement, it is most likely that both Iraq and Iran will strive to maximize oil exports in order to pay for national reconstruction.

While it is difficult to determine the threshold beyond which the US and perhaps Western and Persian Gulf allies might consider more active military intervention to assure access to oil supplies, it has become apparent to close observers that the continued security of Saudi sea lanes and oil facilities continues to represent a likely threshold.[55] Thus, precipitous military action is most unlikely unless Saudi security is directly threatened.[56] To the extent that transfers of anti-aircraft missiles and other military equipment, together with the presence of American early-warning aircraft and naval forces, have improved the prospects for Saudi security, however marginally, the threshold for Western intervention has most likely been raised.[57]

Whatever Soviet motive(s) were in invading Afghanistan, its military presence there has been perceived as a threat to the already delicate balance in the Gulf region—a threat which appears to be waning with the gradual withdrawal of Soviet forces. The events in Afghanistan were, nonetheless, an impressive demonstration that the Soviets have achieved an 'operational mastery' of their increasing capacity for force projection.[58] The invasion advanced the Soviet basing structure some 500 miles, thus bringing such critical areas as the Gulf of Oman and the Strait of Hormuz within unrefuelled reach of Soviet tactical air power. This, together with Soviet bases, anchorages and port facilities in the Red Sea, Gulf of Aden and Persian Gulf, could, in certain circumstances, pose a clear threat to the security of the West's lines of communication for oil.[59]

The Soviet invasion of Afghanistan did not, however, imply that an invasion of Iran was imminent and indeed, the recent agreement for the withdrawal of Soviet forces, makes this an even more remote contingency. The military and political 'price' of occupying Iran would in any case, dwarf that which the Soviet Union has encountered in Afghanistan. The potential for Western military opposition would be much greater as well. In addition, the seizure of any country in the more distant Arabian Peninsula would prove vastly more difficult. Overall, one may conclude that a Soviet invasion of an oil-producing state or an attempt to impede oil shipments from the Gulf represents a rather unlikely case, short of a major East-West crisis or a complete collapse of order in Iran.[60] More apparent is the scope for political leverage which the Soviet Union gained simply from being in a position, *in extremis*, to intervene in the region.

It has been suggested that one possible contingency would be the 'lightning employment' of limited Soviet forces to support a local pro-Soviet group in seizing power within an oil-producing state. Limited forces might also be used to pre-empt the arrival of Western rapid deployment forces in a crisis.

Given the proximity of the Soviet Union to the Gulf, the inherent strategic mobility of airborne forces, and the Soviet military's pronounced doctrinal and operational emphasis on surprise, distant U.S. rapid deployment forces could well arrive in the Persian Gulf only to find their objectives already occupied by Soviet airborne forces which, unlike their U.S. counterparts, possess impressive firepower and a high level of tactical mobility. The choice at that point would be unenviable: to withdraw, or fire the first shot against the Soviet Union.[61]

A strong and early statement of the Soviet threat to Western oil can be found in James Schlesinger's farewell observations as US Secretary of Energy in 1979:

> Of late, Mr. Georgi Arbatov, whose links to the KGB are perhaps not so well known as his ability to influence and pacify American elites, has opined in an interview that the Soviet Union 'would certainly not interfere with Western oil supplies' for these 'would be very hostile acts, close to a declaration of hostilities'. Some will, no doubt, find such off-hand verbal guarantees wholly reassuring. I merely note that the episode provides a clue to those options about which the Soviets have been ruminating—and which, we may hope, they have rejected, at least for the moment . . . For those less complacent, the underlying implications are stark. Soviet control of the oil tap in the Middle East would mean the end of the world as we have known it since 1945 and of the association of free nations . . . That quite clearly implies that we cannot for long acquiesce in a regional preponderance of Soviet military power.[62]

Schlesinger also stressed that the most significant element of the 'energy crisis' was that it represented a new dimension in the ideological and political competition between the West and the Soviet Union, as borne out by Soviet actions in the 1973 October War, the essential point being that the energy security problem must be viewed as 'part of a much larger strategic canvas'.[63]

An important distinction should be drawn between the 'denial' of Persian Gulf oil and the direct or indirect 'control' of oil supplies by an adversary. The control or 'potential denial' of oil by the Soviet Union would clearly place severe and perhaps intolerable strains on the US alliances with NATO Europe and Japan. Although there can be little reason to assume a Soviet plan for the annexation of the oil-producing regions of the Gulf under current circumstances, this might not be the case under quite different conditions.[64] Notably, the Soviet Union might be tempted to take military action in the Gulf if it perceived a general war with the West to be imminent, or if a sudden development (for example, turmoil in Iran or Saudi Arabia) provided a compelling opportunity to gain a dramatic strategic advantage *vis-à-vis* the West.[65] The confluence of these two conditions would clearly increase the likelihood of a Soviet attack, particularly if the Soviet leadership judged an attack on the Gulf to be less risky than a direct attack on NATO in Europe.

As forecasts of an impending Soviet need for overseas oil supplies have been tempered by the realization that the overall energy balance in the Soviet Union is 'likely to remain positive well into the future', the fear of a Soviet drive south for access to oil has receded. Beyond the above conditions, should the Soviets ever perceive a strategic opportunity in curtailing the flow of Persian Gulf oil, it would most likely be due, not to their own energy requirements, but rather to the enormous influence it would bestow over Europe and Japan.[66]

An issue of particular concern to US observers has been the security of the sea lines of communication from the Gulf to the oil-consuming nations. The lines of communication for oil are clearly vulnerable to regional as well as external threats, as the recent 'tanker war' in the Gulf demonstrates. A successful blockade of the Strait of Hormuz could impose substantial costs on the European and Japanese economies.[67] The military consequences could be dramatic as well, as a blockade could hardly remain a 'local' crisis, as it would represent a major challenge to the West which could easily lead to a wider conflict.[68]

As previously noted, Iran appears to be the most likely source of an attempt to disrupt shipping through the Strait of Hormuz through artillery or air attack, naval blockade or mining (although, in a post-war environment there would be very strong incentives for Iran to keep the oil routes open). The threat to close Hormuz was made explicitly in a speech by Ayatollah Khomeini on 22 September 1983, and has been repeated on several occasions, most notably on 18 May 1984 and 22 September 1985 (the fifth anniversary of the start of the Gulf war).[69] Again, Iran has shown little willingness to move beyond rhetoric with regard to the actual closure of the Strait, and it is unlikely that actions to restrict tanker passage, if initiated could be maintained for very long.

Long before the build-up of American and Western naval forces in the Gulf region, US policy-makers expressed a willingness to contemplate the use of force in order to protect the sea lines of communication for oil. White House spokesman Larry Speakes, referring to the Iranian threat to the Strait of Hormuz, stated that 'we would view with grave concern attempts by any party to interfere with the right of passage by non-belligerent shipping through international waters'.[70] President Reagan also told a news conference on 19 October 1983: 'I do not believe the free world could stand by and allow anyone to close the Strait of Hormuz . . . to oil traffic'.[71]

One should also note that technology has progressed to the point that the detection and attack of surface vessels is considerably easier than in the past. So, too, the cost of defending vessels against attack has risen sharply. In addition to the Soviet Union, local states, and perhaps even terrorist groups now possess the capability to attack surface elements and shipping.[72] The experience with mines in the Red Sea and the Gulf, as well as the use of shore and air-launched missiles against a variety of naval targets, confirms the general proliferation of such capabilities.

THE CARTER DOCTRINE AND THE ROLE OF FORCE IN THE PERSIAN GULF

In his January 1980 State of the Union Speech, President Carter declared that the US would be prepared to use force if necessary to protect vital interests in the Persian Gulf, including the supply of oil. The 'Carter Doctrine' identified the Soviet Union as the principal threat:

> Let our position be absolutely clear: an attempt by any outside force to gain control of the Persian Gulf region will be regarded as an assault on the vital interests of the United States of America. And such an assault will be repelled by any means necessary including military force.

On 28 January 1980 Secretary of Defense Harold Brown produced a variant on the Carter theme (some have labelled this the 'Brown Doctrine') stating that he recognized a greater and more likely danger to oil supplies arising from regional turbulence.[73] In short, whether the Soviet Union was likely to intervene or not, 'the threat of violence and the use of force remain widespread'.[74]

The Carter Doctrine found initial military expression in the stationing of a fleet in the Arabian Sea which included 17 warships, seven support vessels and a force of 1800 marines; in the placement of pre-positioning ships at Diego Garcia to support a Marine brigade with weapons, ammunition and supplies; in 'agreed access' to facilities in Kenya, Somalia, Oman and Egypt; and in the development of a Rapid Deployment Force (later the Rapid Deployment Joint Task Force, and now known as Central Command or CENTCOM). The RDF was an 'aggregation' of Marine and Army divisions, Air Force wings, carrier battle groups, and supporting mobility personnel.[75] Most recently, the Reagan Administration has committed itself to improving the rapid reaction element of the force through the charter of additional pre-positioning ships and the procurement of several fast logistics ships.

Given the clear and at least theoretically identifiable threats to Western interests in the Gulf region, and the commitment contained in the Carter Doctrine, it is appropriate to ask what the mission for such rapid deployment forces is to be. This is necessary because the design of the RDF and the terms of the Carter Doctrine both suggested that the force was primarily designed to counter potential Soviet aggression. Yet, as mentioned, the direct Soviet threat may not constitute the sole or even the most likely contingency. Recently, however, an expansion of the force's mission to include domestic and regional contingencies in the Gulf has been emphasized. Following the Gulf War, the focus on regional threats will surely remain.

As originally conceived, the RDF was 'dedicated to missions anywhere outside the NATO area'. In fact, the force came to be viewed almost entirely as a means of intervention in Persian Gulf crises.[76] Moreover, the Carter Doctrine's reference to 'outside force', together with DOD policy guidance, served to define the primary RDF mission as being to 'deter or defend against Soviet intervention in the vital Persian Gulf region'.[77]

The question of whether the mission of the force is to be interpreted in a broad or restrictive manner is an important one indeed. The notion which stresses the force's role as a Soviet counter has drawn a great deal of criticism from analysts who assert that the most likely threats are domestic or regional in nature. Similarly, Gulf sources have reacted with some alarm to the idea of a force tailored for intervention on a local level. Oblique Western references to the seizure of oilfields as a potential response to OPEC actions, common since 1973, reinforce this unease.[78] Unfortunately for the prospects of political acceptability in the Gulf, a rapid deployment force which is responsive to the imperative of protecting Western access to oil must have the capacity to intervene in crises arising from domestic or regional as well as Soviet sources.

Whereas in Europe the objective of an American presence is also to deter Soviet aggression, in the Persian Gulf the purpose is, again, to ensure access to the region's oil supplies. Given this, the US can have no 'single standing and identifiable adversary' in the Gulf.[79] The murky and interactive circumstances under which force may have to be threatened or employed, pose potential political and strategic dilemmas for the US. Political dilemmas may arise because the force might have to be used in response to internal developments in a Gulf

state; strategic dilemmas because action may be required in circumstances difficult to predict.[80]

The consensus of opinion among observers in the US is that
CENTCOM is now granted a fairly broad range of missions. Evidence of this began to emerge early on, with Under Secretary of
Defense Robert Komer's assertion in hearings on the RDF that 'the
most immediate threat to stability in the Indian Ocean area is not an
overt Russian attack, but rather internal instability, coups and
subversion'.[81] Former Secretary of State Alexander Haig's comment
that 'a change in the *status quo* in the region' would be countered
'with the full range of power assets' of the US also appeared to go
somewhat beyond a strict interpretation of the Carter Doctrine.[82]

One may discern a growing consensus throughout the 1970s and
1980s that the cure for the 'insolvency' of US foreign policy with
regard to the Persian Gulf and oil security must be a restoration of,
among other things, the necessary military means. It has been
suggested as well that the temptation will exist to find a substitute for
this need. The experience of the past decade is seen to illustrate the
fact that there can be 'no reliable substitute for Western power in the
Gulf'. The use of regional surrogates, on the model of Iran, or of
'collective non-alignment' may be hampered by the conditions of
domestic instability and regional rivalry which characterize the
Gulf.[83] Some important issues flow from this commitment to bolster
Western military power in the Gulf. These include: the constraints
which may exist with regard to the use of military force in securing oil
fields; conventional and nuclear deterrence in the Gulf; and the
operational doctrine which will govern the composition of rapid
deployment forces.

First, it has been asserted that the Iran-Iraq war illustrates that the
most important Western objective in the region, the security of oil
supplies, cannot be protected by CENTCOM forces regardless of
their strength. In short, oil fields are seen as another example of the
'Vietnam War irony that, to take or hold them, you end up
destroying them'.[84] This view was echoed in a well-respected report
which suggested that 'under no circumstances' would a conflict
between the US and the Soviet Union or between the US and any
regional power aid in preserving the flow of oil. Such action would
result in the immediate halt of exports and perhaps do sufficient
damage to the logistical network to halt production for several years
thereafter. The report concludes that 'in short, there is no military
solution to the problem of securing oil supplies'.[85] While this *may* be

so with regard to the physical occupation of oil fields, the Gulf War surely demonstrates the clear utility of military presence as a deterrent to unrestricted attacks on oil shipments.

Broader arguments questioning the utility of military force in Gulf contingencies have been put forth by former Secretary of State Cyrus Vance and Stanley Hoffmann. The former has stated that increased military power in the region is a 'basis, not a substitute for diplomacy,' and warns against the 'dangerous fallacy of the military solution to non-military problems'.[86] Stanley Hoffmann goes further, presenting in Robert Tucker's words 'the average European view' of the Carter Doctrine as 'militaristic and simplistic'.[87]

Persistent critics of American policy towards the Persian Gulf, such as Michael Klare, perceive an increased emphasis on 'short-term strategic interests'. In this view, the oil and strategic mineral issues have been used by defence planners to justify new strategies of intervention, rather than encouraging domestic policies aimed at reducing American dependence on foreign sources of supply.[88]

While critics of the policy of strengthening the Western ability to intervene militarily in the Gulf clearly exist, one recognizes a broad consensus of opinion on the importance of developing, at a minimum, the capacity to intervene should Western access to Middle Eastern oil be seriously threatened. Further, given the longstanding importance of oil to the military and civilian economies, it would surely be unwise to call access to adequate supplies a 'short-term strategic interest'. With regard to strategic minerals, critics of current policy are on firmer ground (the question of non-fuel minerals is discussed in chapter 7).

The potential objectives of an intervention to secure oil supplies would be conditioned by specific supply requirements. Clearly, the Middle East might not be the sole or even the most promising objective in all cases. To supply US needs alone, Venezuela (Maracaibo) and Nigeria could suffice to meet civilian demand, and would involve only a slight threat of Soviet intervention.[89] Alternatively, the oil fields of Maracaibo and Libya could meet the demands of the US and some allies, although Soviet naval intervention would be a possibility in the latter case.[90] The need to assure supplies to the US plus any significant portion of NATO and Japanese demand, would require consideration of objectives in the Middle East. Only in the states bordering the Persian Gulf can sufficient quantities be found to meet all Western requirements. The choice of specific target areas would, of course, require very careful consideration.[91]

A key 1979 study asserts that the success of action to seize oil supplies from producers (as opposed to countering an attack by Soviet forces or proxies, local states, or a terrorist group) could be assured only if US forces could satisfy all aspects of a five-part mission: (1) seize required oil installations intact; (2) secure them for weeks, months, or years; (3) rapidly restore damaged assets; (4) operate installations without local co-operation; and (5) guarantee safe overseas passage for oil supplies. 'Failure to fulfill any step, despite all opposition, would constitute failure.'[92]

As the German and Japanese experience in World War II reveals, the protection, restoration and operation of captured oil installations can present formidable obstacles. To be most effective, an intervention force would need to pre-empt the destruction of oil facilities, including the sabotage of production and transport equipment.[93] The vulnerability of oil facilities is apparent; some 60 per cent of Persian Gulf oil exports pass through three ports, with eight central pumping stations controlling the flow of oil.[94] The concentration of facilities enhances this vulnerability. The 40-mile wide strip of coast which stretches from Kuwait to Qatar includes some 1700 wells grouped in 31 fields and served by nine refineries and ten ports.[95]

Many oil producers, including Saudi Arabia, Kuwait and Algeria, have hinted that they would rather sabotage oil wells than leave them intact to be operated by a successful intervention force (that is, in the event that the intervention is aimed not at their protection, but rather at the seizure of oil resources). Prince Fahd has stated, in a somewhat ambiguous comment, that 'if U.S. forces ever invade Saudi Arabia to prevent an interruption of oil supplies, the most that can be done is to blow up the oil fields'.[96]

Three methods of sabotage can be envisioned. First, oil wells could be destroyed, either by blocking them with concrete or rubble—an effort requiring time and labour—or by setting them on fire. Such fires could prove very difficult to extinguish in a timely manner. Second, pumping stations could be wrecked to stop the flow of oil to the ports. These complex systems could be repaired or replaced, although this could prove a difficult task for an expeditionary force. Third, pipelines and other facilities could be destroyed. While these too could be repaired, their destruction would be an effective means of denial, achieved with a minimum of effort.[97] Against these considerations, however, it must be said that over time most facilities could be restored to operation and, given a fair degree of surprise, an intervention force could well pre-empt their destruction altogether.[98]

While the threat or use of force to secure oil supplies may be 'highly circumscribed', this does not mean that it is without its effects.[99] The potential which exists for further serious conflict in the region, bringing with it the destruction of oil facilities, will remain. Once this is accepted, 'then at least one of the great and standing objections' to the reassertion of Western power in the region through the continued development of rapid deployment forces 'must be discarded'. Apart from the Soviet reaction, little can be jeopardized by such forces that 'irrespective of our wishes would not be jeopardized through other developments' and a great deal might be gained.[100] Others have argued, however, that the use of force to remove producer-imposed supply constraints should be viewed with caution, lest it unleash a series of 'unexpected and uncontrollable reactions'.[101]

As in Europe, there must be a relationship between conventional and nuclear deterrence and defence in the Persian Gulf region. This question is of concern in considering the role of rapid deployment forces in countering Soviet threats to oil supplies; particularly since doubt exists as to the ability of such forces to oppose the Soviet Union 'in its own backyard'.

An American defence of Iran, a contingency which has received attention by strategists and force planners, would clearly pose formidable problems. Even given sufficient warning, it has been suggested that US forces might, at best, be able to conduct a delaying and interdiction campaign in central Iran, employing tactical air-power and taking advantage of the natural barrier posed by the Zagroz Mountains; gaining enough time to establish defensive enclaves along the Gulf Coast and in Khuzistan.[102] A State Department official involved in the planning of the original RDF suggested that in such an event 'we might have to choose between committing more forces or alternatively going to areas where the U.S. has greater advantage'. It has also been reported that Robert Komer, in a closed session of the Senate Armed Services Committee, referred to tactical nuclear weapons as America's first line of defence in the Persian Gulf.[103]

In theory the US could employ nuclear weapons to attack the Soviet Union's southern military bases and overseas posts; to block Soviet passage through the Zagroz Mountains; to eliminate Soviet surrogate forces in Iraq; or to destroy Soviet naval forces in the Indian Ocean or the Eastern Mediterranean. The US deploys nuclear weapons in its Mediterranean and Indian Ocean fleets, and could launch strikes from bases in Turkey, Diego Garcia and possibly Egypt. Overall, however, these airfields and carrier forces may be 'more vulnerable to preemptive attack than Soviet nuclear weapons which could be dispersed to dozens of separate bases along its southern border'.[104] Clearly, a nuclear conflict in the region is unlikely to remain geographically limited for long.[105]

Considerable controversy exists on the question of whether rapid deployment forces are, or can be modified to be, capable of meeting a conventional challenge from the Soviet Union without resort to nuclear weapons. Albert Wohlstetter rejects the notion of reliance on nuclear escalation to deter Soviet action:

> The threat of using nuclear weapons in response to a conventional incursion—of introducing a trip-wire or plate-glass defense of the Persian Gulf—is likely to frighten allies, especially those in the region, more than it will the Russians. A nuclear trip-wire defense in the European center becomes progressively less persuasive as Soviet nuclear strength increases at short, medium, and intercontinental range. A trip-wire in the Persian Gulf is likely to be even less persuasive.[106]

Others, such as Robert Tucker, suggest that 'in the limiting situation—a Russian assault in the Gulf—we must either rely on the threat of responding with nuclear weapons or concede that . . . there is no effective response we can make'.[107] Yet even here it is acknowledged that a serious effort to enhance US conventional capabilities with regard to the Persian Gulf is crucial. This is so because, as in Europe, a strategy of nuclear deterrence depends for its credibility on the capacity to respond effectively at lower levels of the escalatory ladder. In any event, the threat of a nuclear response must be reserved for the 'limiting situation' of a Soviet attack.

General Richard Ellis of the Strategic Air Command has pointed out that 'the last thing we want is to be the one who has to initiate nuclear weapons to salvage a force'. The organization of 24 B-52H aircraft into a conventionally-armed Strategic Projection Force in 1981 was designed to widen the fire-break between conventional and nuclear war in defence of oil resources in the Persian Gulf region.[108]

The issue of nuclear deterrence in relation to the oil resources of the Persian Gulf differs from the situation in Europe on the very important question of relative interests. The Carter Doctrine and Reagan administration policy notwithstanding, the Soviets are not likely to perceive American stakes in the Gulf to be as uniformly high as those in Western Europe. Thus, the Soviets may view the US as having a high degree of interest in the defence of Saudi Arabia, but not in the defence of northern Iran. So, too, the absence of a permanent land-based American military presence in the region decreases the risks of immediate escalation.[109] One should bear in mind, however, that ultimately it is the relative balance of interests that will influence the credibility of nuclear and conventional deterrence in relation to the Gulf and its oil resources. On this point, it has been asserted that 'there is no equality of interest between the West and the USSR in the Gulf' and it is misleading to suggest otherwise.[110]

That there is a need for an effective rapidly deployable force as the conventional component of deterrence in the Persian Gulf region is not seriously disputed. The doctrine which ought to govern the composition and use of such a force has, however, been the subject of considerable and continuing debate. It has been said that the current CENTCOM force is 'too heavy to lift and too light to fight'. The RDF as originally conceived was composed largely of mechanized or armoured forces, as it was thought that the terrain and the nature of likely opponents in the Persian Gulf made such forces a necessity. Since 'heavy' forces are difficult to lift rapidly by air, time is traded for firepower. The pre-positioning of material—the current emphasis—and the forward deployment of limited forces would help speed deployment times. Any substantial presence ashore, however, may be self-defeating 'because it excites powerful local nationalism, invariably hostile to that presence'.[111] In addition, a substantial presence ashore tends to make the effectiveness of the force conditional on the co-operation of local states in perhaps unpredictable circumstances.

Accordingly, it is argued by some observers that what is needed is a rapidly deployable force capable of protecting Western interests in the Gulf—principally continued access to oil—while maintaining a low political profile in the region. Specifically, it is argued that what is not needed is a 'large unwieldy combat force that, in the classic American expeditionary tradition, is unable to sustain itself without the presence ashore of an even larger logistical infrastructure'.[112] In this view of the situation, a strategy for the protection of Western access to oil and other interests in the region should be centred on sea-based forces, and the application of maritime power generally.[113]

By contrast, it has been suggested that a 'maritime strategy' for the defence of oil resources in the Gulf region is a fundamentally misguided one. As Robert Komer has stated: 'I will make two points about the Persian Gulf: First you cannot defend the oil from behind. Second, this means that you cannot defend the oil from the sea. You can defend the oil access routes from the sea, but if we lose the oilfields, I do not want to defend the access routes, I want to close them'.[114]

One may identify elements of both continuity and discontinuity in reviewing the policies of the Carter and Reagan administrations with regard to oil and security in the Persian Gulf. Whereas the Carter administration placed relatively greater emphasis on domestic policy as a means of improving energy security, the Reagan administration has taken the course of preparing to deter or defeat the threats to continued 'stable access to oil and the maintenance of the sea lines of communication' for its transport.[115] Apart from a policy of de-regulation with regard to domestic petroleum production, existing initiatives such as the Strategic Petroleum Reserve have been given less than enthusiastic support (the Strategic Petroleum Reserve objective of 250 million barrels is widely perceived as inadequate, and the current fill-rate is behind schedule).[116]

Viewed in perspective, the policy of the Reagan administration with regard to safeguarding Western access to Middle Eastern oil supplies descends directly from what may be termed the 'second' policy of the Carter administration (that is, post-Afghanistan). In the words of one Reagan administration official, the post-Afghanistan Carter policy 'had a great number of good features we decided to keep'.[117] For contingencies short of Soviet involvement, the Reagan administration will need to rely heavily on the co-operation of countries in the region. The prospects for such co-operation may be rated as 'good' in the case of Oman and Bahrain, 'fairly good' in the case of Saudi Arabia, and 'marginal' in the case of Kuwait. The attitude of the United Arab Emirates and Qatar is described as 'very ambivalent'.[118] The subject of intervention in response to Soviet action, such as an invasion of Iran, is now discussed less frequently, with attention currently focussing on the issue of naval presence and shipping protection, and the logistical constraints associated with an American response to regional or local threats.[119]

OVERALL OBSERVATIONS ON OIL AND STRATEGY SINCE 1973

Despite the current surplus on the world market, the issue of safeguarding access to oil retains a prominent place on the strategic agenda. Although the question of intervention as a counter to the 'oil weapon' has declined in importance, the spectre of supply interruptions from various quarters looms large, as it has since the Soviet invasion of Afghanistan and the onset of the Iran-Iraq War. Thus, strategic planners have been confronted with a situation with regard to Middle Eastern oil in which there is not, and cannot be, a single identifiable adversary. There is, rather, a range of potential threats arising from domestic instability in oil-producing states, regional turmoil and external pressure or aggression.

The war between Iran and Iraq clearly demonstrated that while oil facilities, individually, may be highly vulnerable to attack, the oil production and shipping infrastructure itself has proven to be quite resilient—at least in the absence of a concentrated campaign against resource-related targets. Developments in the Gulf War thus reinforced the World War II lessons regarding the adaptability of the system of supply for vital resources under wartime conditions, short of the most intensive and sustained attack. In this context, it is worth noting that many of the most productive Middle Eastern oilfields had not yet been developed in World War II. The relatively greater current strategic importance of such fields which this fact implies is, however, offset by the expansion in the number of important centres of oil production (for example, in the North Sea and Alaska) in recent years.

One must also recognize the importance of perceptions of vulnerability with regard to oil supplies. Thus, while the actual degree of Western import 'vulnerability' (beyond the issue of 'dependency') may vary with time—having declined, it is again approaching the serious levels of the mid-1970s—the continuing perception of a high degree of vulnerability has been the most important element in the formation of strategy to safeguard oil supplies. In the case of American policy, the principal concern with regard to Persian Gulf supplies will continue to be the vulnerability of NATO Europe and Japan (and secondarily, of other importing countries) to supply disruptions.

In terms of the military uses of oil, these continue to be of importance for the maintenance of deterrence in peacetime, as well as for the conduct of limited and general conventional war. In this context, the greatly reduced significance of modern military petroleum requirements relative to the quantities of oil consumed in the civilian economy has created a very different background to the direct military uses of oil from that which existed during the two world wars. The potential for shifting demand from the civilian economy in times of crisis or war is now very much greater than it has been in the past—a development which enhances the American ability to meet defence needs in a conventional conflict. For Europe and Japan vulnerability to a disruption of oil supplies at source or in transit will remain.

Finally, one cannot divorce questions of oil supply security from the broader strategic canvas. Particularly in terms of deterrence and defence at the level of a general conventional conflict with the Soviet Union, the objective of securing access to Middle Eastern oil is related, but ultimately subordinate to the defence of Western European and Asian allies. The defence of the Persian Gulf would be of little or no utility if these vital areas were overrun. Nonetheless, the linkage between the oil supplies of the Persian Gulf and the ability to defend Europe or Asia means that a credible deterrent must also exist in the Gulf.

There is clearly an asymmetry of risk and interest between NATO and the Warsaw Pact in the Persian Gulf which will influence the nature of deterrence in that region. As with Allied planning in World War II, preventing the control or denial of oil supplies by an enemy represents a vital Western interest, but one that flows from consideration of broader strategic requirements. Thus, one may conclude that Western, and particularly post-Afghanistan American policy, is very much in the historical tradition of thinking about oil supply as an element of grand strategy in coalition deterrence and warfare.

7 Strategic Minerals Revisited

The issue of Western vulnerability to interruptions in the supply of 'strategic' or 'critical' non-fuel minerals, particularly as a result of direct or indirect Soviet action, has become increasingly prominent in recent years. Concern over strategic minerals supply at the time of the Korean War, and continuing through the Eisenhower Administration, was followed by a period of complacency lasting into the 1960s in which the primary concern was the economic problem of excess supply. By 1973–74, however, US mineral requirements exceeded existing production capacity as a result of Vietnam War demand coupled with substantial growth throughout the OECD economies. Rapidly increasing prices, together with the nationalization of major producing facilities in the Third World (all this in the wake of the OPEC challenge) raised new fears of potential mineral shortages.[1]

It is noteworthy that a Congressional Commission on Supplies and Shortages, established in the wake of these developments, produced 'reassuring' conclusions. The Cabinet level Non-Fuel Minerals Policy Coordinating Committee, founded by President Carter to review mineral supply issues in the face of perceived complacency, presented similarly 'non-alarmist' findings.[2]

Increased Soviet activity in Africa, principally through proxies, together with the general deterioration of Soviet-Western relations in the late 1970s, rekindled concern about the strategic dimensions of mineral supply, and raised the spectre of what former Secretary of State Alexander Haig and others have termed 'resource wars'.[3] Yet, unlike the oil crisis on which there has been some consensus as to strategic importance and Western vulnerability, the minerals issue has given rise to fundamental debate. The debate is of particular relevance to this study because of the frequent and often contradictory uses of historical analogies to support or counter resource vulnerability arguments.

Just as there is a distinction to be made between current, commercially viable 'reserves' and the very much larger category of overall 'resources', it is also important to distinguish between the economic and military implications of mineral scarcity. Under wartime conditions it is likely that changes in supply and demand schedules can be accomplished without threatening military potential, provided adequate stockpiles are available. However, in peacetime, the economic dislocations flowing from severe shortages might well impose unpleasant costs.[4]

Many prominent observers reject the notion of impending 'mineral wars' and suggest that concerns about strategic minerals and their role in strategy are exaggerated.[5] In short, 'the problem of mineral access is not nearly as serious for the U.S. as the problem of oil, unless a war of the magnitude and duration of World War II is contemplated'. For Europe and Japan, however, the stakes may be higher and there is potential scope for disagreement among the Western allies on preferred policies for assuring access.[6] Such strains would be particularly acute in the event of a general conventional war in which US stockpiles might have to serve allied as well as American requirements. In the event that the industrial regions of Europe and Japan were overrun, this consideration would, of course, be irrelevant. Thus, in some senses, the continued concern over strategic minerals and wartime requirements has been divorced from strategic reality. 'If you cannot fight for more than sixty days in Europe, why bother worrying about access to minerals.'[7]

With some exceptions (notably tungsten), the mineral needs of defence industries are rather small compared with consumption in the Western economies as a whole. While wartime demands would surely alter this situation to some degree, 'uncertainties about the scope, duration, and consequences of large-scale military conflict make speculation about possible mineral supply bottlenecks and their impact on the war itself extremely difficult'.[8] 'Historical experience suggests that such bottlenecks would appear—and be overcome.'[9] As has been suggested, this was clearly the case with regard to mineral resources on both sides in the world wars. Another general point, most notable in the case of oil, but relevant to mineral questions as well, is that there are now many more developed centres of resource production than were available during the world wars (although the production of some important minerals remains concentrated in a limited number of regions).

MINERAL VULNERABILITY: CONFLICTING ASSESSMENTS

Broadly, any mineral 'neither found nor produced' domestically in sufficient quantities 'to sustain the nation during a period in which the security of the country is threatened by a foreign power' could be classified as strategic.[10] More specifically, the degree of vulnerability associated with a given material will depend on such factors as (1) the value of the particular application in which it is used; (2) the extent of accessible reserves; (3) government and industry stockpiles; (4) the geographic distribution of foreign sources of supplies; and (5) the availability of alternative or substitute materials.[11] From the perspective of this study, a key element in considering the 'strategic' value of a mineral is its importance in specific defence-related applications.

Although relatively self-sufficient in mineral resources in comparison to most industrialized countries, the US has become increasingly dependent on imported sources of these materials, particularly since the 1960s (the overall percentage has not increased dramatically since 1970).[12] For example, while the US was a net exporter of copper, iron, steel and vanadium in 1960, it is now a net importer of these materials. Dependence on imported bauxite and alumina increased from 74 per cent in 1960 to 94 per cent in 1981. Cobalt dependence increased from 66 per cent to 91 per cent in the same period. Dependence has also increased for zinc, cadmium, tungsten and titanium.[13] The number of materials for which at least 50 per cent dependence must be placed on foreign sources has also increased—from 4 in 1950 to 23 in 1976.[14]

Chromium, manganese, cobalt, tin, titanium and aluminium are the minerals which appear most frequently on lists of strategic or critical materials. Significantly, imports of the first three materials come overwhelmingly from Sub-Saharan Africa.[15] In the case of chromite, Zimbabwe and South Africa together account for 97 per cent of the world's high-grade reserves (chromite is the principal ore of chromium metal).[16]

Statistics of this sort have fuelled concerns about vulnerability to potential interruptions as a result of producer cut-offs, denial at source, or interference with sea lines of communication. One should note, however, that mineral trade statistics can be misleading as they seldom take account of factors such as recycling. More importantly, references to total 'reserves' are often taken to represent the total amount of a resource extant and potentially extractable. In fact, the term 'reserves' refers only to identified mineral concentrations which can be economically exploited given current prices, mining technologies, regulations, and so forth. Under crisis conditions, very much larger volumes of many materials could be extracted, although at higher cost and with varying degrees of delay. Lastly, in the case of the US, substantial amounts of many resources are obtained from near or 'secure' sources (for instance, Canada, Mexico) which would almost certainly remain available in a crisis.

As noted earlier, there is now greater scope for satisfying defence-related material demands from the civilian economy in wartime in comparison to the World War II experience. This must, however, be weighed against the potentially greater intensity of modern conventional warfare. This was clearly demonstrated during the 1973 October War, in which rates of ammunition consumption and matériel attrition were considerably higher than those associated with the World War II and Korean experience.[17] Modern defence production is also more highly dependent on supplies of critical hardening agents, conductive materials and light metals. The importance of such materials is most evident in the case of advanced airframes and jet engines, the basic constituents of which are aluminium, titanium and iron. To produce alloys of these and other metals used in military and commercial aircraft construction, a variety of imported additives are required (for instance, chromium, copper, manganese and cobalt). Total consumption of even trace additives can be significant, and dependence on overseas supplies can be high—97 per cent of US cobalt requirements for 1978 were imported, primarily from Zaire.[18] The US relied on imports for 91 per cent of its cobalt needs in 1982 (the 9 per cent produced domestically is accounted for entirely by recycling as their was no cobalt mining in the US).[19]

The invasion of Zaire's Shaba Province in 1978 by Cuban and East German trained Katangans pointed to the potential risks to Western cobalt supplies. The resulting intervention by French and Belgian forces, with US support, was clearly motivated in large measure by the threat to copper and cobalt mining operations in the region, as well as the need to protect expatriate workers. Yet cobalt production in Zaire was still significantly higher in 1978 than in 1977, and full-mining operations were again underway just 60 days after the incident.[20]

Another notable dimension of the Shaba incident, although of more commercial than strategic interest, concerns Soviet cobalt purchases in 1978, both from Zaire and on the world market, prior to the invasion in the same year. These purchases, together with the sale of material from stockpiles, allowed the Soviet Union to reap substantial profits in the wake of the disruption of Zairean production, suggesting that the Soviet Union knew of the invasion plan beforehand. On the other hand, the Soviet Union has had an on-going requirement for cobalt imports to bridge the demand gap which has been apparent since the early 1970s. Indeed, the Soviets announced another major purchase of Zairean cobalt in 1980.[21]

Apart from the possibility of supply disruptions in peacetime as a result of instability in producing areas (as borne out during the Shaba incident of 1978), more serious security risks would arise in wartime:

> Even more dangerous still would be the sustained interruption of cobalt deliveries to the United States and its allies during, or soon before, the period of mobilization that would necessarily precede a major war. Such a supply disruption might be engineered by the Soviet Union but disguised as a locally inspired event.... A sustained disruption at a time of mobilization almost certainly would mean delays in the nation's ability to prepare for war. And it might even make war more likely if the cobalt shortage (together with potential related shortages in other materials originating in south-central Africa) contributed to an enemy's perception that it was then in an advantageous position that would not persist indefinitely.[22]

Thus, in a protracted crisis or period of mobilization, with demand rising, Soviet inspired or supplier actions could interfere significantly with essential supplies. At the same time, however, technological progress may reduce the extent of Western vulnerability in the future (for example, the use of ceramic composites in place of hardened alloys in aircraft engines).[23]

STOCKPILING, WARTIME REQUIREMENTS AND HISTORICAL 'LESSONS'

The US maintains a National Defense Stockpile containing 93 commodities, including 34 minerals. For 14 of these minerals stocks in the first quarter of 1982 were in excess of the established goals.[24] As discussed in Chapter 4, the origins of the current stockpile may be traced to the Strategic Minerals Act of 1939, and the Strategic and Critical Materials Stockpile Act of 1946 which continued the commitment to maintain stocks of critical materials for use in the event of a national emergency. The 1946 Act was motivated, however, 'as much by concern for the drop in mineral prices that would occur if material stocks held at the conclusion of the war were sold'.[25] Current US stockpile planning is based on the rather arbitrary assumption of a one year threat of war followed by three years of conflict. Target amounts in the stockpile represent 'the difference between these needs and what we have or can get from the economy'. It has also been asserted that roughly 80 per cent of the materials imported for the strategic stockpile programme are available in the US in non-economic quantities.[26] President Reagan's National Materials and Minerals Plan and Report of April 1982 emphasized the need to review and up-grade the materials stockpile and encourage more rapid development of domestic mineral resources.

The possibility and timing of nuclear escalation introduces a major uncertainty into resource planning for war. Indeed, a principal justification for the three year 'major conflict' basis for stockpile planning is the role it plays in supporting conventional deterrence, reducing the likelihood that resource shortages would contribute to a decision to employ nuclear weapons.[27] Of course, shortcomings in the sustainability of conventional forces, arising at a much earlier stage in a general conflict, would undercut any contribution that mineral stockpiles might make to deterrence and defence. As in the case of oil, resort to nuclear weapons would upset any estimate of the defence industrial base available in NATO Europe and Japan to consume materials in support of a war effort. Escalation to the strategic nuclear level would similarly invalidate resource demand estimates for the United States and the Soviet Union.[28] In any event, the prospect of a conflict involving the use of nuclear weapons continuing for a protracted period must be considered remote.

In the current debate over strategic minerals, reference is often made to the problems which German planners faced as a consequence of mineral shortages (for example, chrome and wolfram). Often overlooked is the fact that in no sense did such shortages constitute 'war stoppers'. One observer, for example, has asserted that World War II 'demonstrated that the elimination of even a single critical resource drastically affected the war's outcome. . . . Today the denial of a country's critical resources in either a short or a protracted conflict would prove disastrous'.[29] To be sure, it is important that adequate and readily usable stockpiles exist to support mobilization for a protracted conflict, or for a short war in which the longer-term adaptability of the war economy cannot make itself felt. Surely, however, the appropriate lesson to be drawn from the World War II experience is precisely the opposite of the assertion above—shortages will arise, and they will be overcome through substitution, conservation, increased production, the acquisition or conquest of new sources of supply, and other measures.

Defence policy-makers have not been unaware of the history associated with resource questions and war economy. A former US official has observed that 'we probably underestimate the extent to which we can work around vulnerabilities'.[30] Similarly, during his tenure in the US Department of Defense another prominent official responded to repeated calls for the establishment of a new strategic minerals programme by recalling the German success with substitution and other measures in the two world wars.[31]

THE 'RESOURCE WAR' AND CURRENT POLICY

The debate over strategic minerals has been given new impetus by the Reagan administration and, indeed, criticism of President Carter's less active pursuit of the mineral question played a minor part in the 1980 presidential campaign. Former Secretary of State Alexander Haig has been particularly active in calling attention to the 'mineral threat'. Speaking before the House Subcommittee on Mining in September 1981, he stated: 'I have long been troubled by what is rapidly becoming a crisis in strategic and critical materials'. Haig asserted that not only is the US 'inordinately and increasingly dependent on foreign sources of supply', but it must also compete with the Soviet Union for influence and control over many key producing areas in Asia, Africa and Latin America. In sum, he stated that 'as one assesses the recent step-up of Soviet proxy activity in the Third World . . . one can only conclude that the era of the resource war has arrived'.[32] Critics have characterized this statement (one of many on this theme), together with the former Secretary's views on the use of force to assure supplies of vital resources, as the 'Haig Doctrine'.[33]

Perceptions of a growing Soviet threat to Western mineral supplies arise from the confluence of a number of developments, including the emergence of a rough military parity between the superpowers, the expansion of the Soviet Union's ability to project power to distant areas, more active Soviet political, economic and military involvement in resource-bearing regions, and, not least, the increasing Warsaw Pact need for mineral purchases on the world market.

The notion of a resource war over access to strategic minerals has been at the forefront of arguments in favour of an expanded American navy (that is, 600 ships) to counter the growing threat to 'strategic lifelines'. In explaining the Administration's plan to increase the Navy's shipbuilding account by US$3.8 billion in 1982, Secretary of Defense Caspar Weinberger told Congress that 'we are in a very real sense an island nation . . . Access to vital resources, and the sinews of the Western alliance depend on our ability to control the seas. We must be able to defeat any adversary who threatens such access'.[34] In a similar vein, an April 1977 posture report by the US Chief of Naval Operations had earlier emphasized the importance of the maritime trade protection mission to the security of a 'raw materials deficit nation'.[35]

Parallel to the assessment offered by Former Secretary Haig, James D. Santini, former Chairman of the House Subcommittee on Mines and Mining, has pointed to the threat implicit in the fact that South Africa and the Soviet Union together possess a preponderance of the world's strategic mineral resources.[36] This situation is seen to be all the more disturbing when placed in the context of 'Soviet aggression' in Southern Africa, with Cuban and East German forces playing a key role: 'Control of Southern Africa would give the Soviets complete control of at least 15 of the most strategically important minerals in the world'.[37]

One Administration observer has asserted, in somewhat more measured terms than the above, that while the issue of access to and protection of Southern African resources is 'really only important if they are under Soviet control' or in the event of a 'protracted conflict', neither case 'is beyond the realm of possibility'.[38] Yet any Soviet temptation to interfere with African mineral supply sources would very likely be tempered by the realization that the region has become an increasingly important source of supply for her Eastern European allies (this argument will be developed further in Chapter 8).[39]

WESTERN VULNERABILITY AND AFRICAN RESOURCES

As in the case of oil, the mineral vulnerability of America's European and Japanese allies necessarily plays an important role in the debate over minerals and strategic planning. Despite the heavy mineral import dependence of European countries, 'only France and to a lesser extent Sweden have established firm stockpiling policies'. Japan, reliant on imports for virtually all of its mineral requirements, does not maintain a stockpile of strategic minerals.[40] There have, however, been calls for strategic stockpiling of the US type in Japan as a useful contribution to comprehensive security.[41] Thus, it is likely that in the event of a prolonged conflict with the Soviet Union, the stocks of minerals in the US National Defense Stockpile might have to serve allied as well as US needs.

The active French role in Africa is, to a significant extent, related to the fact that France receives substantial amounts of strategic minerals from that continent. While 'it is true to say that political relations with countries such as Niger and Gabon are maintained *in part* to ensure the continued supply of uranium', this does not necessarily imply that France would consider military intervention in either of these two countries to ensure continued supply.[42] Nonetheless, France clearly possesses the capacity, and should circumstances so dictate, the inclination, to intervene in resource-related crises in Africa, as the Kolwezi episode demonstrated.

Concern over access to African minerals also played a role in the debate over US and allied policy towards Angola in its early stages, as well as towards the Rhodesian conflict and Namibia. In these cases, concern focussed on the denial of potential strategic gains to the Soviet Union and the threat of regional instability and its implications for mineral production and export.[43] The rise of OPEC and the 'oil shock' of 1973 also suggested to many that the cartelization of African mineral resources, with all its implications for Western economic security, could not be far off. In retrospect, this worry has proven to be an exaggerated one, yet it played a significant role in the debate over mineral security in the second half of the 1970s and beyond.[44]

Clearly, as suggested by writing on the topic, significant elements of the American defence community hold the view that the US and its allies are seriously vulnerable to the denial of African mineral supplies, and consider that this vulnerability dictates the preservation of political and economic relations with South Africa.[45] Ironically,

South Africa itself has reportedly been stockpiling strategic materials for more than a decade in preparation for likely interruptions in supply as a consequence of trade sanctions or regional instability.[46] South African efforts in the area of synthetic oil production are well known, and these facilities have been the target of at least one attack by the African National Congress.

In strategic terms, that is, in relation to current or wartime defence concerns, it is the potential for Soviet interference with Western mineral supplies which looms large. Short of the case of crisis or war, however, it is the potential for peacetime political disturbances in supplier countries, especially in South Africa, which poses the most likely threats to mineral supply. Such disturbances might in some instances involve Soviet interference. In terms of economic security, a total and prolonged halt of mineral exports from Southern Africa must be considered unlikely, but even here adjustment would be possible, over time and at some cost.[47]

STRATEGIC MINERALS: SUMMARY OBSERVATIONS

It is clear that there has been a tendency to equate import dependency with vulnerability, together with a parallel tendency to underestimate the scope for substitution and other measures, particularly in a wartime economy. The result has been a general overstatement of the risks relating to strategic minerals, buttressed in the American case by a heightened perception of the Soviet threat to Western resources. An additional factor contributing to the anxiety over strategic minerals has been the recent references to 'lessons' derived from the experience of the world wars. Far from demonstrating the extreme vulnerability of war economies to mineral supply interruptions, the wartime experience actually suggests the broad point that while supply restrictions are likely to arise, it is equally likely that they will be overcome, despite the best efforts of an adversary. This lesson should be recognized as a useful contribution to the current debate over minerals and strategy, and should serve to temper the more extreme assertions on this question. As one prominent observer— and one not noted for his reticence in calling attention to the Soviet threat to vital resources such as oil—has noted, the minerals vulnerability argument is a combination of 'strategic paranoia' and 'industrial naïveté'.[48] To this one might also add historical naïveté.

Nonetheless, one also needs to bear in mind the limitations on extrapolation from historical experience. Factors such as the vastly increased sophistication of defence technology, coupled with the possibility of very much more material-intensive conventional operations, complicate estimates of resource requirements. Substitution and other measures aimed at relieving resource pressures could prove difficult to apply in the absence of a protracted period of mobilization or conflict. In a sense, this may be regarded as a revival of the 'armament in depth' versus 'armament in width' dilemma of the 1930s. The potential for nuclear conflict introduces additional uncertainties. Planning for resource security, including that related to strategic minerals, can, however, play a role in deterrence at the conventional level, and thus contribute to a reduction in the likelihood of a resort to nuclear weapons.

The strategic mineral problem cannot be meaningfully compared to the problem of oil supply. The important resources of Central and Southern Africa notwithstanding, there is no comparable 'focus of vulnerability' such as the Persian Gulf in the case of non-fuel minerals 'or even nearly so'.[49] Even in the current atmosphere of concern with regard to oil and security in the Gulf, one now hears few, if any, references to the prospect of a 'resource war' embracing mineral supply.[50] Finally, drawing resources from distant regions will always imply certain security risks, especially in the context of a conventional conflict with the Soviet Union. Historically, this has been an accepted vulnerability associated with the system of international trade in raw materials, supported by maritime communications. The alternative of measures aimed at greater self-sufficiency, to the extent that these would be practical—and even in the case of the United States this is highly uncertain—while reducing the sources of risk, would surely impose economic costs which might, in the long run, prove more harmful to Western prosperity and, ultimately, defence.

8 Resource Issues and the East-West Strategic Relationship

The confluence of several critical developments has brought into sharper focus the role of resource access and denial in the East-West strategic relationship. First, the reawakening of concern over the historically vital question of oil supply for economic prosperity and defence, brought about by the decade of the energy crisis, has created a continuing legacy of concern. This concern has, in turn, led to less clear, but nonetheless important, perceptions of Western vulnerability with regard to strategic non-fuel minerals.

Second, the perceived decline in the credibility of extended nuclear deterrence as a consequence of changes in the nuclear balance at the strategic level has resulted in increasing emphasis being placed on conventional deterrence and defence. This, in turn, has led to a re-evaluation of the prospects for prolonged, resource-intensive conventional conflict between NATO and Warsaw Pact forces.

Third, the invasion of Afghanistan, coupled with growing Soviet naval activity in areas important to the flow of strategic resources to the West has made vital resource-bearing regions, and particularly the Persian Gulf, potential theatres of East-West conflict. Furthermore, in the event of a NATO-Warsaw Pact conflict in Europe, a parallel battle over Persian Gulf oil supplies, either at source or at sea, must be considered likely.

Following a general discussion of some key aspects of resource factors in the Soviet and American strategic traditions, this chapter will examine the role of resource issues in the current East-West strategic relationship, including their effect on the military balance or 'correlation of forces', naval strategy, economic targeting, theatre interdependence, and the coalition defence of vital resources. It will be seen that while developments in military technology and national economic capabilities, not least the advent of nuclear weapons, have introduced new elements into the strategic calculus, Soviet and Western approaches to resource-related questions continue to reflect, to a marked extent, considerations suggested by historical experience.

RESOURCES AND THE AMERICAN STRATEGIC TRADITION

There is an identifiable American 'strategic culture' flowing from distinctive geopolitical, historical, economic and social influences, which provides the milieu within which defence concepts and policies are formed. The fundamental elements of this strategic culture include: a succession of victories from the Seven Years War (1756–63) to 1945; 'continental insularity'; non-threatening neighbours; the conquest of a vast frontier; and most importantly for this analysis, an abundance of natural resources.[1]

The advantages of material abundance, coupled with a certain 'industrial hubris', encouraged a belief in the power of mobilization to defeat an adversary and the desire to wage technological, production-oriented wars rather than wars of human attrition.[2] As Edward Luttwak has argued, until very recently the US has had little need for 'strategy' as opposed to the technical functions associated with war planning.[3] Throughout the 20th century the US has been a resource-rich country. Victory achieved through the marshalling of superior resources, together with a pragmatic national style, has tended to subsume issues of strategy more narrowly defined (that is, operational strategy).[4] Clearly, this is not necessarily a tradition which lends itself to dealing with actual or perceived resource scarcity. Since the 1950s, there has also been a general increase in reliance on nuclear deterrence and conventional forces-in-being, and correspondingly less interest in the potential for longer-term mobilization. Only recently, with the revival of interest in conventional forces, has the question of resource supply for mobilization returned to the fore.[5]

Another characteristic of the American strategic tradition, particularly relevant to concerns about security in the Persian Gulf, is the phenomenon of the 'security shock'. Such shocks 'occur periodically and serve to rouse the U.S. from ill-preparedness of one sort or another'.[6] The oil shocks of 1973–74 and the invasion of Afghanistan in 1980 which gave rise to the Carter Doctrine and the Rapid Deployment Force (CENTCOM) fit rather well into this tradition. Indeed, to quote one observer:

> The present level of concern around the world is at least partly a consequence of the fact that the last major boom, and the oil price rises which marked its end, coincided with a marked decline in the self-sufficiency of the United States, the biggest consumer of

almost everything, whose praiseworthy habit of discussing her national worries in public has helped to focus attention on raw material questions.[7]

The pragmatic national style as a component of the American strategic tradition has also affected the way in which defence practitioners consider questions of longer-term resource planning, as opposed to battlefield logistics, and this may work to reduce the importance accorded to resource issues. It should not be surprising that defence policy-makers will be more concerned about threats which may have to be faced tomorrow than threats which may arise at some indeterminate time in the future. In this sense, immediate questions of 'sustainability' in Europe and elsewhere will naturally take precedence over longer-term issues of resource access.[8]

Despite some recent interest, the geopolitical tradition, with its emphasis on resource-bearing areas, really has no parallel in American strategic thought.[9] As Henry Kissinger has complained, Americans do not, as a rule, think geopolitically.[10] Much of the American thinking on such questions as access to strategic minerals and stockpiling derives from notions of beleaguered isolation and hemispheric self-sufficiency prevalent in the 1930s and 1940s. By contrast, current concerns with regard to safeguarding Western access to oil presuppose that the US will remain deeply committed to world affairs. Thus, the American tradition in thinking about resources and strategy is marked by certain 'irrational and contradictory' elements.[11] There is broad consensus, however, on the consistent and influential role of the US Navy in highlighting the importance of assured access to imported resources and, not surprisingly, the need to safeguard vital sea lines of communication for these resources.

The tradition of state intervention in the organization of the supply and distribution of critical resources, with the exception of wartime exigencies, is rather weak in the American experience. Thus, the balance between measures aimed at reducing dependence on a scarce resource through domestic controls or the development of substitutes, and measures designed to enhance the security of supply from abroad, will often lean heavily in favour of the latter. By contrast, the Soviet general staff surely takes the question of domestic resource planning more seriously as a consequence of their long experience with economic planning for autarky in war and peace.[12]

With regard to economic, including resource-related targeting as a component of nuclear strategy, American planning has been strongly influenced by the 'independent strategic bombing tradition' flowing from the World War II experience. Initially, this meant that a massive blow against a variety of economic targets was thought necessary in order to thwart an invasion by destroying the Soviet industrial base. As the Soviet capacity to inflict similar damage in exchange came to be recognized, 'economic attack was transformed into a withholdable option'.[13] The development of more accurate delivery systems, as well as more sophisticated intelligence gathering and targeting systems, has naturally created new possibilities for 'discriminating' attacks on resource-related targets, as dictated by the location of specific bottlenecks in supply and production.[14] This, too, may be regarded as a natural evolution based on the strategic bombing campaigns of World War II.

Another aspect of the economic targeting problem suggested by historical experience concerns the possibility of 'outside aid' in the form of resources purchased, volunteered, coerced or seized from territory outside the Soviet Union.[15] Thus, as in World War II, target planners must consider the possible necessity of pre-empting or denying Soviet access to resources on the 'rimlands' of the Eurasian landmass. This raises the question of utilizing nuclear forces not only in defence of resources such as those in the Persian Gulf, but also in terms of their denial to the Soviet Union and her allies. Such a contingency is not a likely one, as the use of nuclear weapons for such a purpose would imply a degree of escalation which would call into question the possibility of any prolonged conventional conflict in which longer-term resource access would be of importance.

RESOURCES AND MODERN SOVIET STRATEGY

Soviet references to resources in strategic thought and action may be divided into several broad categories. First, one may identify the notion of resources as a cause of war, that is, war as a means by which the capitalist states obtain or protect raw material sources and markets.[16] The Western dependence on overseas trade in resources is, further, seen as a source of strategic vulnerability to be exploited by Soviet strategists. Second, defensive and offensive measures related to resources as a component of war economy are stressed in discussion of both conventional and nuclear war. Finally, the notion of resource denial and operations against Western sea lines of communication forms a significant, although clearly not a predominant, part of Soviet naval strategy.

V. D. Sokolovsky, in *Soviet Military Strategy*, states that every war is a 'product of social and economic relations', citing Engels' assertion that 'the victory of force is based on the production of weapons, and the production of weapons in turn, is based on productivity in general, and consequently on "economic strength", on the "situation of the enemy" and on the material means at the disposal of that force'.[17] Sokolovsky emphasizes that developments in military strategy 'depend completely' on economic conditions and the prevailing 'level of productive forces'. Specifically, he points to raw material constraints and motivations as major determinants of German and Soviet strategy in World War II:

> In order to execute military attacks against the economy of the enemy according to strategic plans, frequently special operations are executed to capture and destroy strategically important regions or raw material sources. In this sense, we can refer to Hitler's operation 'Blue Fox', whose main purpose was the capture of the nickel deposits of the Kola Peninsula.[18]

In the view of another prominent Soviet writer, the military power of the state is held to be an expression 'of the degree of its ability to wage a war against other states by straining all the material . . . forces of society', including natural resources. Moreover, it is asserted that the nature of these 'material forces' is historically conditioned.[19]

> The qualitatively new relation between the economy and the course of military operations during the two world wars consisted in the fact that the course and outcome of the armed struggle depended largely on the economic possibilities of the warring sides, on how effectively they used their possibilities for developing the constantly growing mass production of the means of armed struggle in order to secure their military/technical supremacy over the opponent. . . . In these wars, economic victory was a material pre-requisite for military victory.[20]

Soviet observers note the inherent disadvantage of capitalist states in bringing about a rational organization of resource acquisition, distribution and use, in direct contrast to the Soviet capacity for centralized control. So, too, the Soviet system is perceived to possess distinct advantages in terms of the planned distribution of centres of production with a view towards regional economic development and, not least, strategic dispersal.[21] The latter, while its utility has surely diminished since World War II, is still not without relevance in considering the vulnerability of economic targets in nuclear war.

Sokolovsky draws specific attention to the importance of petroleum supplies in wartime, noting the rapid increase in fuel and lubricant requirements for Russian forces over the two world wars: 'Under present day conditions, due to the complete motorization and mechanization of the Armed Forces and the continuous increase in their technical equipment, the importance of fuels and lubricants in supporting the combat operations of troops has increased even more'.[22]

Perhaps the most outspoken Soviet commentator on resource questions is a now relatively obscure strategist and economic warfare specialist, Major-General A. N. Lagovsky. His 'weak link' principle was based on the assumption that the West would continue to be very heavily dependent on imported sources of raw materials critical to the manufacture of modern military hardware, including jet engines and armour-piercing projectiles (the familiar list of chrome, manganese, cobalt, nickel and titanium). By contrast, Lagovsky argued that the Warsaw Pact nations are, 'given the continuing development of Soviet resources', largely self-sufficient (the increasing Eastern European reliance on imports actually calls this assertion into question).[23] Indeed, Lagovsky suggests that the Soviet Union possesses 'inexhaustible resources of every conceivable strategic raw material', even under an expanded war production programme.[24]

The overall theme of Lagovsky's work concerns the grooming of the Soviet war economy for a future conflict (in essence, similar to World War II—'only more so') and the 'economic potential' and the means by which it might be exploited. Western reviewers at the time were struck by Lagovsky's perplexing image of World War III as 'a much magnified and intensified version of its predecessor', despite the availability of nuclear weapons.[25]

Lagovsky's vision is that of a protracted war, in which the 'maritime communications lines of the Western powers, which convey an extensive foreign trade, will become . . . the most vulnerable point in the entire system of supplying war production with strategic raw materials'.[26] Particular stress is therefore laid on operations against sea lines of communication, including blockade operations, among the main objectives of which would be the reduction of 'the enemy's war production, by drastically reducing his imports of strategic raw materials'.[27] It is noteworthy that these arguments are virtually identical to those put forth by German strategists prior to the two world wars in advocating a submarine *guerre de course* against British trade. One may regard such assertions, together with suggestions regarding the merits of strategic dispersal, as flowing directly from the experience of the world wars, at a time when notions of 'economic potential' and 'mobilization' were being actively reassessed in the West in light of the changes wrought by nuclear weapons. Finally, Lagovsky emphasizes the importance of protecting economic regions and objectives from attack by air, sea and land forces, including the possible use of nuclear weapons.[28] The imperative of protecting key resource-producing areas, reinforced by the World War II experience, was also cited by Western analysts in the early post-war years as providing the basis for Soviet policy towards Iran. In this case, Soviet planners were clearly concerned to prevent the development of a potential base of operations against important resource-bearing areas of the Soviet Union, and particularly the Baku oilfields.[29] This concern was surely even more prominent in the calculations of Soviet planners in the years immediately following 1945, as Soviet oil production had declined by nearly 40 per cent during the war.[30]

The decline in Soviet oil production as a result of wartime disruptions may also have encouraged Soviet planners to consider the possibility of a drive south, aimed at seizing control of additional oil-producing areas.[31] This possibility was clearly noted by Western analysts at the time, and can be viewed as a harbinger of the arguments put forth more recently as a result of overly-pessimistic Western forecasts of Soviet oil production levels.[32] Overall, earlier Western analyses concluded that while the denial of oil supplies to the West represented a potential objective of Soviet strategy, an actual drive for access to Middle Eastern oil supplies would be hindered by formidable transportation problems, rendering the bulk of Middle Eastern oil production unavailable for timely use in the Soviet Union unless secure shipment by sea could be arranged (an unlikely prospect).[33] The question of exploiting captured oil resources in the absence of adequate transportation echoes the German experience in both world wars, of which Soviet planners are well aware. Such considerations, perhaps of less importance today given better technology and increased Soviet capabilities, are still not without relevance for Soviet planners.

The Soviet Union has, on occasion, advanced proposals for East-West co-operation to ensure the 'free flow of oil from the

Persian Gulf'. Most notable of these was the 'Portugalov Statement' of February 1980, which was aimed primarily at encouraging European support for a Soviet role in security arrangements in the Persian Gulf in the wake of the Carter Doctrine. The proposal aroused little interest in Europe or the Gulf.[34]

Soviet objectives and interests in the Gulf region have been couched in essentially defensive terms, embracing domestic resource considerations such as the security of the Baku area cited earlier. In this context, Soviet observers mention the 1921 Treaty with Iran, under which the Soviet Union is permitted to deploy troops in Iran under circumstances threatening Soviet security. An active strategy of resource denial in the Gulf, outside of a period of crisis or general war, is probably unlikely given the apparent Soviet recognition that Middle Eastern oil is a vital Western interest 'that cannot be lightly challenged'. Indeed, Soviet commentators have expressed the concern that regional instability threatening continued access to oil supplies could 'provide a pretext for American intervention'.[35] Of course, the ability to threaten actions directed against Western access to oil, implicit in the Soviet position, has its political and strategic uses, particularly with regard to Soviet relations with Western Europe and Japan. This too is surely recognized by Soviet planners.

Soviet writing asserts that under 'modern conditions' the potential for attacking and undermining the economies of warring states has been radically transformed by the advent of modern delivery systems for nuclear weapons. In addition to strategic systems, theatre and tactical delivery systems may be used to attack economic targets in the rear, including those related to resource production, distribution and use. In the wake of an initial nuclear exchange at the strategic level, it is suggested that pronounced changes may occur in 'the relation of combatants' economic potentials'.[36] This is not, however, interpreted as implying that the economic base will have little importance in the course of the war following such an initial stage. Even after a nuclear exchange, the opposing economies may prove resilient enough to support a lengthy war whose course and outcome will be 'enormously affected' by supply considerations. Factors such as strategic dispersal, hardening of facilities, and the ability to restore resource-related production and supply would still be critical.[37]

With regard to resource-related targeting for nuclear forces, it is clear that the Soviet approach differs substantially from that of the US. While acknowledging the role of attacks on economic targets in rear areas, based on the considerations outlined above, as a rule,

Soviet planners have not placed as great an emphasis on such target systems. This difference in approach may be explained in two ways. First, the Soviet Union lacks a strategic bombing tradition of the sort developed by the US as a result of the World War II experience. The corresponding Soviet tradition, by contrast, emphasizes a strategy based on the direct engagement of opposing forces, rather than attacks on economic targets. The Soviet disdain for the bombing practices of the US and Britain in World War II has been termed 'a classic case of making a virtue of necessity, since the Soviet airforce almost completely lacked the strategic reach needed to carry the air war to the German heartland'.[38] The Soviet argument, at least in the pre-nuclear years, was that economic attacks short of virtual complete devastation, could not be assured of exploiting an enemy's industrial and resource-related vulnerabilities, particularly in the absence of 'high-confidence' intelligence regarding key supply bottlenecks. In support of this, Soviet strategists pointed, not unreasonably, to the demonstrated resilience of the German war economy.[39]

The deployment of nuclear weapons of increasing power and range by the Soviet Union naturally led to a re-evaluation of the utility of 'comprehensive rear-area targeting', and such targeting was raised to a level of considerable importance, although a counter-military strategy continues to dominate Soviet thinking in this area. The Soviet tendency to view nuclear strategy from a perspective which is not necessarily defined by the 'assured destruction' model, provides a second explanation for the assymetries in US and Soviet approaches to the question of economic targeting. The object of Soviet industrial and resource-related targeting would be the impairment of the enemy's ability to support an extended conflict, rather than a desire to inflict devastating damage with very long-term implications for recovery and military potential.[40] Such an approach is not very different from that which governed the conduct of economic warfare, including strategic bombing in World War II.

RESOURCE ISSUES AND THE EAST-WEST BALANCE

Any assessment of the relative positions of NATO, Japan, and the Warsaw Pact in terms of the capacity for resource access and denial must consider a range of factors, including the degree of dependence on overseas sources of raw materials, the vulnerability of lines of communication for these resources, the adaptability of economies, and the ability to interrupt or safeguard the flow of resources, principally through the application of naval power. While in the broadest terms it is true that the NATO member countries and Japan are heavily dependent on external, sea lines of communication for vital resources, while the Warsaw Pact enjoys the benefit of internal lines, this is not so in all cases. In particular, the growth of Warsaw Pact raw material imports from Africa and other areas represents a potential constraint on Soviet action.

As a review of historical experience demonstrates, resource factors will inevitably influence defence priorities and plans. In addition to imposing limits on what can be undertaken in the strategic sphere, they can suggest new targets for attack and protection, and they can significantly affect economic capacity, both during a conflict and as an element of military potential over extended periods in peacetime.[41] Of particular importance is the manner in which the relationship between resources, technology and strategy may evolve over time. For example, technological and capital 'inputs' are becoming increasingly important in OECD economies, whereas raw material 'inputs' have declined in relative importance, with potential implications for future defence priorities.[42] While industrial equipment built in the West since the experience of the oil crises has generally been designed to reduce energy consumption, there are indications that new weapons systems (for example, main battle tanks) are actually more inefficient in this regard.[43] Overall, the NATO countries and Japan have devoted greater effort to improving energy efficiency than have the Warsaw Pact states, a fact which will continue to influence the energy positions of both alliance systems in the future. A similar assymetry of effort exists with regard to the development of alternative materials as substitutes for potentially vulnerable minerals in such applications as jet engines.

In the wake of the oil crises, the US significantly reduced its dependence on oil imports (although it is again on the rise), Western Europe made considerable headway in energy security (largely due to North Sea oil—the strategic vulnerability of which has not been widely recognized), with Japan remaining 'very much at risk'.[44] There is now general agreement among Western observers that the Soviet oil sector is in decline, although the rate of decline is a subject of controversy. If, as suggested at a 1981 NATO colloquium, Soviet oil production peaks sometime during the 1980s, and declines or stagnates thereafter, then the Soviet Union would be hard pressed to maintain, let alone expand deliveries to her Eastern European allies.[45]

In the case of mineral resources, there are indications that the Soviet Union and, even more certainly, Eastern Europe face the prospect of increasing requirements for overseas supplies. Currently, the Soviet Union is dependent on imports only for supplies of aluminium, tin, antimony, tungsten, barium and molybdenum.[46] There are, however, indications that the Soviet position is deteriorating with regard to the production of other important ores, including titanium, vanadium, manganese and chromite. As a consequence, it is likely that 'only by reducing and, in some cases, terminating the supply of minerals' to its Eastern European allies 'will the Soviet Union be able to remain self-sufficient in certain basic raw materials into the 1990s and beyond'.[47] Thus, Eastern European imports of Middle Eastern oil, of increasing importance since 1974, are likely to be followed by expanding imports of vital minerals from Africa and elsewhere.[48] These developments may have important implications for intra-alliance as well as inter-alliance relations in peacetime, and would affect the formation of crisis or wartime strategy. One consequence of this new dependence will be that the Eastern European members of the Warsaw Pact will increasingly look to their superpower ally as a guarantor of continued access to resource supplies in the Middle East and Africa, a relationship with clear parallels in the case of NATO.[49] Thus, in the context of resource access, 'the Middle East, like Southern Africa, reflects a peculiar looking-glass world in which both the Soviet and the Western alliance systems have come to see each other as a threat, each threat being a reflection of the other'.[50]

The resource fate of the Eastern European countries for the remainder of the 1980s and beyond will be much more strongly influenced by Soviet policy than will their counterparts in NATO Europe be affected by American policy (and American policy is likely to have a considerable influence). It is possible that relations between the Soviet Union and its Warsaw Pact allies, all of which may face economic and political problems, may be strained by energy and mineral factors. This is all the more likely as the Soviets continue to raise the real price, while limiting the amount of their resource exports to Eastern Europe.[51] As a result, the Soviet Union may be forced to move further from the objective of self-sufficiency in order to forestall harmful discord within the Soviet bloc.

The potential for serious discord springing from resource issues within the Atlantic Alliance has been evident since the 1973 October War (indeed, it can be seen as early as the Suez Crisis of 1956). Clearly, this danger must be viewed in the context of the East-West strategic relationship. It has been asserted that the Soviet Union regards Western disarray on resource questions as evidence of a 'profound crisis' of the capitalist system and Western democracy.[52] By contrast, recent US-European co-operation on the protection of shipping in the Gulf strikes a very positive note.

The effects of resource issues on alliance relations can be seen not only in the experience of competition for bilateral oil agreements in the Middle East, but also in disputes surrounding claims to offshore resources, such as that between Greece and Turkey over the exploitation of Aegean oil. Further problems of alliance cohesion and effectiveness may arise as a consequence of arms-for-oil agreements (and the effect of arms exports to the Middle East on the prospects for NATO weapons standardization), as well as friction over divergent policies on the export of nuclear materials and technology.[53] There is also the potential for conflict between individual members of opposing alliances flowing from conflicting resource claims (for example, the dispute between Norway and the Soviet Union over oil and gas in the Barents Sea).[54]

It is clear that the overall balance between the two alliance systems in terms of resource access and use 'depends crucially on the context within which it has to be measured'. In wartime, or in a period of crisis in which access to supplies is interrupted, the Warsaw Pact would, at least initially, be in a position of considerable relative strength based on a comparatively greater degree of self-sufficiency and largely internal lines of communication. Short of such conditions, or over the course of a prolonged conflict in which Western sea lines of communication have been successfully secured, it is likely that NATO and Japanese assets in resource technology, productivity and overall economic strength, 'provided such assets are consistently and effectively exploited', will redress the resource balance.[55]

As noted, the existence of rough 'parity' at the strategic nuclear level has focussed attention on the need for strengthened conventional defences, as well as stimulating a general reassessment of the likely nature of a conventional conflict in Europe. Such a war might well be characterized by a slower movement of forces than had previously been supposed—a prospect made more likely by NATO plans for the attack of follow-on forces in rear areas, and developments in military technology (for example, 'brilliant munitions') which greatly increase the firepower which can be brought to bear on the battlefield.[56] Should a conventional conflict in Europe extend beyond two or three months, the need to secure access to and communications for Middle Eastern and African oil and mineral resources will be evident. In the view of one observer:

> Uncertainty in estimating the outcome of a battle for the sea lines of communication from the Persian Gulf stems from the inability to estimate the effect attrition in the battle for the North Atlantic would have on the relative strength of the opposing sides, and whether the Southern Oceans claim on assets could await the outcome of that battle, which might last several months.[57]

The supply of essential civilian petroleum needs in the event of a general non-nuclear war would present additional problems. Conservation measures, expanded domestic production, and the maintenance of access to some Western Hemisphere resources would probably allow the US to meet civilian demand. The countries of NATO Europe and Japan, would, however, be faced with the prospect of serious shortages. Even with North Sea production, it is apparent that stockpiles and imports would have to be called on for the European economies to continue to function 'even at austerity levels'.[58] The Japanese position would be even more precarious.

Comparatively little attention has been paid to the vulnerability of North Sea oil production. This production is dependent on a very limited number of pipelines carrying a high volume of oil. Indeed, the Sullom Voe terminal on the Shetlands now handles more oil than the port of Rotterdam which has been the principal European oil centre since World War II. Attacks on North Sea facilities would be of strategic significance if coupled with the simultaneous interdiction of oil from the Middle East, Africa or the Western Hemisphere. As one observer has stated: 'Such a purely British choke point reminds us that the Strait of Hormuz is not the only vulnerable point in the oil chain'.[59]

The question of European vulnerability to an interruption of Soviet natural gas exports, which led to considerable discord between the US and its NATO allies in the early 1980s, while of limited relevance to a discussion of wartime planning, remains a factor in peacetime relations. The consensus of expert opinion suggests that Western Europe could cope with a disruption of these supplies. Such a disruption must be considered unlikely in conditions short of crisis and war as a cut-off of exports would involve significant costs to the

Soviet Union in terms of hard currency earnings and access to Western technology. Moreover, Soviet policy-makers surely recognize that an attempt to use gas exports as a political weapon runs the risk of provoking a major East-West crisis.[60] Nonetheless, it would be imprudent to assume that a peacetime cut-off is impossible, and, indeed, there have been instances in which the Soviet Union has employed resource restriction as a political instrument (for instance, in relations with Yugoslavia, China and Israel).[61]

RESOURCE ACCESS AND DENIAL—MARITIME ASPECTS

As discussed in earlier chapters, the interdiction and protection of sea-borne resources has a long and important history in strategic thought and action. Such considerations continue to shape strategic concerns in the nuclear era, particularly in light of the continuing Western perception of vulnerability with regard to petroleum and mineral resources, and the growth of Soviet maritime power.

The priority assigned to the interdiction of Western sea lines of communication in Soviet naval planning has been a matter of considerable debate. The relative importance of the interdiction task has clearly fluctuated over time, in response to Soviet assessments of the likely nature and duration of a NATO-Warsaw Pact conflict. In the event of a war of short duration in which nuclear weapons are employed, it is probable that attacks on maritime trade would be assigned a relatively low priority, and would consist mainly of bombing and mining attacks on key port installations. The expectation of a prolonged conflict would raise the importance of the interdiction mission, and would suggest an active open-ocean campaign against Western shipping, including shipments of vital oil and mineral resources. In this context, Soviet attack submarines would pose the principal threat.[62]

Even in the case of a conventional war in Europe, the attack and protection of shipping intended for initial reinforcement and resupply would probably be the principal priority, with a more general campaign against resources important for longer-term supply emerging only later as the prospects for a prolonged conflict become more apparent. Yet another possibility would be some form of 'trade war' fought out 'beneath a nuclear umbrella'.[63] The interdiction of resource shipments could be expected to figure prominently in such a scenario.

Most prominent Western observers acknowledge that the Soviet Union would almost certainly engage in a *guerre de course* under appropriate circumstances, but assert that other missions, in particular strategic nuclear attack (SSBN) and the countering of Western sea-based nuclear forces, are assigned a higher priority.[64] Admiral Gorshkov, in his writings, has referred to the importance of trade interdiction, noting that the German submarine campaign in World War II might have been decisive had greater resources been devoted to the task from an earlier date. So, too, Sokolovsky has stated that 'among the primary missions of the Navy in a future war will be the disruption of enemy ocean and sea shipping and the interdiction of his communication lines'.[65] Another Soviet commentator has stated: 'Western strategists recognize that in the event of war the severing of these [oil] communications would be fraught with the most serious consequences for the countries of NATO'.[66]

Western, and particularly American, concern has focussed on the perceived vulnerability of resource flows on the Cape Route and the potential for a Soviet strategy of resource denial based on threats to critical 'choke points' along Western sea lines of communication.[67] Such choke points include the Strait of Hormuz, the Bab-el-Mandeb Strait at the entrance to the Red Sea, the Cape itself, the sea lanes off West Africa, and the Malacca, Sunda and Macassar straits in the Pacific. In the case of oil supplies *en route* from the Middle East to Europe, the US or Japan, the great size of modern very-large and ultra-large crude carriers makes these ships vulnerable and high value targets.

In a press conference in February 1986, President Reagan highlighted the importance of maritime 'choke points', asserting that Soviet forces, through the acquisition of key bases 'have placed themselves to be able to intercept the 16 choke points in the world' through which supplies and raw materials are shipped to Western nations.[68] The Soviet development of the former US base at Cam Ranh Bay as a major naval and air facility, in particular is cited as posing a significant threat to vital shipping lanes for oil and other commodities in the Pacific.[69]

The notion of a 'choke point' strategy is, in reality, a 'two-way street' in that the naval forces which the Soviet Union would require to implement such a strategy depend for their operational freedom on passage through other vulnerable choke points (for example, the Greenland-Iceland-UK Gap, the Dardanelles, and similarly restrictive points in the Sea of Japan) subject to control by Western naval and air forces. Moreover, the Soviet Union clearly has a growing interest in safeguarding the free passage of merchant shipping, both as a means of resource access, particulary for her Eastern European allies, and as a consequence of her substantial and hard-currency earning merchant marine.

The expansion of the Soviet naval presence off West Africa reflects the very large amount of Soviet and East European shipping in this area.[70] West Africa, for example, represents the area of greatest activity for Polish shipping in the Third World, 'as well as a major transit route for its material and liquid fuel imports'.[71] Thus:

> In its strategic planning, Moscow is in no position totally to disregard the interests of its allies which are so tied to developments south of the tropic of Cancer that one Soviet writer [Dmitri Volsky] has questioned whether the strategy of interdiction has a future. Other Soviet writers have laid great stress on the fact that the Cape route carries a substantial percentage of East European shipping which is in constant risk of interdiction by the West. NATO may well fear an armed attack along the Cape route, but the Warsaw Pact faces a threat at the Cape itself—for its members have no doubt on whose side South Africa will be counted were war to break out.[72]

The likely expansion of Soviet and East European oil and mineral imports from the Middle East and Southern Africa will undoubtedly complicate any attempt to assess which alliance system poses the greater threat to the other in terms of resource denial. One consequence of this may be that a Soviet strategy of resource denial would be best pursued 'at source', that is, in the Persian Gulf or the Indian Ocean in the case of oil.[73] With regard to Middle Eastern oil supplies, a Soviet strategy of denial at source could also be pursued without challenging Western naval superiority. Indeed, this is a danger identified by a prominent American strategist in the context of an out-of-area strategy which relies to an unreasonable extent on maritime power as a means of containing the Soviet Union and protecting Western access to vital raw materials: 'A peripheral maritime strategy gives up the chief prize of any U.S.-Soviet global contest—the resources of Eurasia'.[74]

THEATRE INTERDEPENDENCE AND THE COALITION DEFENCE OF RESOURCES

It is worthwhile to consider the essential interdependence of the Middle Eastern, European and Asian theatres, as this issue has become increasingly important to the debate over American and allied policy. Closely related is the question of 'burden-sharing' as part of a coalition approach to assuring continued access to oil and other resources. The US Congress, in particular, has begun to question the perceived imbalance between the European and Japanese stake in Middle Eastern oil and the absence of any commensurate commitment to its defence. Resource security concerns are of tremendous relevance to the prosperity and broader security of NATO member countries and Japan, yet NATO itself is limited in its ability to address out-of-area threats. As James Schlesinger has observed:

> In 1949 we needed to protect the land mass of Western Europe against the possibility of Soviet invasion and to provide for the recovery of Western Europe. Those requirements were met through the creation of NATO and the Marshall Plan. Today, the security problem has taken on an altered form. The easiest route to the domination of Western Europe by the Soviet Union is through the Persian Gulf. And it is to be noted that NATO is a defensive alliance. It cannot in terms of its own charter respond to what may be the more serious threat against the security of Western Europe.[75]

In the post Afghanistan period it has become increasingly difficult to separate the Gulf region's own internal conflicts from the wider issues of Soviet-Western military rivalry. 'Concern about the shifting military balance in the Middle East and the Persian Gulf is related to overall unease about the military balance between the superpowers.'[76] It is recognized that serious problems could arise unless a defensive balance is maintained in each theatre, since 'swinging' forces to a threatened theatre may encourage aggression in other areas. Similarly, a swing strategy may prove impossible when threats appear on two fronts simultaneously. Thus, 'if Soviet forces in Central Europe were placed on alert just as an attack on the Gulf commenced, the Allies would be hard put to determine priorities'.[77] The Soviets, by confronting the West in the Gulf would, in effect, confront the West in Europe as well. This problem is exacerbated by the fact that the forces currently available to CENTCOM are drawn largely from units already committed to NATO.[78]

One may identify two classes of options—apart from a unilateral American effort—to strengthen Western defences with regard to resource access and, in particular, Middle Eastern oil. First, the European members of NATO, together with Japan, might increase their defence efforts in their own regions, thus allowing the US to shift some forces to the defence of interests in the Middle East. In the event, however, US forces might still be stretched 'too thinly' in the three areas. As an example, the diversion of attack carriers from the Mediterranean to the Indian Ocean would leave a gap which only the US can fill.[79]

The second option would be for the US together with NATO Europe and Japan, to undertake a strengthening of overall defence capabilities so as to permit the commitment of 'allied' forces to the Indian Ocean-Persian Gulf region.[80] Clearly, this option does not imply that commitments will be of a uniform nature. Because of limited resources for long-range operations, and political concerns over such a role—as in the case of Japan and Germany—a mixed policy could be pursued in which the US would bear the main burden of assembling a rapidly-deployable ground force, with allied contributions to naval and transport requirements.[81]

Some have argued that an expanded conception of NATO security must be central to the development of any multilateral or coalition approach to safeguarding resource access. The problem of European security has, in some sense, always included perceived threats to the Alliance from outside its technical geographic perimeter. Whereas in many resource-related contingencies it would be impossible or inappropriate for NATO as a whole to act, it may still be possible and desirable for individual allies to act in concert.[82] As noted earlier, however, potential disagreement over who constitutes 'the enemy' in such vital resource-bearing regions as the Persian Gulf, is likely to hamper a coalition approach 'out-of-area'. Certainly, the formal integration of 'out-of-area' issues in NATO planning would threaten cohesion on 'core' questions of European security.

Lastly, it should be clear that individual NATO states, together with Australia and perhaps Japan, are prepared to contribute limited military assets to protect vital interests outside their own theatres. In the Indian Ocean-Persian Gulf region, Britain, France and Australia maintain a significant naval presence. The French presence in Africa has already been cited in the context of strategic minerals. The war between Iraq and Iran has stimulated further Western naval activity in the Indian Ocean and the Gulf.[83] Informal efforts toward a coalition approach to resource security may serve to prevent such issues from contributing to the risk of a 'de-coupling' of US, European and Japanese security interests on a wider level.

RESOURCE ISSUES AND THE EAST-WEST STRATEGIC RELATIONSHIP—CONCLUDING OBSERVATIONS

Considerations of resource access and denial continue to play an important role in the East-West strategic relationship in the nuclear age. Moreover, Soviet and Western thinking in this area has been strongly influenced by the experience of the two world wars, and the 'lessons' which have been derived from this history. Resource factors have contributed to shaping US and Soviet nuclear strategy, both in terms of the defence of resource-bearing regions, and in the context of attacks on economic targets in rear areas.

The weight of historical precedent is most readily seen in planning for the prospect of a prolonged conventional conflict in which the capacity for mobilization and economic potential would be important. Indeed, planning for resource supply and restriction in such a war is likely to become a more active concern of strategists as part of the general renaissance in thinking about conventional deterrence and defence. Sharp reductions in the level of strategic and short-range nuclear weapons as a result of new arms control agreements post-INF, or significant progress in strategic defences, would provide additional incentives for the consideration of resource issues in conventional war.

Safeguarding access to vital oil and non-fuel resources in peacetime, and during periods of crisis or conflict short of general war, has been an enduring concern of Western strategists, and is likely to be an increasingly important concern for the Warsaw Pact. Here, there is a parallel between the positions of the United States and the Soviet Union as the ultimate guarantors of resource access for their respective alliance partners. The resource-related concerns of Eastern European allies may well constitute a constraint on a Soviet strategy of resource denial or, at the very least, serve to modify such a strategy in favour of denial 'at source'. Overall, the overwhelming Western dependence on seaborne imports of raw materials suggests that the best targets for a *guerre de course* are still Western—although growing Warsaw Pact imports may well alter this situation.

Finally, the evident interdependence which exists between deterrence and defence in the European and Asian theatres, and the protection of Western interests in vital resource-bearing areas, suggests that resource considerations continue to merit a place in 'grand strategy' in the nuclear age. Moreover, both Soviet and Western strategists, influenced by historical experience, *perceive* resource access and denial to be an important aspect of warfare and, consequently, deterrence.

9 Contemporary Issues in Historical Perspective

The evolution of resource access and denial in strategic thought and practice has followed a pattern of increasing scope and intensity, keeping pace with the expanding scope and intensity of conflict generally, and the increasing dependence of war economies on raw material imports, particularly since the rise of industrial or 'mobilization' warfare. Early instances of the attack or protection of trade, with the object of restricting or securing sources of revenue, and thus the capacity for financing military establishments and operations, led to campaigns and policies aimed directly at restricting or assuring the flow of militarily important materials—for instance, naval timber in the 18th century, oil and strategic minerals in the 20th. Ultimately, resource-related strategy during the two world wars came to embrace the attack and protection of resources vital for the functioning of war economies and societies as a whole.

Resource denial in the 20th century emerges as a 'counter-value' strategy; a means of attacking an opponent's economy and society without having first defeated his forces in the field. Moreover, the attack on resources was seen as a means of carrying forward the offensive in situations of strategic stalemate, or where opportunities for the direct engagement of enemy forces were restricted or unavailable. While nuclear weapons and ballistic missiles have replaced the blockade instrument as the ultimate counter-value weapon, considerations of resource access and denial are still relevant to military strategy, and will continue to be of central importance at many levels of conflict and crisis short of full-scale nuclear war.

Throughout this study, it has been asserted that *perceptions* of resource vulnerability—including the vulnerability of adversaries—have played an important role in the formation of strategic plans and policies; they continue to do so today. Most frequently, it has been the perception of vulnerability, rather than the reality of vulnerability which thrust resource issues into the forefront in the determination of strategic priorities for offence and defence.

It was the perception of Britain's vulnerability to even brief interruptions in her sea-borne imports of raw materials which stimulated the development of French naval doctrine aimed at exploiting this vulnerability. In the years leading up to World War I, increasing British concern with regard to dependence on imported food and other raw material resources, and the threat posed to this trade by French and later German naval forces, lent considerable weight to arguments for a continuing expansion of naval power. The vision of economic chaos and widespread starvation which was seen as the likely result of a successful *guerre de course* against British trade is echoed in current concerns about the consequences of the interdiction of Western sea lines of communication for vital resources, particularly at critical 'choke points'. The possession of appropriate bases and adequate naval forces to control areas essential to the flow of resources clearly continues to shape Western, and particularly American strategy in the nuclear era. The protection of Western access to resources, and the associated sealines of communication, constitutes a vital interest of the Western allies, the historical antecedents of which are very much in the minds of contemporary strategists.

While considerations of resource access and denial in strategy have been closely tied to perceptions regarding resource vulnerability and the potential for effective supply restriction, these perceptions have quite frequently been false. Study of economic warfare in the two world wars, together with earlier experience, clearly demonstrates that a strategy of resource denial faces great obstacles and is rarely as straightforward as perceived. Even the most active efforts to disrupt the supply and use of resources (for instance, the German submarine campaigns in the Atlantic, and the Allied strategic bombing campaigns against resource-related targets) could not be decisive in their own right—although in some respects both campaigns came close to achieving their objectives. A clear lesson of the World War II experience is that a strategy of resource restriction will be most effective where adequate intelligence is available with regard to raw material supply and distribution bottlenecks. With the development of more sophisticated intelligence gathering capabilities, prospects for the effective attack of resource-related targets may be very much better than they have been in the past.

The most significant lesson to be derived from the experience of the two world wars concerns the remarkable flexibility and adaptability of modern industrial economies to resource constraints and the scope for technical and strategic counter-measures. Here, again, resource vulnerabilities have rarely been as great as anticipated. The range of potential responses to supply restrictions is wide, and includes substitution, the use of synthetics, conservation and territorial expansion. The extension of state control and planning with regard to raw material supply, distribution and use has also proven to be a potent means of stretching a society's economic potential in wartime. In practice, most 'strategic' materials have proven to be neither particularly vital nor absolutely irreplaceable, *with some important exceptions, most notably oil.* The implications of this are clear: with regard to both offensive and defensive strategy, claims about the likely effects of the disruption of the supply of many 'vital' resources, and particularly strategic minerals, should be treated with a great deal more scepticism than has commonly been the case.

A strategy of resource denial does have applications, as the consequences of the allied campaign against German synthetic aviation fuel and the *guerre de course* against Japanese maritime communications demonstrated. So, too, campaigns against resource supply may compel an adversary to devote assets in response which otherwise might be available for more central tasks. The costs of waging a campaign of resource-denial must, however, be weighed carefully against the potential effect on an adversary. In the absence of accurate intelligence about the most vulnerable components of an enemy's war economy, the prospects for a successful strategy of denial are poor.

Since 1945 a number of fundamental changes have taken place which will continue to influence the role of resource factors in strategy. First, it is clear that many materials will not retain their overwhelming importance for defence production and the conduct of military operations. Rubber, once a strategic commodity of the highest importance, has ceased to be so. Advances in the use of ceramics and other composite materials will undoubtedly lead to the replacement of 'critical' minerals in a variety of defence applications. Overall, there has been a noted decline in the importance of raw material 'inputs' in the Western economies, and a commensurate increase in the importance of technology and capital. Second, civilian consumption of raw materials has grown enormously in comparison to military and defence-related demand in the period since World War II. Thus, there is now far greater scope for supplying military needs from the economy as a whole. Moreover, more sophisticated economies—and here the Western and Soviet bloc economies are in no sense equal—will be capable of a more effective use of substitution and other counter-measures to resource denial.

Third, there are now many more areas of resource production than there were during the two world wars (for instance, most Middle Eastern oil production had not yet been developed, and extensive new reserves in the North Sea, Canada, Mexico and elsewhere had not yet been identified). New resource discoveries, coupled with changes in civilian and military technology, will undoubtedly present new objectives for attack and defence. The evolution in the focus of concern with regard to resource access and naval power, from timber to coal, and finally to oil, provides an excellent example of this process.

There has been an evident tendency to equate dependence on overseas sources of raw materials with 'vulnerability' to supply restriction or denial. To be sure, these two elements may overlap; however, this will not be so in many cases. Past experience provides numerous examples of systems of wartime supply dependent largely on overseas trade, and the ability to draw on far-flung raw material sources has proved a source of military and economic strength for the traditional maritime powers. In historical terms, this dependence has been a potent strategic assumption, dictating that considerations of overseas resource access and secure sea communications are assigned a high priority in the formation of plans and policies.

An alternative tradition, which has its routes in neo-mercantilist and autarkic doctrine, regards the system of international trade in raw materials as fraught with threats to national security and prosperity. Here, the objective is the full development of indigenous 'secure' resources, the extension of territorial control to expand the available resource base, and the consolidation of these resources within a larger, integrated economic system (for instance, Napoleon's Continental System, the National Socialist 'Greater Space Economy', and the Japanese Greater East-Asia Co-Prosperity Sphere). This is an essentially 'continental' strategy of access to resources which might be adapted, as in the Japanese case in the 1930s, to the maritime environment. Of course, 'autarky' in the literal meaning of the term has proven to be an illusory concept, and policies directed towards this end have most often amounted to little more than a self-imposed blockade.

The pursuit of resource self-sufficiency also forms an important part of the Soviet strategic tradition, based largely on the experience of World War II, in which the mobilization of domestic resources provided the key to Soviet military power. This autarkic tradition will be strained by an expanding need for imported sources of various raw materials, largely to satisfy requirements in Eastern Europe. As a consequence, it is likely that the Soviet Union will be increasingly concerned with safeguarding Warsaw Pact access to oil and mineral supplies from the Middle East and Africa. Thus, not all the targets for resource restriction or denial in a future conflict or crisis would be Western, although the most attractive targets undoubtedly will be.

In the nuclear age, access to resources can no longer be considered the ultimate determinant of military power and potential. At the level of nuclear conflict, the utility of economic warfare, in general, including actions directed against resource supply, is largely irrelevant, with the exception of the limited role resource factors might be expected to play in targeting strategies. As one moves across the spectrum of potential conflicts, however, the continuing relevance of resource issues is evident. Resource access and denial will be of great importance to strategic planning in the event of a protracted conventional war, or in the event of a prolonged period of crisis and mobilization. Included here would be the possibility of interference with resource production or sea lines of communication conducted under a nuclear umbrella. Developments at the nuclear level (continuing parity or 'equivalence', further substantial arms reductions, or the prospect of an effective defence against ballistic missiles) will almost certainly lead to even greater emphasis on conventional deterrence and defence, and a correspondingly increased possibility of a protracted non-nuclear conflict. Already, concern with regard to bolstering conventional deterrence has fuelled existing worries over the security of Western oil and non-fuel mineral supplies, raising questions of longer-term resource supply strongly reminiscent of the pre-nuclear era.

In addition, the issue of assuring access to resources for economic prosperity and security in peacetime has been an important strategic concern in the West, and particularly in the US, in the wake of the events of 1973–74, 1979–80, and the recent war in the Persian Gulf. The attack on, and protection of, oil resources has occupied a unique place in strategy since World War I, and has grown enormously in importance as a result of the ever increasing demands of air, sea and land forces for fuel and lubricant supplies. To this one must also add the vast increase in the level of oil consumption in civilian economies worldwide. While the question of strategic minerals vulnerability is the subject of heated debate, oil will continue to be a *unique* case in terms of its importance and vulnerability in peace and war.

The consideration of resource questions in terms of 'geopolitics', which forms an important part of the historical experience, has undergone a revival in recent years, principally as a result of the Soviet invasion of Afghanistan and the perception of a Soviet threat to the oil-producing regions of the Persian Gulf. Just as the German threat to Middle Eastern oil supplies and lines of communication was intimately connected with the maintenance of the Allied position in other theatres during World War II, a Soviet threat to the oil supplies of the Persian Gulf would clearly threaten the Western position in other areas. In this context, the Carter Doctrine, and subsequent American policy towards the Gulf, is a manifestation of an enduring vital interest, the defence of which may require the use of force. The point here is that, as in the past, resource-related questions must be viewed as part of a broader canvas, in which the East-West strategic relationship, as well as regional balances, will play a central role.

Short of regional or general conflict, there is a continuing fear that the extension of Soviet 'continental' control over vital resources on the periphery of the Eurasian landmass will place the Soviet Union in a position to exert substantial political leverage over Western Europe and Japan, leading to a weakening of the Western alliances, and resulting in a long-term shift in the strategic balance. Analyses of this nature have noteworthy historical precedents, not least the commanding position and influence afforded Britain by her control over the supply of naval coal prior to 1914. Ensuring access to the oil resources of the Middle East has been a strategic imperative since the revolution in naval technology brought about by the Admiralty's oil conversion decision in 1911. The overwhelming importance of oil to the functioning of economies in peacetime as well as the conduct of military operations, ensures that safeguarding its supply will remain a high priority for strategic planning.

OVERALL REFLECTIONS ON RESOURCES, STRATEGY AND WAR

Beyond the foregoing observations on the evolving role of resource factors in strategy, some broader reflections can be offered on resource issues as a cause of war, and the extent to which resource questions can be separated from geostrategic ideas.

First, in none of the instances surveyed in this study can resource issues be identified as the primary *cause* of war in their own right. The Napoleonic conflict was certainly not fought over access to naval timber or other materials; Germany did not go to war in 1914 or 1939 specifically to secure access to raw materials, although the conquest of resource-rich regions played an important role in the formation of strategy over the course of the war. Even in the case of Japan in World War II, the decision for war was the result of a quest for a much broader political, military and economic hegemony in Asia. Secure access to vital resources was perceived as a necessary condition for the pursuit of broader aims, and as such exerted a considerable influence over the timing and objectives of strategic action. The key question here, as elsewhere, must be 'resources for what end?' In the German, Italian and Japanese cases, it is clear that the 'inadequacy' of available resources was in reality a perceived shortfall in what would be needed in order to play a greater world role or, indeed, to embark on a course of expansion and war.

· Ultimately, resource-related needs and objectives, like other aspects of strategy, have tended to be determined by broader political aims, and not *vice versa*. Where the resource aspects of strategy have been pursued without regard to broader policy, the results have often been counter-productive; witness Hitler's obsession with the conquest and defence of resource-bearing regions in the face of more urgent strategic imperatives elsewhere.

Second, the consideration of resource issues has historically been closely linked to 'geostrategic' notions. While perceptions about resources, trade, autarky, and strategy have developed along different lines in the maritime and continental traditions, these lines have never been entirely fixed. Japanese strategists drew on essentially continental notions of geography and war economy in pursuing the creation of a 'greater space economy' in Asia. Similarly, some contemporary American observers refer, in a much less systematic way, to the 'geopolitics' of raw materials in a manner reminiscent of continental theorists.

Generally, the maritime approach to resource access has focussed on pragmatic, *ad hoc* policies. Here, resource issues have rarely assumed the guiding role or mystical significance which they have often had in German and Soviet planning. Geopolitical thinking, certainly in the sense of interwar German 'geopolitics', is largely alien to the Anglo-American strategic tradition. For the traditional maritime powers, resource-related strategy has been concerned with the most effective exploitation of worldwide access to raw material sources in war, that is, the management of strategic dependencies and strategic assets in relation to sea-borne trade. It has been far less concerned with the promotion of self-sufficiency as an objective of policy.

At the highest levels of strategic analysis, and especially in relation to 'grand strategy', varying geostrategic traditions have shaped, and continue to shape the manner in which resource issues are perceived. At the operational level, resource factors will have a much more pragmatic quality (for example, the effect of fuel shortages on the mobility of forces), and as the experience of the two world wars demonstrates, strategies of resource *denial* have tended to cut across traditional maritime and conventional lines. The intimate connection between the production and transport of resources and geographic reality (that is, the location of raw material reserves, and the lines of communication available for access to them) suggests that consideration of resource issues cannot be divorced from 'geostrategic' ideas, although there will be significant differences in the extent to which such ideas are explicitly formulated and systematically introduced into strategic planning.

Finally, while the evolution of military technology and doctrine and, most significantly, the advent of nuclear weapons, have brought about revolutionary changes in the nature of warfare, they have not eliminated the role of resource factors, which continue to influence strategic perceptions and plans across a broad spectrum of conflicts and crises. An understanding of the elements of continuity and change, and the lessons to be derived from historical experience, will be essential to understanding the relationship between resources and strategy in the future.

Notes

1 Introduction
1. Quincy Wright, *A Study of War* (Chicago: University of Chicago Press, 1964, first published 1942) pp. 65–7.
2. Raymond Aron, *Peace and War* (London: Weidenfeld & Nicolson, 1966) p. 244.
3. Aron, p. 24.
4. Aron, p. 243.

2 Resources and Strategy to 1914
1. See Martin van Creveld, 'The Origins and Development of Mobilization Warfare' in Gordon H. McCormick and Richard E. Bissell (eds) *Strategic Dimensions of Economic Behavior* (New York: Praeger, 1984) pp. 26–43.
2. Arnold Toynbee, *Mankind and Mother Earth* (Oxford: Oxford University Press, 1976) p. 88.
3. Geoffrey Kemp and John Maurer, 'The Logistics of *Pax Britannica*' in Uri Ra'anan *et al.* (eds) *Projection of Power: Perspectives, Perceptions and Problems* (Hamden: Archon, 1982) p. 30.
4. See Geoffrey Parker, *The Army of Flanders and the Spanish Road 1567–1659* (Cambridge: Cambridge University Press, 1972).
5. Raymond Aron, *Peace and War* (London: Weidenfeld & Nicolson, 1966) pp. 244–5.
6. John Evelyn, *Navigation and Commerce* (1674). Quoted in Aron, p. 245.
7. Gordon H. McCormick 'Strategic Considerations in the Development of Economic Thought' in McCormick and Bissell, p. 4.
8. McCormick, p. 5. See Eli F. Heckscher, *Mercantilism* (London: Allen & Unwin, 1955); 'Revisions in Economic History, V, Mercantilism', *The Economic History Review*, vol. vii, 1936; and Jacob Viner, 'Policy versus Plenty as Objectives of Foreign Policy in the 17th and 18th Centuries', *World Politics*, vol. i (1948–49).
9. Heckscher, *Mercantilism*, vol. ii, p. 43.
10. See John H. Maurer, 'Economics, Strategy and War in Historical Perspective', in McCormick and Bissell, pp. 73–4.
11. See Henry Guerlac, 'Vauban: The Impact of Science on War' in Edward Mead Earle (ed.) *Makers of Modern Strategy* (Princeton: Princeton University Press, 1943) p. 39.
12. Herbert W. Richmond, *The Navy as an Instrument of Policy* (Cambridge: Cambridge University Press, 1953) p. 43.
13. See Maurer, 'Economics, Strategy and War', p. 75.
14. Quoted in E. M. Earle, 'The Economic Foundations of Military Power, in E. M. Earle (ed.) *Makers of Modern Strategy*, p. 130.
15. *Works of Alexander Hamilton*, Henry Cabot Lodge (ed.) (New York: Putnam & Sons, 1904) vol. iv, p. 70.
16. Earle, 'Economic Foundations', p. 131.

17. Robert G. Albion, *Forests and Sea Power; The Timber Problem of the Royal Navy 1652–1862* (Cambridge: Harvard University Press, 1926), p. vii. See also P. W. Bamford, *Forests and French Sea Power 1660–1789* (Toronto: University of Toronto Press, 1956).
18. Albion, p. viii.
19. Albion, p. ix.
20. Albion, p. x.
21. Albion, pp. xi–xii.
22. Adam Smith, *An Inquiry into the Nature and Causes of the Wealth of Nations* (London: G. Bell & Sons, 1908) p. 693.
23. Aron, pp. 248–9.
24. Paul M. Kennedy, *The Rise and Fall of British Naval Mastery* (London: Macmillan, 1976) p. 130.
25. Alfred Thayer Mahan, *The Influence of Sea Power Upon the French Revolution and Empire* (London, 1892) vol. i, pp. 202–203.
26. D. T. Jack, *Studies in Economic Warfare* (London: P. S. King, 1940) p. 2.
27. Kennedy, *Rise and Fall*, p. 131.
28. Kennedy, *Rise and Fall*, p. 131.
29. Bryan Ranft, 'The Protection of British Seaborne Trade and the Development of Systematic Planning for War, 1860–1906', in Ranft (ed.) *Technical Change and British Naval Policy 1860–1939* (London: Hodder & Stoughton, 1977) p. 14.
30. Eli F. Heckscher, *The Continental System: An Economic Interpretation* (Oxford: Clarendon Press, 1922) p. 364.
31. Jack, p. 41.
32. See George Lefebvre, *Napoleon* (New York: Columbia University Press, 1965) vol. ii, pp. 253–62.
33. The Convoy Acts of 1793, 1798 and 1803 imposed this system on the bulk of British merchant ship owners.
34. Quoted in Martin Doughty, *Merchant Shipping and War* (London: Royal Historical Society, 1982) p. 3.
35. By 1800 French trade with Asia, Africa and America had been reduced to less than $356,000. See Mahan, *The Influence of Sea Power Upon the French Revolution and Empire*, vol. ii, pp. 218–20; and Lefebvre, *Napoleon*, vol. i, p. 43.
36. See Heckscher, *The Continental System*.
37. Jack, p. 17.
38. Mahan, *The Influence of Sea Power Upon the French Revolution and Empire*, vol. ii, p. 289.
39. Aron, p. 250.
40. Quoted in Earle, 'Economic Foundations', p. 142.
41. Gottlieb Fichte, *Der geschlossene Handelsstaat* (Berlin: Brockhans, 1800) p. 480. Quoted in McCormick, p. 16.
42. See Friedrich List, *The National System of Political Economy* (New York: A. M. Kelley, 1977, first published 1841).
43. See Earle, 'Economic Foundations', pp. 144–53.
44. See J. A. Hobson, *Imperialism: A Study* (London: George Allen & Unwin, 1948, first published 1902).

45. Gerhard Ritter, *The Sword and the Scepter: The Problem of Militarism in Germany* (Coral Gables: University of Miami Press, 1970) vol. i, p. 188.

46. V. I. Lenin, *Imperialism, The Highest Stage of Capitalism* (London: Martin Lawrence, 1934, first published 1917) pp. 69, 71.

47. Lenin, *Imperialism*, p. 111.

48. William L. Langer, *The Diplomacy of Imperialism, 1840–1902* (New York: Knopf, 1965) p. 68.

49. Ritter, vol. ii, p. 108.

50. Jean De Bloch, from a prefatory interview with the author in *The Future of War in its Technical, Economic and Political Relations* (New York: Doubleday & McClure, 1899), pp. xvi–xvii.

51. Bloch, pp. xlii–xliv.

52. Idem.

53. Bloch, pp. lix–lx.

54. Maurer, 'Economics, Strategy and War in Historical Perspective', p. 63.

55. Michael Howard, 'Men Against Fire: The Doctrine of the Offensive in 1914', in Peter Paret (ed.) *Makers of Modern Strategy; From Machiavelli to the Nuclear Age* (Princeton: Princeton University Press, 1986) p. 512. In the same volume, see also the discussion of Bloch by Walter Pintner, 'Russian Military Thought: The Western Model and the Shadow of Suvorov', pp. 365–6.

56. Arthur J. Marder, *British Naval Policy 1880–1905* (London: Putnam, 1940) pp. 50–61.

57. Ranft, 'The Protection of British Seaborne Trade', p. 2.

58. Quoted in Ranft, 'The Protection of British Seaborne Trade', p. 2.

59. Marder, *British Naval Policy 1880–1905*, pp. 84–5.

60. *Report of the Royal Commission on Supply of Food and Raw Materials in Time of War*, Cd. 2643 (1905) pp. 4 and 17.

61. Arthur J. Marder, *Anatomy of British Sea Power* (New York: Knopf, 1940) p. 65.

62. Kennedy, *Rise and Fall*, p. 200.

63. David French, *British Economic and Strategic Planning 1905–1915* (London: Allen & Unwin, 1982) p. 12. See *Report of the Royal Commission*, Cd. 2643, p. 3.

64. *Report of the Royal Commission*, Cd. 2643, p. 3.

65. Quoted in Maurer, 'Economics, Strategy and War', pp. 75–6.

66. Russell F. Weighley, *The American Way of War: A History of U.S. Military Strategy and Policy* (Bloomington: Indiana University Press, 1973) p. 180.

67. Doughty, p. 4.

68. Marder, *Anatomy of British Sea Power*, pp. 163–4.

69. *Report of the Royal Commission*, Cd. 2643, p. 28.

70. Idem.

71. Idem.

72. *Report of the Royal Commission*, Cd. 2643, p. 29.

73. Marder, *British Naval Policy 1880–1905*, p. 481.

74. A. Temple Patterson (ed.) *The Jellicoe Papers, Vol. I, 1893–1916* (London: Navy Records Society, 1968) p. 34.

75. *Jellicoe Papers*, Vol. I, p. 35.
76. Mahan, *The Influence of Sea Power Upon History, 1660–1783* (Boston: Little, Brown & Company, 1890) p. 138.
77. H. J. Mackinder, 'The Geographical Pivot of History', *Geographical Journal*, xxiii (1904) p. 434.
78. Kennedy, *Rise and Fall*, p. 198.
79. See Ranft, 'Protection of British Seaborne Trade', p. 1.
80. Langer, p. 434; and Ritter, vol. ii, pp. 137–58.
81. Bernard Brodie, *Sea Power in the Machine Age* (Princeton: Princeton University Press, 1941) p. 116.
82. Brodie, *Sea Power in the Machine Age*, p. 116; and John D. Alden, *The American Steel Navy* (Annapolis: Naval Institute Press, 1971) pp. 129–30.
83. See Lamar J. R. Cecil, 'Coal for the Fleet That Had to Die', *The American Historical Review*, vol. 69 (1964) no. 4.
84. Kemp and Maurer, p. 39. See Winston Churchill, *The World Crisis 1911–1914* (London: Thornton Butterworth, 1923) pp. 129–34.
85. Churchill, *The World Crisis*, p. 132.
86. Quoted in Leonard Mosley, *Power Play: Oil in the Middle East* (Baltimore: Penguin, 1974) p. 23.
87. Michael Lewis, *The Navy of Britain: A Historical Portrait* (London: Allen & Unwin, 1948) p. 127.
88. E. M. Earle, *Turkey, the Great Powers and the Baghdad Railway* (New York: Macmillan, 1924) pp. 46–7.
89. C. M. Cipola (ed.) *Fontana Economic History of Europe*, vol. iv, Part 2 (London: Fontana, 1973) Statistical Appendix. Cited in Van Creveld, 'Mobilization Warfare', p. 27.
90. Earle, *Baghdad Railway*, p. 50.
91. Earle, *Baghdad Railway*, p. 50.
92. Ibid., p. 51.
93. Earle, *Baghdad Railway*, p. 51.
94. Idem.
95. Fritz Fischer, *Germany's Aims in the First World War* (New York: Norton, 1961) p. 21.
96. Earle, *Baghdad Railway*, p. 205.

3 Resource Access and Denial in World War I

1. Van Creveld, 'The Origin and Development of Mobilization Warfare' in McCormick and Bissell, p. 25.
2. Van Creveld, 'Mobilization Warfare', p. 27.
3. Van Creveld, 'Mobilization Warfare', pp. 27–8. See also John Terraine, 'The Achievements of World War I'; lecture given at the RUSI, London, 23 June 1982. Published in the *RUSI Journal*, vol. 127 (December 1982) no. 4. Terraine points to the very considerable achievement of the professional military in adapting to rapid technological change over the course of the war.
4. Based on Van Creveld, 'Mobilization Warfare', pp. 28–9.
5. F. P. Chambers, *The War Behind the War 1914–1918* (London: Faber & Faber, 1934) p. 21.

6.   W. G. Jensen, 'The Importance of Energy in the First and Second World Wars', *The Historical Journal*, XI (1968) pp. 538–9.
7.   Van Creveld, 'Mobilization Warfare', p. 31.
8.   Van Creveld, 'Mobilization Warfare', p. 30.
9.   Jensen, p. 539.
10. Chambers, pp. 22 and 64.
11. Jensen, p. 539.
12. Arthur Fontaine, *French Industry During the War*, Carnegie Series (New Haven: Yale University Press, 1926) p. 21.
13. Jensen, pp. 539–40.
14. Chambers, p. 22.
15. S. O. Zegorsky, *State Control of Industry in Russia During the War*, Carnegie Series (New Haven: Yale University Press, 1928) p. 37.
16. Jensen, p. 540.
17. Jensen, p. 541.
18. Boris E. Nolde, *Russia in the Economic War*, Carnegie Series (New Haven: Yale University Press, 1928) p. 1. See also Norman Stone, *The Eastern Front 1914–1917* (London: Hodder & Stoughton, 1975).
19. Chambers, p. 184.
20. Ritter, vol. iv, pp. 112–13.
21. Chambers, p. 64.
22. Quoted in Fritz Fischer, *War of Illusions: German Policies from 1911 to 1914* (London: Chatto & Windus, 1975) p. 450.
23. Chambers, pp. 141–3.
24. Ibid., p. 145.
25. Chambers, p. 153.
26. Kennedy, *The Rise and Fall of British Naval Mastery*, p. 252.
27. See James T. Shotwell, *What Germany Forgot* (New York: Macmillan, 1940) p. 21.
28. Quoted in L. Farago (ed.) *Axis Grand Strategy* (New York, 1941) p. 499.
29. Chambers, pp. 145 and 152.
30. Shotwell, p. 25.
31. Jensen, p. 542.
32. See C. H. Ellis, *The Transcaspian Episode 1918–1919* (London: Hutchinson, 1963).
33. Jensen, p. 542.
34. Chambers, p. 523.
35. J. A. Salter, *Allied Shipping Control* (Oxford: Clarendon Press, 1921) p. 1.
36. Alan S. Milward, 'Restriction of Supply as a Strategic Choice', in McCormick and Bissell, p. 44.
37. Milward, 'Restriction of Supply', p. 44.
38. Chambers, p. 137.
39. Margaret Tuttle Sprout, 'Mahan: Evangelist of Sea Power', in Earle, *Makers of Modern Strategy*, p. 435.
40. Jack, p. 108.
41. Elmo R. Zumwalt, 'Blockade and Geopolitics', *Comparative Strategy*, vol. 4 (1983) no. 2, p. 171.

42. Chambers, pp. 152–3.
43. M. W. W. P. Consett, *The Triumph of Unarmed Forces 1914–1918* (London: Williams & Norgate, 1923) p. ix.
44. Quoted in Consett, p. 78.
45. W. K. Hancock and M. M. Gowing, *British War Economy* (London: HMSO, 1949) p. 20.
46. Jack, p. 122.
47. Kennedy, *Rise and Fall*, pp. 254–5.
48. Kennedy, *Rise and Fall*, p. 259.
49. Conversation between Bethmann-Hollweg and Pohl, quoted in Fritz Fischer, *World Power or Decline* (New York: W. W. Norton, 1974) p. 40.
50. Diary entry, 1 February 1917. Quoted in Maurer, 'Economics, Strategy and War', p. 78.
51. Chambers, p. 412.
52. Ibid., p. 413.
53. Chambers, p. 417.
54. Kathleen Burk, *Britain, America and the Sinews of War 1914–1918* (Boston: Allen & Unwin, 1985).
55. Burk, pp. 62 and 10.
56. Jensen, p. 542.
57. Pierre L'Espagnol de la Tramerye, *The World Struggle for Oil* (London: Allen & Unwin, 1923) p. 80.
58. de la Tramerye, p. 81.
59. Jensen, p. 542.
60. General Ludendorff, *The Nation at War* (London: Hutchinson, 1936) pp. 78–9. See also Ludendorff's comments with regard to oil in his *Memoirs*, quoted in de la Tramerye, p. 81.
61. Fritz Sternberg, *Germany and a Lightning War* (London: Faber & Faber, 1938).
62. Quoted in Sternberg.
63. Jensen, p. 542.
64. Address by Lord Curzon to the Inter-Allied Petroleum Council, London, 21 November 1918. Quoted in Ludwell Denny, *We Fight for Oil* (New York: Knopf, 1928) p. 27.
65. Address to the Inter-Allied Petroleum Council, London, 21 November 1918. Quoted in Benjamin Shwadran, *The Middle East, Oil and the Great Powers* (New York: Praeger, 1955) p. 39.
66. de la Tramerye, p. 82.
67. Denny, p. 27.
68. Quoted in Kemp and Maurer, p. 43. See also C. Gareth Jones, 'The British Government and the Oil Companies 1912–1924', *The Historical Journal*, vol. 20 (1977) no. 3, p. 661.
69. de la Tramerye, p. 82.
70. Jones, p. 664.
71. Note of 15 December 1917. Quoted in Denny, pp. 27–8.
72. Address to the Inter-Allied Petroleum Council, London, 21 November 1918. Cited in Denny, p. 28.
73. Jones, p. 664.

74. See, for instance, Fritz Fischer, *Germany's Aims in the First World War* (New York: Norton, 1961).
75. Jensen, p. 544.
76. Fischer, *Germany's Aims in the First World War*, p. 556.
77. US Department of Defense (OASD/PA&E), 'Capabilities for Limited Contingencies in the Persian Gulf', Washington, 15 June 1979, Part I, p. 10. (Declassified Doc.)
78. F. J. Moberly, *The Campaign in Mesopotamia*, vol. i (London: HMSO, 1923) pp. 80–1.
79. US Department of Defense, 'Capabilities for Limited Contingencies in the Persian Gulf', Part I, p. 10.
80. Kennedy, *Rise and Fall*, p. 258.
81. V. H. Rothwell, 'Mesopotamia in British War Aims 1914–1918', *The Historical Journal*, XII, 2 (1970) p. 288.
82. Admiralty Memo (Cab., 24/60 G.T. 5313), cited in Rothwell, p. 288.
83. Rothwell, p. 290.
84. F.O. 800/204, Hankey to Balfour, 1 August 1918. Quoted in Rothwell, p. 289.
85. Herbert Richmond, *Statesmen and Sea Power* (Oxford: Clarendon Press, 1946) p. 284.

4 Resource Access and Denial in World War II

1. It is noteworthy that League of Nations statements made frequent reference to the need for consideration of the resource endowment of states in determining defence and armament requirements. See Brooks Emeny, *The Strategy of Raw Materials: A Study of America in Peace and War* (New York: Macmillan, 1944) pp. 2–4.
2. Milward, 'Restriction of Supply as a Strategic Choice', in McCormick and Bissell, p. 48.
3. The interactive nature of resources as *objectives* and resources as *means* in relation to strategy should be noted. Cases such as the German offensive in the Caucasus point to the influence of both.
4. This question is examined in detail in Albert T. Lauterbach, *Economics in Uniform* (Princeton: Princeton University Press, 1943), and Alan S. Milward, *War, Economy and Society 1939–1945* (London: Allen Lane, 1977).
5. Lauterbach, p. 29.
6. Lauterbach, p. 30.
7. D. C. Watt, *Too Serious a Business* (London: Temple Smith, 1975) p. 110.
8. Fritz Sternberg, *Germany and a Lightning War* (London: Faber & Faber, 1938) p. 14.
9. These concepts are developed in Ratzel's principal works, *Anthropo-Geographie* (Stuttgart: Engelhorn, 1882) and *Politische und Geographie* (Munich: Oldenburg, 1897).
10. Derwent Whittlesey, 'Haushofer: The Geopoliticians' in Earle, *Makers of Modern Strategy*, p. 389.
11. See Johannes Mattern, *Geopolitik* (Baltimore: Johns Hopkins Uni-

versity Press, 1942) pp. 95–106; and Robert Strauz-Hupe, *Geopolitics* (New York: Putnam, 1942) pp. 40–7.

12. See Friedrich Naumann, *Mitteleuropa* (Berlin: George Remer Varlag, 1916).

13. Strausz-Hupe, p. 37.

14. A. G. B. Fisher, 'Economic Self-Sufficiency', *Oxford Pamphlets on World Affairs*, no. 4 (1939) p. 8.

15. Quoted in Fisher, p. 10.

16. Quoted in Maxwell H. H. Macartney and Paul Cremona, *Italy's Foreign and Colonial Policy 1914–1937* (New York: Howard Fertig, 1972, originally published 1938) pp. 2–3.

17. *Sanctions*, Information Department Papers, no. 17 (London: Royal Institute for International Affairs, 1935) p. 39.

18. Macartney, p. 3. The problem of Italy's resource position, particularly with regard to energy supplies, was also a source of concern to German planners in the late 1930s. See Robert Goralski and Russell N. Freeburg, *Oil and War* (New York: William Morrow, 1987) pp. 24–38.

19. As asserted by Mussolini in a speech of 16 May 1937 to the Third General Assembly of the Council of the Corporations. Quoted in Macartney, p. 5.

20. Quoted in Fisher, p. 9.

21. Macartney, p. 5.

22. See *Sanctions*, Appendix IX, 'Procedures Adopted by the League for the Application of Sanctions Against Italy', pp. 70–2; and M. Mugger-idge (ed.) *Ciano's Diplomatic Papers* (London: Odhams Press, 1948) p. xv. See also, Herbert Feis, *Seen from E.A.: Three International Episodes* (New York: Knopf, 1947), 'Supplementary Note on Sanctions', pp. 297–308.

23. William O. Scroggs, 'Oil for Italy', *Foreign Affairs*, vol. 14 (April 1936) no. 3. After the Abyssinian crisis, Mussolini reportedly told Hitler that an extension of the League sanctions to include oil would have forced him to withdraw. See Gorolski and Freeburg, pp. 23–4.

24. Lauterbach, p. 98.

25. Fisher, p. 17.

26. Derwent Whittlesey, *German Strategy of World Conquest* (New York: Farrar & Rinehart, 1942) p. 172.

27. Quoted in Whittlesey, *German Strategy of World Conquest*, p. 172.

28. Whittlesey, 'Haushofer', p. 389.

29. Strausz-Hupe, p. 59.

30. Strausz-Hupe, p. 60. Haushofer expressed considerable interest in the work of the British geographer James Fairgrieve, including his assertion that the quest for energy resources, for instance, coal and oil, would dictate the pattern of modern geopolitical relationships. See Fairgrieve, *Geography and World Power* (London: 1920). The German version of the book, published in 1925, contains an introduction by Haushofer.

31. Berenice A. Carroll, *Design for Total War: Arms and Economics in the Third Reich* (The Hague: Mouton, 1968) pp. 101–2.

32. *Volkischer Beobachter*, 13 September 1936. Quoted in Carroll, p. 104.

33. Quoted in Mattern, p. 120.
34. Strausz-Hupe, pp. 92–3.
35. *New York Times*, 24 July 1926. Quoted in Parker T. Moon, 'Raw Materials and Imperialism', *International Conciliation*, no. 226 (January 1927).
36. See Strausz-Hupe, pp. 109–10.
37. Ewald Banse, *Germany Prepare for War!* (London: Lovat Dickson, 1934, originally published as *Raum und Volk in Weltkriege* in 1933) p. 43.
38. Banse, p. 46.
39. Ibid, p. 48.
40. See Ludendorff, *The Nation at War*, pp. 55–85.
41. B. H. Liddell Hart, *Europe in Arms* (London: Faber & Faber, 1937) p. 286.
42. Hans Speier, 'Ludendorff: The German Concept of Total War' in Earle, *Makers of Modern Strategy*, p. 315.
43. Lauterbach, p. 36.
44. Idem.
45. See, for example, R. J. Overy, *Goering: The 'Iron Man'* (London: Routledge & Kegan Paul, 1984); and by the same author, 'Hitler's War and the German Economy: A Reinterpretation', *Economic History Review*, 2nd ser., vol. 35 (1982).
46. Watt, p. 111.
47. Quoted in Watt, p. 111.
48. Georg Thomas, *'Operatives und Wirtschaftiches Denken', Kriegswirtschaftliches Jahresberichte*, 1936, p. 14. Quoted in Sternberg, p. 73.
49. Quoted in Sternberg, p. 77.
50. Carroll, p. 47. This sceptical view of attempts at economic autarky was shared by Hjalmar Schacht, and contrasted sharply with the outlook of Goering and other 'autarkists'. See Overy, *Goering: The 'Iron Man'*, pp. 48–75.
51. Carroll, p. 47.
52. Burton H. Klein, *Germany's Economic Preparations for War* (Cambridge: Harvard University Press, 1959) p. 28.
53. Charles Webster and Noble Frankland, *The Strategic Air Offensive Against Germany 1939–1945* (London: HMSO, 1961) vol. i, p. 273.
54. Klein, p. 35.
55. Quoted in Klein, p. 36.
56. 1936 Directive to Goering. Quoted in Klein, p. 18.
57. Alan S. Milward, *The German Economy at War* (London: Athlone, 1965) pp. 3–4.
58. Milward, *The German Economy at War*, pp. 12–13. The process for the production of synthetic rubber (I. G. Farben's 'Buna S') was also available by 1930. As with synthetic oil, however, the product was very expensive due to the enormous amount of electric power required. Thus, Germany continued to rely almost exclusively on imports of natural rubber. See Klein, p. 33.
59. United Kingdom Ministry of Fuel and Power, *Report on the Petroleum and Synthetic Oil Industry of Germany* (London: HMSO, 1947); see

also Ronald C. Cooke and Roy Conyers Nesbit, *Target: Hitler's Oil: Attacks on German Oil Supplies 1939–1945* (London: William Kimber, 1985) p. 15.

60. *The Effects of Strategic Bombing on the German War Economy*, United States Strategic Bombing Survey (USSBS), Overall Economic Effects Division (Washington: GPO, 1945) pp. 73–83.
61. Idem.
62. Idem.
63. Klein, p. 49.
64. Milward, *War, Economy and Society*, p. 261.
65. Klein, pp. 49–50.
66. Sternberg, p. 210.
67. See Klein, pp. 59–63.
68. Lauterbach, p. 44.
69. Joachim Joesten, 'The Scramble for Swedish Iron Ore', *Political Quarterly*, I (1938) p. 58.
70. Milward, *War, Economy and Society*, p. 294.
71. W. N. Medlicott, *The Economic Blockade* (London: HMSO, 1952) vol. i, pp. 17–18.
72. Watt, pp. 111–12.
73. Medlicott, vol. i, p. 113.
74. Stephen Roskill, *Naval Policy Between the Wars* (London: Collins, 1976) vol. ii, p. 335.
75. W. K. Hancock and M. M. Gowing, *British War Economy* (London: HMSO, 1949) p. 211.
76. During the mid-1930s it was estimated that Britain imported annually some 20 million tons (mt) of foodstuffs, 12 mt of metals and ores, 10 mt of oil, and 2 mt of non-metallic materials. Sternberg, pp. 112–13; and R. W. B. Clarke, *The Economic Effort of War* (London: Allen & Unwin, 1940) p. 118.
77. *The Times*, 25–27 October 1937. Cited in Irving Gibson, 'Maginot and Liddell Hart: the Doctrine of Defense' in Earle, *Makers of Modern Strategy*, p. 381.
78. Milward, *War, Economy and Society*, p. 295.
79. See Jack, *Studies in Economic Warfare*: and Milward, *War, Economy and Society*, p. 296.
80. See, for example, Sternberg, *Germany and a Lightning War*; and Ferdinand Friedensburg, *Die Mineralischen Bodenschatze als weltpolitik und militarische Machfaktoren* (Stuttgart: Ferdinand Enke Verlag, 1936).
81. Milward, *War, Economy and Society*, p. 296.
82. Clarke, pp. 118–19.
83. See, for example, Emeny, *The Strategy of Raw Materials*; Eugene Staley, *Raw Materials in Peace and War* (New York: 1937); G. A. Roush, *Strategic Mineral Supplies* (New York: 1939); and C. K. Leith, *World Minerals and World Peace* (Washington: The Brookings Institution, 1943).
84. Emeny, p. 168.
85. Wallace T. Buckley, 'The Strategic Raw Materials' in George A.

Steiner (ed.) *Economic Problems of War* (New York: John Wiley, 1942) p. 3.
86. Idem.
87. Buckley, p. 6.
88. Ibid., pp. 18–20.
89. Nicholas J. Spykman, *America's Strategy in World Politics* (New York: Harcourt, Brace & World, 1942) p. 296.
90. Spykman, p. 296.
91. Quoted in Spykman, p. 292.
92. J. Hurstfield, *The Control of Raw Materials* (London: HMSO, 1953) p. 161.
93. Ibid., p. 158.
94. Hurstfield, p. 167.
95. *Fifth Annual Report of the U.S. Senate Committee Investigating the National Defense Program*, 79th Congress, 2nd Session, Report No. 110, Part 7, p. 15. Cited in H. Duncan Hall and C. C. Wrigley, *Studies of Overseas Supply* (London: HMSO, 1956) p. 263.
96. The Canadian contribution to Allied requirements included 95 per cent of nickel, 75 per cent of asbestos, 30 per cent of aluminium, and 20 per cent of zinc. See Hall and Wrigley, p. 263.
97. Jean Monnet, *Memoirs* (New York: Doubleday, 1978) p. 128.
98. Hall and Wrigley, pp. 263–4.
99. Similar machinery was put in place for the co-ordination of food supply with the establishment of the Combined Food Board on 9 June 1942.
100. *Documents on American Foreign Relations*, vol. vi (July 1943–June 1944) p. 241.
101. Hall and Wrigley, p. 271.
102. Emeny, p. 15.
103. Einzig, pp. 132–4.
104. Sternberg, p. 297.
105. See Max Werner, *The Military Strength of the Powers* (New York: Left Book Club, 1939).
106. E. M. Earle, 'Lenin, Trotsky, Stalin: Soviet Concepts of War' in Earle, *Makers of Modern Strategy*, p. 353.
107. Fisher, 'Economic Self-Sufficiency', p. 13.
108. V. D. Sokolovsky, *Soviet Military Strategy*, Harriet Fast Scott (ed.) (New York: Crane Russak, 1975, first published 1968 p. 131.
109. John Erickson, *The Soviet High Command: A Military-Political History 1918–1941* (London: Macmillan, 1962) pp. 283, 295 and 303.
110. Raymond Garthoff, *How Russia Makes War; Soviet Military Doctrine* (London: Allen & Unwin, 1954) pp. 30–4.
111. Erickson, *The Soviet High Command*, p. 303.
112. Ibid.
113. Ibid., p. 425.
114. Alexander Werth, *Russia at War 1941–1945* (London: Barrie & Rockliff, 1964) pp. 213–15.
115. Earle, 'Soviet Concepts of War', p. 353.
116. Erickson, *The Soviet High Command*, p. 608.
117. As early as July 1941, the Soviet Academy of Sciences was engaged in a vast surveying operation aimed at exploiting new sources of energy and

raw materials in the Urals. See John Erickson, *The Road to Berlin* (Boulder: Westview, 1983) p. 77.

118. Werth, pp. 220–1.
119. Benjamin T. Brooks, *Peace, Plenty and Petroleum* (Lancaster: Jacques Cattel Press, 1944) pp. 83–4.
120. Garthoff, p. 291.
121. Werth, p. 223.
122. Erickson, *The Soviet High Command*, pp. 628 and 665.
123. See 'Soviet War Economy', *The Economist*, CXLI (1941) pp. 3 and 17–18.
124. Broadcast quoted in Earle, 'Soviet Concepts of War', pp. 361–2.
125. Garthoff, p. 161.
126. Werth, p. 216.
127. Werth, pp. 113–14.
128. The loss of the Lorraine steel industry, based on lower-grade ores, increased German dependence on imports to roughly 70 per cent, of which Sweden supplied the greatest amount in terms of tonnage and iron content. See Alan S. Milward, 'Could Sweden Have Stopped the Second World War?', *Scandinavian Economic Review*, XV (1967).
129. See Rolf Karlblom, 'Sweden's Iron Ore Exports to Germany, 1933–1944', *Scandinavian Economic History Review*, XII (1965).
130. Ibid., p. 71.
131. See Jorg-Johannes Jagar, 'Sweden's Iron Ore Exports to Germany 1933–1944', *Scandinavian Economic History Review*, XV (1967); and Martin Fritz, 'Swedish Iron Ore and German Steel 1939–1940', *Scandinavian Economic History Review*, XXI (1973).
132. Milward, 'Could Sweden Have Stopped the Second World War?'
133. Alan S. Milward, *The German Economy at War*, pp. 47–8.
134. As asserted by General von Falkenhorst in his testimony at the Nuremberg Trials. See Churchill, *The Second World War*, vol. i, p. 446.
135. Idem.
136. Lauterbach, p. 41.
137. Walter J. Levy, 'The Paradox of Oil and War', in *Oil, Strategy and Politics 1941–1981*, Melvin A. Conant (ed.) (Boulder: Westview Press, 1982, article reprinted from *Fortune*, September 1941) p. 9.
138. Webster and Frankland, vol. i, p. 275.
139. Ibid.
140. W. N. Medlicott, *The Economic Blockade* (London: HMSO, 1952) vol. ii, p. 652.
141. See Royal Institute for International Affairs, *Occupied Europe: German Exploitation and its Post-War Consequences* (London: Oxford University Press, 1944).
142. Medlicott, vol. ii, p. 653.
143. Speier, p. 312.
144. Overy, *Goering: The 'Iron Man'*, pp. 76–108.
145. Milward, 'Restriction of Supply', pp. 47–8.
146. David L. Gordon and Roydon Dangerfield, *The Hidden Weapon* (New York: Harper Brothers, 1947) p. 208.
147. Gordon and Dangerfield, p. 209.

148. Overy, *Goering: The 'Iron Man'*, p. 131.
149. Barry Leach, *German Strategy Against Russia 1939–1941* (Oxford: Clarendon Press, 1973) p. 144.
150. Idem.
151. Quoted in Leach, p. 151.
152. Leach, p. 156.
153. Directive from Hitler, 5 April 1942. Quoted in Michael Howard, *Grand Strategy*, vol. iv, April 1942–September 1943 (London: HMSO, 1972) p. 31.
154. Webster and Frankland, vol. i, p. 479.
155. Medlicott, vol. ii, pp. 652–3.
156. Overy, *Goering: The 'Iron Man'*, pp. 216–17.
157. See USSBS, *Overall Economic Effects*, pp. 73–83.
158. Sokolovsky, p. 138.
159. In Romania, Soviet requisitioning involved the wholesale removal of oil production equipment for use in the Soviet Union. See Erickson, *The Road to Berlin*, p. 370.
160. Gordon and Dangerfield, p. 209.
161. Howard, *Grand Strategy*, p. 325.
162. Gordon and Dangerfield, pp. 209–10. See also Erickson, *The Road to Berlin*, pp. 380, 446, 459.
163. Webster and Frankland, vol. iii, p. 234.
164. Levy, 'Paradox of Oil and War', p. 18.
165. Brooks, pp. 87–8.
166. Webster and Frankland, vol. iii, p. 239; Milward, *War, Economy and Society*, p. 317.
167. F. H. Hinsley, *Hitler's Strategy* (Cambridge: Cambridge University Press, 1951) pp. 214–15.
168. See Howard, *Grand Strategy*, pp. 64–5.
169. Admiral Doenitz, *Memoirs* (London: Weidenfeld & Nicolson, 1959) p. 40.
170. Doenitz, p. 44.
171. Levy, 'The Paradox of Oil and War', p. 38.
172. Maurer, p. 78.
173. Michael B. Stoff, *Oil, War, and American Security; The Search for a National Policy on Foreign Oil, 1941–1947* (New Haven: Yale University Press, 1980) p. 72.
174. Stoff, pp. 72–3.
175. See *A Documentary History of the Petroleum Reserves Corporation 1943–1944*, Subcommittee on Multinational Corporations, Senate Committee on Foreign Relations, 93rd Congress, 2nd Session, 1974.
176. Joseph E. Pogue, 'Oil in Peace and War' (New York: Chase National Bank, 1944) p. 7.
177. Hurstfield, p. 173.
178. Quoted in Medlicott, vol. ii, p. 13.
179. Medlicott, vol. ii, p. 13.
180. Quoted in Howard, *Grand Strategy*, p. 54.
181. Howard, *Grand Strategy*, p. 55.
182. Hancock and Gowing, pp. 435–6.

183. Hancock and Gowing, p. 214.
184. F. H. Hinsley, *British Intelligence in the Second World War* (London: HMSO) vol. i, pp. 60 and 71. See also Robert J. Young, 'Spokesmen for Economic Warfare: The Industrial Intelligence Centre in the 1930's', *Europe Studies Review*, 6 (1976) p. 483.
185. Gordon and Dangerfield, p. 6.
186. See Howard, *Grand Strategy*, pp. 610 and 161; E. L. Woodward, *British Foreign Policy in the Second World War* (London: HMSO, 1962) pp. 129 and 371–4; and Wallace E. Pratt and Dorothy Good (eds) *World Geography of Petroleum* (Princeton: Princeton University Press, 1950) p. 394.
187. Milward, 'Restriction of Supply', p. 46.
188. Medlicott, vol. ii, p. 632.
189. Webster and Frankland, vol. i, pp. 280 and 282.
190. Ibid., p. 289.
191. Webster and Frankland, vol. i, p. 294. See also W. F. Craven and J. L. Cate, *The Army Air Forces in World War II* (Chicago: University of Chicago Press, 1949) vol. ii, p. 356; and Webster and Frankland, vol. ii, pp. 285–98.
192. Cooke and Nesbit, p. 18.
193. Ibid. See also Craven and Cate, vol. ii, pp. 477–83.
194. War Cabinet Memo on Anglo-American Strategy in 1943, 31 December 1942. Cited in Howard, *Grand Strategy*, pp. 611–12.
195. Webster and Frankland, vol. iii, p. 229.
196. Woodward, pp. 29–30; Cooke and Nesbit, p. 19.
197. Cooke and Nesbit, p. 19.
198. Ibid. The devastating effect of the 347 USAAF and 158 Bomber Command attacks on German oil plants between May 1944 and April 1945 is made clear in a series of memos from Speer to Hitler reporting on damage and possible counter-measures. See Webster and Frankland, vol. iv, Appendix 32.
199. See USSBS, *Powder, Explosives, Special Rocket and Jet Propellants, War Gases and Smoke Acid* (Ministerial Report 1), no. 111; and USSBS, Oil Division, *Final Report*, p. 57.
200. See USSBS, Oil Division, *Final Report*.
201. Webster and Frankland, vol. iii. p. 237. This is substantially the same conclusion expressed in USSBS, *Overall Economic Effects*, p. 83.
202. Webster and Frankland, vol. i, p. 295.
203. Milward, 'Restriction of Supply', p. 46.
204. Extracts from the interrogation of Albert Speer, 18 July 1945. Quoted in H. R. Allen, *The Legacy of Lord Trenchard* (London: Cassell, 1972) pp. 214–15.
205. Roskill, *Naval Policy Between the Wars*, vol. ii, p. 26.
206. As suggested by Professor J. A. A. Stockwin, St. Antony's College, Oxford. Interview, 1 May 1985.
207. Hans W. Weigert, *Generals and Geographers* (New York: Oxford University Press, 1942) pp. 168–77. See also, Strausz-Hupe, pp. 127–9.
208. Weigert, p. 178.
209. Idem.

210. Sternberg, p. 278.
211. Ibid., p. 279.
212. O. Tanin and E. Yohan, *When Japan Goes to War* (London: Lawrence & Wishart, 1936) p. 252.
213. See I. H. Anderson, *The Standard-Vacuum Oil Company and U.S. East Asian Policy 1933–1941* (Princeton: Princeton University Press, 1975).
214. Raymond Vernon, *Two Hungry Giants: The U.S. and Japan in the Quest for Oil and Ores* (Cambridge, Mass.: Harvard University Press, 1983) pp. 89–90.
215. Walter Levy, 'Japanese Strategy' in *Oil, Strategy and Politics 1941–1981*, p. 24. Article reprinted from *World Petroleum* (1942).
216. Milward, *War, Economy and Society*, pp. 256–7.
217. Ibid., p. 256.
218. Herbert Feis, *The Road to Pearl Harbor; The Coming of the War Between the U.S. and Japan* (Princeton: Princeton University Press, 1950) pp. 108–9.
219. Ibid., p. 109.
220. Ibid., p. 157.
221. Nagoka Shinjiro, 'Economic Demands on the Dutch East Indies' in J. W. Morley (ed.) *The Fateful Choice: Japan's Advance in to Southeast Asia 1939–1941* (New York: Columbia University Press, 1980) pp. 125–53. This volume is one of a series of translations from the Japanese Official History.
222. Quoted in Feis, *Road to Pearl Harbor*, pp. 231–2.
223. Shinjiro, p. 153.
224. See 'Sale of Oil to Japan', Informal talk of President Roosevelt, Washington, 24 July 1941, *Documents on American Foreign Relations*, vol. iv, July 1941–June 1942, p. 500.
225. Vernon, p. 41. See also, Anderson, pp. 171–92.
226. Paul Kennedy, *Strategy and Diplomacy 1870–1945* (London: Fontana, 1983) p. 183.
227. Milward, 'Restriction of Supply', p. 45.
228. Arthur J. Marder, *Old Friends, New Enemies: The Royal Navy and the Imperial Japanese Navy; Strategic Illusions, 1936–1941* (Oxford: Clarendon Press, 1981) p. 166.
229. Quoted in Marder, *Old Friends, New Enemies*, pp. 166–7.
230. Ibid., p. 167.
231. Quoted in Marder, *Old Friends, New Enemies*, p. 168.
232. Ibid.
233. Quoted in Nobutaka Ike (ed.) *Japan's Decision for War: Records of the 1941 Policy Conferences* (Stanford: Stanford University Press, 1967) pp. 139–40.
234. Quoted in Nobutaka Ike, p. 247.
235. See Robert J. C. Butow, *Tojo and the Coming of the War* (Princeton: Princeton University Press, 1969).
236. Kennedy, *Strategy and Diplomacy*, p. 184.
237. Article by William Maghretti in *Pacific Affairs*, vol. 14 (1941), republished in Joyce C. Lebra, *Japan's Greater East Asia Co-prosperity*

Sphere in World War II; Selected Documents (Kuala Lumpur: Oxford University Press, 1975) pp. 44–5.

238. Comment by Foreign Minister Toyoda. Cited in Feis, *Road to Pearl Harbor*, p. 283.

239. J. B. Cohen, *Japan's Economy in War and Reconstruction* (Minneapolis: University of Minnesota Press, 1949) p. 140. Cited in Vernon, p. 91.

240. See Paul S. Dull, *A Battle History of the Imperial Japanese Navy, 1941–1945* (Annapolis: Naval Institute Press, 1978), pp. 281–7; Maurer, p. 79.

241. Gordon and Dangerfield, pp. 138–9.

242. Ibid., p. 138.

243. Milward, 'Restriction of Supply', p. 55.

244. See Hatwood Hansell, Jr., *Strategic Air War Against Japan* (Washington: U.S. GPO, 1980).

245. USSBS, *The War Against Japanese Transportation*, cited in Hansell, p. 77.

246. Milward, 'Restriction of Supply', p. 46.

5 Resource Issues and Strategic Planning, 1945–73

1. Van Creveld, 'Mobilization Warfare', p. 37.

2. Ibid.

3. Paul Bracken, 'Mobilization Dynamics in the Nuclear Age', in McCormick and Bissell, pp. 232–3.

4. Van Creveld, 'Mobilization Warfare', p. 38.

5. Alan C. Brownfeld, 'The Growing United States Dependency on Imported Strategic Materials', *The Atlantic Community Quarterly*, vol. 20 (Spring 1982) no. 1, p. 62.

6. NSC–138, 'National Security Problems Concerning Free World Petroleum Supplies and Potential Demand', 8 December 1952, p. 6.

7. International Economic Studies Institute, *Raw Materials and Foreign Policy* (Washington: IESI, 1976) p. 15.

8. *Raw Materials and Foreign Policy*, pp. 15–16.

9. Aaron David Miller, *Search for Security; Saudi Arabian Oil and American Foreign Policy 1939–1949* (Chapel Hill: University of North Carolina Press, 1980) p. 177. The prospect of coal shortages arising in Western Europe was widely noticed at the time.

10. Charles K. Ebinger, *et al.*, *The Critical Link; Energy and National Security in the 1980's* (Washington: Center for Strategic and International Studies, 1982) p. 1.

11. Miller, pp. 195–7.

12. John Lewis Gaddis, *Strategies of Containment* (New York: Oxford University Press, 1982) p. 30.

13. 'X' [George F. Kennan], 'The Sources of Soviet Conduct', *Foreign Affairs*, xxv (July 1947) p. 581.

14. Gaddis, pp. 58–60 and 90.

15. 'Petroleum Crisis in Venezuela', *Intelligence Review*, 23 May 1946, pp. 2–7. Quoted in Miller, p. 177.

16. Kemp and Maurer, p. 29.

17. David A. Rosenberg, 'The U.S. Navy and the Problem of Oil in a Future War; The Outline of a Strategic Dilemma 1945–1950', *Naval War College Review* (Summer 1976) p. 53.
18. Report to the JCS, 'Petroleum Reserves in the Western Hemisphere', 19 June 1947, p. 1.
19. JCS 1725/1, 1 May 1947 (JCS Records, National Archives, Washington, D.C.), in Thomas H. Etzold and John Lewis Gaddis, *Containment: Documents on American Foreign Policy and Strategy 1945–1950* (New York: Columbia University Press, 1978) pp. 303–6.
20. JCS 1725/1, 1 May 1947, in Etzold and Gaddis, pp. 308–11.
21. Etzold and Gaddis, p. 312.
22. JCS 626/3, 3 February 1948, 'Formula for the Determination of a National Stockpile'. Quoted in Etzold and Gaddis, pp. 312–13.
23. JCS 626/3, 3 February 1948. Quoted in Etzold and Gaddis, pp. 313–15.
24. JCS 1844/13, 21 July 1948. Quoted in Etzold and Gaddis, p. 323.
25. Ibid., p. 324.
26. Anthony Cave Brown (ed.) *Dropshot: The American Plan for World War III Against Russia in 1957* (New York: Dial Press, 1978) p. 156.
27. Interview with Professor Robert Tucker, School of Advanced International Studies, Johns Hopkins University, Washington, D.C., 17 September 1984.
28. NSC–29, 26 August 1948, Report to the NSC by the Executive Secretary on 'Security of Strategically Important Industrial Operations in Foreign Countries', pp. 1–5.
29. Michael Shafer, 'Mineral Myths', *Foreign Policy*, no. 47 (Summer 1982) p. 162.
30. *Resources for Freedom: A Report to the President by the President's Materials Policy Commission* (Washington: G.P.O., 1952) vol. i, p. 3.
31. Ibid., p. 17.
32. Ibid.
33. Ibid., pp. 153–4.
34. Ibid., p. 155.
35. Ibid.
36. H. J. Barnett, 'The Changing Relationship of Natural Resources to National Security', *Economic Geography*, xxxiv (July 1958) pp. 193–4.
37. Klaus Knorr and Frank N. Trager (eds) *Economic Issues and National Security* (Lawrence: Regents Press of Kansas, 1977) p. 187.
38. Ibid., pp. 89–90.
39. *Resources for Freedom*, vol. I, pp. 155–6.
40. Ibid., p. 156.
41. Ibid., pp. 157–9.
42. Ibid., p. 162.
43. Ibid., p. 163. The Commission recommended that the existing National Security Resources Board undertake a continuing review of resource security. In the event, the Board was abolished within the year. As a partial consequence of this, the Ford Foundation was prompted to fund an unofficial research organization, Resources for the Future, to carry forward work of this nature. See *Raw Materials and Foreign Policy*, p. 30, footnote.
44. Brownfeld, p. 63.

45. US Senate, Committee on Interior and Insular Affairs (83rd Congress, 2nd session), 'Accessability of Strategic and Critical Materials to the U.S. in Time of War and for Our Expanding Economy' (Washington: G.P.O., 1954) pp. 5–7.

46. 'Accessability of Strategic and Critical Materials', pp. 13–14.

47. Ibid., pp. 18–19.

48. It is noteworthy that with the brief exception of the Korean mobilization, US industrial production increased by roughly 50 per cent between 1947 and 1956 without a serious threat of resource shortage. See Percy W. Bidwell, 'Raw Materials and National Policy', *Foreign Affairs*, vol. 37 (October 1958) no. 1, p. 145.

49. Comment by Alfred E. Eckes, Jr. quoted in Brownfeld, p. 63. See also William Gutteridge, 'Mineral Resources and National Security', *Conflict Studies*, no. 182 (London: Institute for the Study of Conflict, 1984) p. 7.

50. See Bernard Brodie, 'Foreign Oil and American Security', Memorandum no. 23 (New Haven: Yale Institute of International Studies, 1947).

51. Donald J. Goldstein (ed.) *Energy and National Energy: Proceedings of a Special Conference* (Washington: National Defense University, 1981) pp. 27–8. See also John E. Gray, *et al.*, *U.S. Energy Policy and U.S. Foreign Policy in the 1980's* (Washington: Atlantic Council/Ballinger, 1981) p. 114.

52. NSC–138, 8 December 1952, p. 8.

53. Leonard M. Fanning, *Foreign Oil and the Free World* (New York: McGraw-Hill, 1954) pp. 273–4; and Ebinger, *The Critical Link*, p. 2.

54. Herbert Feis, 'Oil for Peace and War', *Foreign Affairs*, vol. 32 (April 1954) no. 3, pp. 428–9.

55. Fanning, p. 272.

56. See 'Capabilities for Limited Contingencies in the Persian Gulf' (OASD).

57. David A. Deese, 'Oil, War and Grand Strategy', *Orbis* (Autumn 1981) p. 543; and Goldstein, p. 28.

58. Deese, 'Oil, War and Grand Strategy', pp. 543–4.

59. *London Star*, 26 July 1956. Quoted in Deese, 'Oil, War and Grand Strategy', p. 545.

60. Deese, 'Oil, War and Grand Strategy', p. 545.

61. Walter J. Levy, 'Issues in International Oil Policy', *Foreign Affairs*, vol. 35 (April 1957) no. 3, pp. 454–5.

62. P. H. Frankel, 'Oil Supplies During the Suez Crisis', *Journal of Industrial Economics*, February 1958, p. 86. The supply of petroleum products to the US military from non-Western Hemisphere sources also became problematic as a result of the canal closure. See JCS memo (DDLM–223–56) from the Deputy Director for Logistics, 5 November 1956; and memo for the Chief of Naval Operations (OP 404c/rw), 'World Oil Situation', 10 November 1956.

63. Deese, 'Oil, War and Grand Strategy', p. 550.

64. Hanson, W. Baldwin, 'Strategy of the Middle East', *Foreign Affairs*, vol. 35 (July 1957) no. 4, p. 655.

65. Ibid., p. 660.

66. JCS Report, 25 June 1957, 'The Protection and Conservation of Middle East Oil Resources and Facilities' (Discussion of NSC-5714).

67. Halford L. Hoskins, 'Needed: A Strategy for Oil', *Foreign Affairs* (January 1957) pp. 235–7.

68. Walter J. Levy, 'Western Security and International Oil', Lecture delivered before the Council on Foreign Relations, New York, 11 June 1958. Quoted in Levy, *Oil, Politics and Strategy*, p. 125.

69. Levy, 'Western Security and International Oil', pp. 127–8.

70. See Harold Lubell, 'Security of Supply and Energy Policy in Western Europe', *World Politics*, vol. xiii (April 1961) no. 3, p. 403; and Goldstein, p. 29.

71. JCS, note by Joint Logistics Plans Committee (JLPC 446/152) on petroleum supply implications for Joint Strategic Objectives Plan for period beginning 1 July 1961.

72. David A. Deese and Joseph S. Nye (eds) *Energy and Security* (Cambridge: Ballinger, 1981) p. 8.

73. This section is based on an interview with Ambassador Robert Komer, former chief US pacification advisor in Vietnam, Washington, D.C., 21 January 1985. It is noteworthy that the total US military petroleum usage during the Korean and Vietnam Wars amounted to only 6–8 per cent of US national consumption. See John Storr, *et al.*, *The Impact of Energy on Strategy; A Consolidated Report* (ORAE Report No. R64) (Ottawa: Department of National Defense, June 1977).

74. Deese and Nye, p. 8.

75. For discussion of the role of conflict over water resources, notably the headwaters of the Jordan River, in the 1967 Arab-Israeli War, see Roy L. Thompson, 'Fresh Water Scarcity: Implications for Conflict; An Overview', paper prepared for conference on 'Scarce Resources and International Conflict', International Security Studies Program, Fletcher School of Law and Diplomacy, Tufts University, 4–6 May 1977; and John K. Cooley, 'The War over Water', *Foreign Policy*, no. 54 (Spring 1984).

76. Ebinger, *et al.*, *The Critical Link*, p. 2.

77. Goldstein, p. 29.

78. Ebinger, *et al.*, *The Critical Link*, p. 3.

79. *The Oil Import Question*, U.S. Cabinet Task Force on Oil Import Control (Washington: G.P.O., February 1970) p. 36.

80. Charles L. Schultze, 'The Economic Content of National Security Policy', *Foreign Affairs* (April 1973) p. 36.

81. Ibid., pp. 528–9.

6 Oil and Strategic Planning Since 1973

1. Deese, 'Oil, War and Grand Strategy', pp. 525–6.

2. Ibid., p. 526.

3. Edward N. Luttwak, 'Intervention and Access to Natural Resources', in Hedley Bull (ed.) *Intervention in World Politics* (Oxford: Clarendon Press, 1984) p. 79.

4. Henry Kissinger, 'The Energy Crisis: Strategy for Cooperative Action', speech delivered in Chicago, 14 November 1974. Quoted in Roy

A. Werner, 'Oil and U.S. Security Policies', *Orbis*, vol. 21 (Autumn 1977) no. 3, p. 651.

5. See Thomas Schelling, *Thinking Through the Energy Problem* (New York: Committee for Economic Development, 1979). Cited in Ray Dafter, 'World Oil Production and Security of Supplies', *International Security*, vol. 4 (Winter 1979/80) no. 3, p. 156.

6. See James E. Akins, 'The Oil Crisis: This Time the Wolf is Here', *Foreign Affairs* (April 1973).

7. Werner, p. 65; and Robert J. Lieber, *The Oil Decade: Conflict and Cooperation in the West* (New York: Praeger, 1983) p. 2.

8. Lieber, *The Oil Decade*, p. 2.

9. *Oil: Strategic Implications and Future Supplies*, Report of a seminar held at the Royal United Services Institute for Defence Studies, London 21 March 1973.

10. Ebinger, *Energy and National Security*, p. 4.

11. Deese and Nye, pp. 10–11.

12. Lieber, *The Oil Decade*, p. 2.

13. Ebinger, *Energy and National Security*, p. 9.

14. C. L. Jefferies, 'NATO and Oil: Conflict and Capabilities', *Air University Review* (January-February 1980) p. 44.

15. Storr, *et al.*, *Impact of Energy on Strategy*, p. 20.

16. Jefferies, p. 44.

17. Memorandum from the Office of the Assistant Secretary for Logistics, 5 November 1973, re: 'Military Petroleum Situation'.

18. Deese and Nye, p. 15. On the question of intervention to safeguard economic security, see Luttwak, 'Intervention and Access to Natural Resources', in Hedley Bull (ed.) *Intervention in World Politics* (Oxford: Clarendon Press, 1984).

19. *Strategic Survey* (London: IISS, 1974) p. 31.

20. Robert W. Tucker, 'Oil: The Issue of American Intervention', *Commentary*, vol. 59 (January 1975) p. 25.

21. Tucker: 'Oil: The Issue of American Intervention', p. 22.

22. Ibid., p. 26.

23. Gray, *et al.*, *U.S. Energy Policy and U.S. Foreign Policy in the 1980's*, pp. 18–19, 35.

24. See Edward J. Laurance, 'An Assessment of the Arms-for-Oil Strategy' in Donald J. Goldstein (ed.) *Energy and National Security: Proceedings of a Special Conference* (Washington: National Defense University, 1981) pp. 59–91.

25. Ebinger, *Energy and National Security*, pp. 12–23.

26. Ibid., p. 32.

27. These are essentially the objectives outlined in the 1982 US 'Defense Guidance' paper. Administration officials assert that these goals remain unchanged. See *New York Times*, 2 September 1986, p. A6.

28. Robert W. Tucker, 'American Power and the Persian Gulf', *Commentary* (November 1980) p. 26.

29. Amos A. Jordan, 'Energy and the Future of NATO', unpublished manuscript, p. 514.

30. Melvin Conant, 'Resources and Conflict: Oil—The Likely Contingen-

cies' in 'Third World Conflict' *Adelphi Paper* No. 167 (London: IISS, 1981) p. 45.

31. *World Oil Trade*, December 1983, p. 10. Quoted in Robert L. Bamberger and Clyde R. Mark, 'Escalation of the Conflict in the Persian Gulf', paper prepared for the US Congressional Research Service, Washington, D.C., 30 May 1984, p. 1.

32. As suggested by Geoffrey Kemp, US National Security Council. Interview, Washington, D.C., 20 September 1984.

33. David A. Deese, 'Oil and Security: The Mobilization Dilemma'. Paper prepared for the Tenth Annual Conference of the International Security Studies Program of the Fletcher School of Law and Diplomacy, Tufts University, 4–6 May 1981, p. 1.

34. Deese, 'Mobilization', p. 3.

35. Ibid., p. 5.

36. Ibid., p. 5.

37. Ibid., p. 8.

38. Interview with Charles K. Ebinger, Center for Strategic and International Studies, Washington, D.C., 14 September 1984.

39. Nonetheless, the amounts required to sustain such activities as sealift and airlift would be considerable. One million barrels of fuel would be required to move four army divisions from the US to Europe. See Jordan, 'Energy and the Future of NATO', p. 508; and SIPRI, *Energy and Security*, p. 58.

40. See Deese, 'Mobilization', p. 12.

41. SIPRI, *Energy and Security*, p. 58.

42. Deese, 'Mobilization', p. 12.

43. Shahram Chubin, 'U.S. Security Interests in the Persian Gulf in the 1980's', *Daedalus* (Autumn 1980) p. 36.

44. Ibid.

45. Walter J. Levy, 'Oil and Decline of the West', *Foreign Affairs* (Summer 1980) p. 1008.

46. Shahram Chubin, 'Repercussions of the Crisis in Iran', *Survival* (May-June 1979) p. 106.

47. Abdul Kasim Mansur (pseudonym), 'The American Threat to Saudi Arabia', *Survival* (January 1981) p. 39.

48. See Michael Sterner, 'The Iran-Iraq War', *Foreign Affairs* (Autumn 1984).

49. Shahram Chubin, 'Reflections on the Gulf War', *Survival* (July/August 1986) pp. 317–18; and Edward Luttwak, *On the Meaning of Victory* (New York: Simon & Schuster, 1986) pp. 139–40.

50. See *The Economist*, 2 November 1985, p. 58; Luttwak, *On the Meaning of Victory*, p. 140.

51. Chubin, 'Gulf War', p. 318.

52. *International Herald Tribune*, 19 May 1986, p. 2.

53. *Strategic Survey 1985–1986* (London, IISS, 1986) p. 126.

54. Ibid., p. 128.

55. Bamberger, p. ii.

56. Ibid.

57. Ibid., p. iii.

58. Jeffrey Record, *The Rapid Deployment Force and U.S. Military*

Intervention in the Persian Gulf (Cambridge: Institute for Foreign Policy Analysis, 1981) p. 9.

59. Ibid.
60. Record, *Rapid Deployment*, p. 11. Other observers are less sanguine; see, for instance, Luttwak, *On the Meaning of Victory*, pp. 261–3; and Dennis Ross, 'Considering Soviet Threats to the Persian Gulf', *International Security*, vol. 6 (Autumn 1981) no. 2.
61. Record, *Rapid Deployment*, p. 12.
62. Schlesinger, 'Energy Risks and Energy Futures: Some Farewell Observations', address before the National Press Club, Washington, D.C., 16 August 1979, p. 2.
63. Ibid., pp. 1–7.
64. 'Capabilities for Limited Contingencies in the Persian Gulf—Part One', declassified US Department of Defense Study, 15 June 1979.
65. Ibid.
66. Douglas R. Bohi and William B. Quandt, *Energy Security in the 1980's: Economic and Political Perspectives* (Washington: Brookings, 1984) p. 42.
67. A 1982 Study suggested that a cut-off of Persian Gulf oil would produce significant economic consequences for the US but, in isolation from other economic factors, markedly less severe than would have been the case in 1980. Today, the consequences would certainly be even less severe. See 'Western Vulnerability to a Disruption of Persian Gulf Oil Supplies: U.S. Interests and Options' (Washington: Congressional Research Service, 1983).
68. Paul Nitze and Leonard Sullivan, *Securing the Seas: Soviet Naval Challenge and Western Alliance Options* (Boulder: Westview, 1979) p. 156.
69. Bamberger, p. 11; *Guardian*, 23 September 1985.
70. Quoted in Bamberger, p. 6.
71. Quoted in Bamberger, pp. 6–7. A more detailed discussion of sealanes issues in relation to resource access is to be found in Chapter 8.
72. Nitze and Sullivan, p. 424.
73. Sir John Hackett, 'Protecting Oil Supplies: The Military Requirements' in 'Third World Conflict and International Security' (Part I), *Adelphi Paper* No. 166. (London: IISS, 1981) p. 41.
74. Ibid.
75. Tucker, 'American Power', p. 28.
76. A fact which probably does little to relieve Mexican, Venezuelan or Nigerian uneasiness.
77. Robert W. Komer, 'Bigger, Better and More Rapid Response', *Washington Post*, 4 March 1981.
78. Most notable was Henry Kissinger's statement on the use of military force in response to another severe price increase: 'It is one thing to use it in the case of a dispute over price . . . its another when there is some actual strangulation of the industrialized world', Interview in *Business Week*, 23 January 1975.
79. Robert W. Tucker, 'The Purpose of American Power', *Foreign Affairs* (Winter 1980/81) p. 253.
80. Ibid.

81. Statement of Robert W. Komer before the Committee on Armed Service, US Senate. Quoted in Record, *Rapid Deployment*, p. 12.
82. 'Haig Says U.S. Would Respond to a Persian Gulf Shift', *Washington Post*, 19 March 1981, p. A30.
83. Tucker, 'The Purpose of American Power', pp. 251–2.
84. Claudia Wright, 'Implications of the Iran-Iraq War', *Foreign Affairs* (Winter 1980/81) p. 303.
85. Charles K. Ebinger, *et al.*, *The Critical Link: Energy and National Security in the 1980's* (Cambridge: Ballinger, 1982) p. 170.
86. Speech by Cyrus Vance at Harvard University, as reported in the *New York Times*, 6 June 1980, p. A12. Quoted in Robert Tucker, *The Purposes of American Power* (New York: Praeger, 1981) p. 76.
87. Tucker, *The Purposes of American Power*, p. 77. See Stanley Hoffman, 'The Crisis in the West', *New York Review of Books*, 17 July 1980, p. 41.
88. See Michael T. Klare, *Beyond the Vietnam Syndrome: U.S. Interventionism in the 1980's* (Washington: IPS, 1982).
89. Hackett, p. 42.
90. Ibid.
91. Ibid., pp. 42–3.
92. John M. Collins, 'Petroleum Imports from the Persian Gulf: Use of U.S. Armed Force to Ensure Supplies' (Washington: Congressional Research Service, 1979, up-dated 1982) p. 16.
93. Robert L. Pfaltzgraff, *Energy Issues and Alliance Relationships: The U.S., Western Europe and Japan* (Cambridge: Institute for Foreign Policy Analysis, 1980) p. 34.
94. Levy, 'Oil and the Decline of the West', p. 1010. The use of overland pipelines to the Red Sea and the Mediterranean will be of increasing importance in the future.
95. Tucker, 'Oil: The Issue of American Intervention', p. 25.
96. Levy, 'Oil and the Decline of the West', p. 1009. See also Stockholm International Peace Research Institute, *Oil and Security* (Stockholm: Almquist & Wiksell, 1974) p. 38.
97. *Strategic Survey 1974*, p. 31.
98. See Luttwak, 'Intervention and Natural Resources', pp. 88–93.
99. Christoph Bertram, 'The Global Security Balance: Theses for Discussion', opening remarks at Trilateral Commission meeting, 24 March 1980, p. 3.
100. Tucker, 'American Power', p. 26.
101. Hans W. Maull, *Raw Materials, Energy and Security* (London: IISS, 1984) p. 389.
102. Record, *Rapid Deployment*, p. 12. For an optimistic assessment of the prospects for a successful defence of Iran, see Joshua M. Epstein, 'Soviet vulnerabilities in Iran and the RDF Deterrent', *International Security*, vol. 6 (Autumn 1981) no. 2. A rebuttal of Epstein's arguments may be found in W. Scott Thompson, 'The Persian Gulf and the Correlation of Forces', *International Security*, vol. 7 (Summer 1982) no. 1.
103. Thomas Toch, 'Rapid Deployment: A Questionable Trump', *Para-*

meters, vol. 10, no. 3, p. 89.

104. Geoffrey Kemp, 'Military Force and Middle East Oil', in David A. Deese and Joseph S. Nye (eds) *Energy and Security* (Cambridge: Ballinger, 1981) p. 382.
105. James G. Roche, 'Projection of Military Power to Southwest Asia: An Asymmetrical Problem', in Ra'anan, *et al.*, *Projection of Power*, p. 221.
106. Albert Wohlstetter, 'Half Wars and Half Policies in the Persian Gulf', in W. Scott Thompson (ed.) *National Security in the 1980's: From Weakness to Strength* (San Francisco: Institute for Contemporary Studies, 1980) p. 164.
107. Tucker, 'Purposes of American Power', p. 253.
108. George C. Wilson, 'Anytime, Anywhere: A New Conventional Role for B-52 Bombers', *Washington Post*, 31 March 1981, p. A2.
109. *Challenges for U.S. National Security, Part II* (Washington: Carnegie Endowment, 1981) p. 157.
110. Tucker, *The Purposes of American Power*, p. 93.
111. Record, *Rapid Deployment*, p. 2.
112. Ibid., p. 3.
113. On the flexibility of maritime power in this context, see Elliot Richardson, 'Power, Mobility and the Law of the Sea', *Foreign Affairs* (Spring 1980) p. 907.
114. Robert W. Komer, 'Coalition Defense versus Maritime Strategies', paper presented at National Security Issues Symposium, Mitre Corp., Bedford, Mass., 4–5 October 1982, p. 40.
115. See 'The Persian Gulf: Are We Committed? At What Cost?: A Dialogue with the Reagan Administration', Joint Economic Committee, US Congress (Washington: GPO, 1981).
116. Interview with James R. Schlesinger, Washington, 21 September 1984.
117. Interview with Geoffrey Kemp, Washington, 20 September 1984.
118. Ibid.
119. Ibid.

7 Strategic Minerals Revisited

1. Michael Shafer, 'Mineral Myths', *Foreign Policy* (Summer 1982) no. 47, p. 154.
2. Ibid., p. 156.
3. A widely cited study from a somewhat earlier period is Yuan-li Wu, *Raw Material Supply in a Multipolar World* (New York: Crane Russak, 1973).
4. Kemp, 'Scarcity and Strategy', p. 409.
5. Interviews with James Schlesinger and Robert Komer; see also Shafer, 'Minerals Myths'; and Hanns Maull, *Raw Materials, Energy and Western Security*, pp. 8–9.
6. Kemp, 'Scarcity and Strategy', p. 405.
7. Interview with Robert Komer.
8. Maull, *Raw Materials, Energy and Western Security*, pp. 8–9.
9. Ibid., p. 9.
10. David J. Kroft, 'The Geopolitics of Non-Energy Minerals', *Air Force Magazine*, June 1979, p. 76.

11. See Kroft, p. 76.
12. *Strategic and Critical Non-Fuel Minerals: Problems and Alternatives* (Washington: Congressional Budget Office, 1983) p. 7.
13. *Strategic and Critical Non-Fuel Minerals*, p. 7.
14. William B. Hankee and Alwyn H. King, 'The Role of Security Assistance in Maintaining Access to Strategic Resources', *Parameters*, vol. viii (September 1978) no. 3, p. 44.
15. Hankee and King, p. 45.
16. Idem.
17. Amos A. Jordan and Robert A. Kilmarx, *Strategic Mineral Dependence: The Stockpile Dilemma* (Beverley Hills: Sage/CSIS, 1979) pp. 61–2.
18. Kroft, p. 78; see also Council on Economics and National Security, *Strategic Minerals: A Resource Crisis* (Washington: CENS, 1981).
19. Barry M. Blechman, *National Security and Strategic Minerals; An Analysis of U.S. Dependence on Foreign Sources of Cobalt* (Boulder: Westview, 1985) p. xiii.
20. *Sub-Saharan Africa, Its Role in Critical Mineral Needs of the Western World*, Report by the Subcommittee on Mines and Mining, Committee on Interior and Insular Affairs, US House of Representatives (Washington: GPO, 1980) p. 9.
21. Maull, p. 294.
22. Blechman, *National Security and Strategic Minerals*, pp. xiii–xiv.
23. Interview with Barry Blechman, Washington, D.C., 12 September 1984.
24. *Strategic and Critical Non-Fuel Minerals*, pp. 7–8.
25. Ibid., p. 8.
26. Interview with former US Assistant Secretary of Defense, Leonard Sullivan, Washington, D.C., 13 September 1984.
27. See Jordan and Kilmarx, p. 60.
28. See ibid.
29. Alan J. Bergstrom, letter to the editor in response to Shafer, 'Mineral Myths', *Foreign Policy* (Spring 1983) no. 50, pp. 173–4.
30. Interview with Leonard Sullivan, Washington, D.C., 13 September 1984.
31. Interview with Ambassador Robert Komer, Washington, D.C., 17 September 1984.
32. US Congress, House Subcommittee on Mines and Mining, *Non-Fuel Minerals Policy Review*, Hearings, second session, 96th Congress, 1980, Part III, p. 5.
33. Klare, p. 51.
34. Statement before the House Budget Committee, US Congress, 20 March 1981 (Department of Defense Transcript). Quoted in Klare, p. 62.
35. Office of the Chief of Naval Operations, US Department of the Navy, *U.S. Lifelines: Imports of Essential Materials—1967, 1971, 1975 and the Impact of Waterborne Commerce on the Nation* (Washington: GPO, 1978).
36. James D. Santini, 'An Island Nation', *Sea Power*, January, 1983, p. 25.

37. Santini, p. 25.
38. Interview with Geoffrey Kemp, US National Security Council. On this question see also William Gutterridge, 'Mineral Resources and National Security', *Conflict Studies No. 162* (1984).
39. As suggested by Dr. Christopher Coker, London School of Economics and Political Science, Interview, 9 May 1986.
40. Kroft, p. 79.
41. Rae Weston, *Strategic Minerals: A World Survey* (London: Croom Helm, 1984) p. 6.
42. John Chipman, 'French Military Policy and African Security', *Adelphi Paper* No. 201 (London: IISS, 1985) p. 31.
43. On US policy towards Namibia, see *Namibia: The United Nations and U.S. Policy*, Hearings before the Subcommittee on International Organizations of the Committee on International Relations, US House of Representatives. 94th Congress, 2nd Session (Washington: GPO, 1978). See also *Resources in Namibia: Implications for U.S. Policy*, Hearings before the Subcommittee on International Resources, Food and Energy of the Committee on International Relations, US House of Representatives, 94th Congress, June 1975 and May 1976 (Washington: GPO, 1975, 1976).
44. See, for instance, statement of Elizabeth Landis in *Resources in Namibia* (1975) p. 30.
45. Neil MacFarlane, 'Intervention and Regional Security', *Adelphi Paper* No. 196 (London: IISS, 1985) p. 15. See Robert J. Hanks, *Southern African and Western Security* (Cambridge: IFPA, 1983). See also *Resource Development in South Africa and U.S. Policy*, Hearings before the Subcommittee on International Resources, Food and Energy of the Committee on International Relations, US House of Representatives, 94th Congress, 2nd Session, May 25, June 8–9, 1976 (Washington: GPO, 1976).
46. *New York Times* 24 August 1986, p. 7.
47. See Maull, p. 304.
48. Interview with James R. Schlesinger, Washington, D.C., 21 September 1984.
49. Tucker, *The Purposes of American Power*, p. 176.
50. See Jock A. Finlayson and David G. Haglund, 'Whatever Happened to the Resource War?', *Survival*, September/October 1987.

8 Resource Issues and the East-West Strategic Relationship

1. Colin S. Gray, 'National Style in Strategy: The American Example', *International Security*, vol. 6 (Autumn 1981) no. 2, pp. 22–4.
2. Gray, 'National Style in Strategy', p. 28.
3. See Edward Luttwak, 'On the Meaning of Strategy for the U.S. in the 1980's' in W. Scott Thompson (ed.) *National Security in the 1980's; From Weakness to Strength* (San Francisco: Institute for Contemporary Studies, 1980) pp. 260–3.
4. Gray, 'National Style in Strategy', p. 26.
5. Hardy L. Merritt and Luther F. Carter (eds) *Mobilization and the*

National Defense (Washington: National Defense University Press, 1985) p. 9.

6. Gray, 'National Style in Strategy', p. 43.

7. Robert Perlman and Anthony Murray, 'Resources and Conflict: Requirements and Vulnerabilities of the Industrialized World', in 'Third World Conflict and International Security, II', *Adelphi Paper* No. 167 (London: IISS, 1981) p. 51.

8. As suggested in an interview with former US Under Secretary of Defense for Policy, Ambassador Robert Komer, Washington, 17 September 1984.

9. The writings of Nicholas Spykman in the 1940s provide a notable exception. More recent works such as Colin Gray's *The Geopolitics of the Nuclear Era* point to a revival of interest in this area.

10. Henry Kissinger, *The White House Years* (Boston: Little Brown, 1979) p. 914.

11. As suggested in an interview with James R. Schlesinger, Washington, 21 September 1984.

12. As suggested in an interview with Ambassador Robert Komer, Washington, 17 September 1984. See also David Deese, 'The Vulnerability of Modern Economies', in McCormick and Bissell, pp. 149–79.

13. Benjamin S. Lambeth and Kevin N. Lewis, 'Economic Targeting in Modern Warfare', in McCormick and Bissell, pp. 256–7.

14. See Lambeth and Lewis, p. 256.

15. Ibid.

16. See, for example, Col. B. Byely, *Marxism-Leninism on War and Army* (Moscow: Progress Publishers, 1972) p. 49.

17. V. D. Sokolovsky, *Soviet Military Strategy* (New York: Crane Russak, 1968) p. 25.

18. Sokolovsky, p. 28.

19. Byely, p. 278.

20. Ibid., p. 288.

21. See, for example, Sokolovsky, pp. 32–3.

22. Ibid., p. 314.

23. Andrei N. Lagovsky, *Strategy and Economics* was published by the USSR Ministry of Defence in September 1957. Cited in William Gutteridge, 'Mineral Resources and National Security', *Conflict Studies*, No. 162 (1984).

24. Quoted in Oleg Hoeffding, 'Strategy and Economics: A Soviet View', *World Politics*, vol. xi (January 1959) no. 2, p. 323. See also Demitri Shimkin, *Minerals: A Key to Soviet Power* (Cambridge, Mass.: Harvard University Press, 1953).

25. See Hoeffding, p. 318.

26. Quoted in Hoeffding, p. 323.

27. Quoted in Hoeffding, p. 320.

28. Ibid., p. 321.

29. US National Intelligence Estimate, 'Soviet Capabilities and Intentions' (NIE-3), November 1950, p. 19.

30. See Walter Levy, 'Middle Eastern Oil as an Objective of World Power', lecture delivered at the National War College, Washington,

D.C., 22 January 1947. Republished in Levy, *Oil, Politics and Strategy*, p. 60.

31. Levy, 'Middle Eastern Oil as an Objective of World Power', p. 60.
32. See, for instance, National Foreign Assessment Center (CIA), *Prospects for Soviet Oil Production* (Washington: CIA, 1977); and Bernard Gwertzman, 'CIA Revises Estimate, Sees Soviet as Oil Independent Through 1980's', *New York Times*, 19 May 1981, p. 1.
33. CIA Report, 'USSR Petroleum Industry', 5 January 1950. Truman Papers (Secretary's Files 24401) p. 47; NIE–3, 'Soviet Capabilities and Intentions', p. 19.
34. Nicholas Portugalov Commentary, 'An Alternative', *Tass*, 29 February 1980, in 'Portugalov Calls for European Conference on the Persian Gulf', Foreign Broadcast Information Service, *Daily Report* (Soviet Union), 3 March 1980, pp. G1–G2. Cited in Bohi and Quandt, p. 44.
35. Bohi and Quandt, p. 45.
36. Byely, p. 290.
37. Ibid., p. 291.
38. Lambeth and Lewis, p. 258.
39. Ibid., pp. 258–9.
40. Lambeth and Lewis, p. 266. It is reported that the oil industry is ranked second only to electric power as an economic/strategic target in Soviet planning; see R. E. Hansen, 'The Strait of Hormuz and Secure Oil Routes', *Conflict*, vol. 2 (1980) no. 2, p. 124.
41. Louis Turner, 'Energy, Technology and Vulnerability', unpublished paper, RUSI, April 1985, p. 1.
42. Comment by Hon. Edward Streator, US Ambassador to the OECD, RUSI Annual Conference, London, 15 May 1986.
43. Ebinger, Interview, 19 September 1984.
44. Turner, p. 3.
45. Maull, *Raw Materials, Energy and Western Security*, p. 132; Ebinger, Interview, 19 September 1984.
46. Christopher Coker, *NATO, the Warsaw Pact and Africa* (London: Macmillan, 1985) p. 166.
47. Coker, *Nato, the Warsaw Pact and Africa*, p. 166.
48. See Christopher Coker, 'Eastern Europe and the Middle East: The Forgotten Dimension of Soviet Policy', in Robert Cassen (ed.) *Soviet Interests in the Third World* (London: RIIA, 1985) p. 60.
49. As suggested by Dr Christopher Coker, Interview, London School of Economics and Political Science, 9 May 1986.
50. Coker, 'Eastern Europe and the Middle East', p. 47.
51. Paul H. Nitze, 'Strategy in the Decade of the 1980's', *Foreign Affairs* (Autumn 1980) p. 88.
52. Karl Kaiser, 'The Energy Problem and Alliance Systems: Europe', *Adelphi Paper* No. 115 (London: IISS, 1975) p. 17.
53. Robert L. Pfaltzgraff, Jr., 'Resource Issues and the Atlantic Community', in W. F. Hahn and R. L. Pfaltzgraff, *The Atlantic Community in Crisis* (New York: Pergamon, 1979) p. 307.
54. Pfaltzgraff, 'Resource Issues and the Atlantic Community', p. 307.
55. This point is made with reference to energy in Ian Smart, 'Energy and

Power', draft paper for AIIA, Paris, p. 29.

56. See, for example, Lawrence Freedman, 'Logistics and Mobility in Modern Warfare', *Armed Forces*, February 1986, p. 70.

57. Jordan, 'Energy and the Future of NATO', p. 510. Uncertainty with regard to tanker loss factors is reflected in at least one early analysis; see 'Tanker Loss Factors', Report by the Joint Strategic Plans Committee, US JCS 1741/113, 4 April 1955.

58. See Jordan, 'Energy and the Future of Nato', p. 511.

59. Turner, 'Energy, Technology and Vulnerability', p. 4. This point was also suggested by Charles Ebinger, Interview, Washington, 19 September 1984.

60. Maull, *Raw Materials, Energy and Western Security*, p. 19. See also, Thane Gustafson, 'Energy and the Soviet Bloc', *International Security*, vol. 6 (Winter 1981–82) no. 3; and Marshall I. Goldman, 'Will the Soviet Union be an Autarky in 1984?', *International Security*, vol. 3 (Spring 1979) no. 4.

61. Maull, *Raw Materials, Energy and Western Security*, p. 159.

62. Office of the Chief of Naval Operations, US Department of the Navy, *Understanding Soviet Naval Developments* (Washington: Department of the Navy, 1985) p. 16.

63. Geoffrey Till, *Maritime Strategy and the Nuclear Age* (New York: St. Martin's Press, 1982) p. 194.

64. See, for example, Michael McGwire, 'The Rationale for the Development of Soviet Seapower', in J. Baylis and G. Segal (eds) *Soviet Strategy* (London: Croom Helm, 1981); R. W. Herrick, *Soviet Naval Strategy* (Annapolis: Naval Institute Press, 1968); and Bryan Ranft and Geoffrey Till, *The Sea in Soviet Strategy* (London: Macmillan, 1983).

65. Quoted in Ranft and Till, p. 182.

66. A. Lagovsky, quoted in Till, *Maritime Strategy*, p. 193.

67. See, for instance, Robert J. Hanks, *The Unnoticed Challenge: Soviet Maritime Strategy and the Global Choke Points* (Cambridge: Institute for Foreign Policy Analysis, 1980); and Charles Perry, *The West, Japan, and Cape Route Imports: The Oil and Non-Fuel Mineral Trades* (Cambridge: Institute for Foreign Policy Analysis, 1982).

68. Transcript of news conference given by President Reagan, Washington, 11 February 1986.

69. See Michael R. Gordon, 'Naval Choke Points', *International Herald Tribune*, 15–16 February 1986; and Clyde Haberman, 'Challenge in the Pacific', *New York Times*, 9 September 1986.

70. Interview with Dr Christopher Coker, London, 9 May 1986.

71. Christopher Coker, 'The Cape Route and the Persian Gulf: A Warsaw Pact Perspective', in *RUSI/Brassey's Defence Yearbook* (London: Brassey's, 1985) p. 87.

72. Coker, 'The Cape Route and the Persian Gulf', p. 87.

73. Coker, Interview, 9 May 1986.

74. Robert W. Komer, *Maritime Strategy or Coalition Defense?* (Cambridge: ABT Books, 1984) p. 67.

75. James R. Schlesinger, 'The Geopolitics of Energy', *The Washington Quarterly*, vol. 2 (Summer 1979) no. 3, p. 7.

76. Kemp, 'Military Force', p. 367.
77. Tucker, 'American Power', p. 35.
78. Record, *Rapid Deployment*, p. 13.
79. Joint Working Group of the Atlantic Council of the US and the Research Institute for Peace and Security, Tokyo, *The Common Security Interests of Japan, the U.S. and NATO* (Cambridge: Ballinger, 1981) p. 15.
80. Joint Working Group, p. 15.
81. Japan, in particular, possesses substantial sealift assets in the form of Roll-On/Roll-Off and container ships, as well as cargo aircraft. Questions remain as to whether such a contribution would contravene Japanese constitutional restrictions on military activity abroad. On Japanese efforts in the resource access and sealane protection sphere, see Mike M. Mochizuki, 'Japan's Search for Strategy', *International Security*, vol. 8 (Winter 1983–84) no. 3; and M. Leifer, 'Security of Sea-lanes in South-East Asia', *Survival*, January/February 1983.
82. The Working Group on Security Affairs of the Atlantic Council of the US, *After Afghanistan—The Long Haul: Safeguarding Security and Independence in the Third World* (Washington: The Atlantic Council, 1980) p. 48.
83. See Dov S. Zakheim, 'Towards a Western Approach to the Indian Ocean', *Survival*, January/February 1980.

Bibliography

PRIMARY SOURCES

I. **Declassified Government Documents** (US National Security Council, Joint Chiefs of Staff, Department of Defense and others) released under the Freedom of Information Act, and available on microfilm through the Declassified Documents Reference System, Retrospective Collection (New Carolton); additional documents available through the Declassified Documents Quarterly Catalog (Research Publications).

II. **Hearings and Reports**

Bamberger, Robert L. and Mark, Clyde R. 'Escalation of the Conflict in the Persian Gulf'. Paper prepared for the Congressional Research Service. Washington, 30 May 1984.

British Petroleum, *B.P. Statistical Review of World Energy* (London: British Petroleum, 1985).

Collins, John M. *et al.*, *Petroleum Imports from the Persian Gulf: Use of U.S. Armed Force to Ensure Supplies* (Washington: Congressional Research Service, 1979, up-dated 1982).

Congressional Research Service, *Western Vulnerability to a Disruption of Persian Gulf Oil Supplies; U.S. Interests and Options* (CRS: Washington, 1983).

Congressional Budget Office, *Strategic and Critical Non-Fuel Minerals* (Washington: CBO, 1983).

Lee, J. Richard and Lecky, James, US Congress, Joint Economic Committee, *Soviet Economy in a Time of Change, Vol. I* (Washington: GPO, 1979).

The Oil Import Question, US Cabinet Task Force on Oil Import Control (Washington: GPO, February, 1970).

President's Materials Policy Commission, *Resources For Freedom—A Report to the President* (Washington: GPO, June 1952).

Report of the Royal Commission on Supply of Food and Raw Materials in Time of War (three vols). Cd. 2643/2644/2645 (1905).

Storr, John W., Solem, Erik and Cromie, M. V., *The Impact of Energy on Strategy: A Consolidated Report*. ORAE Report No. R64 (Ottawa: Operational Research and Analysis Establishment, Department of National Defense, Canada, June 1977).

United Kingdom Ministry of Fuel and Power, *Report on the Petroleum and Synthetic Oil Industry of Germany* (London: HMSO, 1947).

US Congress, Senate Committee on Interior and Insular Affairs, Minerals, Materials and Fuels. 83rd Congress, 2nd Session. Report 1627, *Accessability of Strategic and Critical Materials to the United States in Time of War and for Our Expanding Economy* (Washington: GPO, 1954).

US Congress, Senate Subcommittee on Military Affairs. Hearings. 79th

Congress, *Elimination of German Resources for War* (Washington: GPO, 1945).

US Congress, Joint Economic Committee, *The Persian Gulf: Are We Commited? At What Cost?; A Dialogue with the Reagan Administration* (Washington: GPO, 1981).

US Congress, House Subcommittee on International Resources, Food and Energy, Committee on International Relations. 94th Congress, *Resources in Namibia: Implications for U.S. Policy* (Washington: GPO, 1975).

US Congress, House Subcommittee on Mines and Mining. Hearings. 96th Congress, 2nd Session. *Non-Fuel Minerals Policy Review* (Washington: GPO, 1980).

US Congress, House Subcommittee on Mines and Mining. *Sub-Saharan Africa, Its Role in Critical Mineral Needs of the Western World* (Washington: GPO, 1980).

US Department of Defense, *Soviet Military Power: 1985* (Washington: GPO, April 1985).

US Maritime Commission, *Essential U.S. Foreign Trade Routes* (Washington: GPO, 1949).

US Maritime Administration, *Essential U.S. Foreign Trade Routes* (Washington: GPO, 1983).

US Navy, Office of Chief of Naval Operations, *Understanding Soviet Naval Developments* (Washington: GPO, April 1985).

US Navy, Office of Chief of Naval Operations, *U.S. Lifelines: Imports of Essential Materials—1967, 1971, 1975—and the Impact of Waterborne Commerce on the Nation.* OpNav-09D-PIA (Washington: GPO, January 1978).

US Strategic Bombing Survey, Overall Economic Effects Division, *The Effects of Strategic Bombing on the German War Economy* (Washington: GPO, 1945).

US Strategic Bombing Survey, Oil Division, *Powder, Explosives, Special Rockets and Jet Propellants, War Gases and Smoke Acid* (Washington: GPO, 1947).

US Strategic Bombing Survey, Transportation Division, *The War Against Japanese Transportation, 1941–1945* (Washington: GPO, 1947).

III. Official Histories and Related Publications

Bartholdy, Albrecht Mendelssohn, *The War and German Society* (New Haven: Yale University Press, Carnegie Series, 1937).

Bell, A. C., *The Blockade of the Central Empires 1914–1918* (London: HMSO, 1937).

Coakley, Robert W. and Leighton, Richard M., *Global Logistics and Strategy 1940–1945*, two vols (Washington: Office of Chief of Military History, 1968).

Corbett, Julian Stafford, *Official History of the Great War: Naval Operations*, three vols (London: HMSO, 1920).

Craven W. F. and Cate, J. L., *The Army Air Forces in World War II* (Chicago: University of Chicago Press, 1949).

Dull, Paul S., *A Battle History of the Imperial Japanese Navy 1941–1945* (Annapolis: Naval Institute Press, 1978).

Etzold, Thomas H. and Gaddis, John Lewis, *Containment: Documents on American Policy and Strategy 1945–1950* (New York: Columbia University Press, 1978).

Fontaine, Arthur, *French Industry During the War* (New Haven: Yale University Press, Carnegie Series, 1926).

Foot, Dingle, *Economic Warfare* (London: HMSO, 1943).

Hall, Duncan and Wrigley, G. C., *Studies of Overseas Supply* (London: HMSO, 1956).

Hancock, W. K. and Gowing, M. M., *British War Economy* (London: HMSO, 1949).

Hinsley, F. H. *et al.*, *British Intelligence in the Second World War* (London: HMSO, 1979).

Howard, M. E., *Grand Strategy, Vol. IV, August 1942—September 1943* (London: HMSO, 1972).

Hurstfield, J., *The Control of Raw Materials* (London: HMSO, 1953).

Ike, Nobutaka (ed.), *Japan's Decision for War; Records of the 1941 Policy Conferences* (Stanford: Stanford University Press, 1967).

Lebra, Joyce C. (ed.), *Japan's Greater East Asia Co-Prosperity Sphere in World War II; Selected Documents* (Kuala Lumpur: Oxford University Press, 1975).

Matloff, M., *Strategic Planning for Coalition Warfare*, two vols (Washington: GPO, 1959).

Medlicott, W. N., *The Economic Blockade*, two vols (London: HMSO, 1952).

Moberly, F. J., *The Campaign in Mesopotamia 1914–1918* (London: HMSO, 1923).

Morley, James William, *The Fateful Choice; Japan's Advance into Southeast Asia 1939–1941*. Selected translations from the Japanese official series *The Road to the Pacific War* (New York: Columbia University Press, 1980).

Nolde, Boris, E., *Russia in the Economic War* (New Haven: Yale University Press, Carnegie Series, 1928).

Roskill, S. W., *The War at Sea*, four vols (London: HMSO, 1954–1961).

Salter, J. A., *Allied Shipping Control; An Experiment in International Administration* (Oxford: Clarendon Press, Carnegie Series, 1921).

Stembridge, Jasper H., *The Oxford War Atlas. Vol. II, September 1941— January 1943* (Oxford: Oxford University Press, 1943).

US Office of War Information, *A War Atlas for Americans* (New York: Simon and Schuster, 1944).

Webster, Charles and Frankland, Noble, *The Strategic Air Offensive Against Germany 1939–1945*, three vols (London: HMSO, 1961).

Woodward, Sir Llewellyn, *British Foreign Policy in the Second World War* (London: HMSO, 1962).

IV.   **Speeches, Memoirs and Unpublished Manuscripts**

Bertram, Christoph, 'The Global Security Balance; Theses for Discussion'.

Opening Comments at a meeting of the Trilateral Commission (24 March 1980).

Churchill, Winston, *The Second World War*, six vols (London: Cassell, 1948–54).

Churchill, Winston, *The World Crisis 1911–1914* (London: Thornton Butterworth, 1923).

Ciano, Galleazo, *Diplomatic Papers*, edited by Malcolm Muggeridge (London: Odhams Press, 1948).

Deese, David A., 'Oil and Security; The Mobilization Dilemma'. Paper prepared for the Tenth Annual Conference of the International Security Studies Program of the Fletcher School of Law and Diplomacy, Tufts University, Medford, Mass. (4–6 May 1981).

Doenitz, Admiral K., *Memoirs*, trans. R. H. Stevens (London: Weidenfeld & Nicolson, 1959).

Ebinger, Charles K., 'Resource Access and Conflict Potential in the Southern Hemisphere; A Preliminary Assessment'. Paper prepared for Conference on Scarce Resources and International Conflict. International Security Studies Program, The Fletcher School of Law and Diplomacy, Tufts University. Medford, Mass. (4–6 May 1977).

Feis, Herbert, *Seen From E.A.; Three International Episodes* (New York: Alfred A. Knopf, 1947).

Franssen, Herman T., 'The Geopolitics of Soviet Resources'. Paper prepared for Conference on Scarce Resources and International Conflict. International Security Studies Program, The Fletcher School of Law and Diplomacy, Tufts University. Medford, Mass. (4–6 May 1977).

Hankey, Lord, *The Supreme Command 1914–1918*, two vols (London: Allen & Unwin, 1961).

Hayes, James H., 'Indian Ocean Geopolitics'. Rand Report No. P–5325 (1974).

Hitler, Adolph, *Mein Kampf*, trans. R. Manheim (Boston: Houghton Mifflin, 1971, originally published 1925).

Institute for Foreign Policy Analysis, 'The U.S. Defense Mobilization Infrastructure—A Conference Report'. IFPA. Cambridge (1981).

Jordan, Amos A., 'Energy and the Future of NATO'. Unpublished draft.

Kidd, Admiral Isaac, 'For Want of a Nail: The Logistics of the Alliance'. Paper prepared for conference sponsored by the Center for Strategic and International Studies, 'NATO: The Second Thirty Years'. Brussels (1–3 September 1979).

Kissinger, Henry, *The White House Years* (Boston: Little Brown, 1979).

Komer, Robert W., 'Coalition Defense Versus Maritime Strategies'. Paper prepared for 'National Security Issues Symposium'. Mitre Corporation, Bedford, Mass. (4–5 October 1982). Mitre Doc. M82–64.

Levy, Walter J., *Oil, Strategy and Politics 1941–1981*, edited by Melvin A. Conant (Boulder: Westview Press, 1982).

Lodge, Henry Cabot (ed.), *The Works of Alexander Hamilton* (New York: Putnam & Sons, 1904) federal edition.

Ludendorff, Erich von, *The Nation at War*, trans. A. S. Rappaport (London: Hutchinson, 1936).

Monet, Jean, *Memoirs* (New York, Doubleday, 1978).

Roosevelt, Franklin D., 'Sale of Oil to Japan; an Informal Talk by the President'. Washington, D.C., 24 July 1941. *Documents on American Foreign Relations*, vol. iv (July 1941–June 1942).

Schlesinger, James A., 'Energy Risks and Energy Futures: Some Farewell Observations'. Address before the National Press Club, Washington, D.C. (16 August 1979).

Smart, Ian, 'Energy and Power'. Unpublished draft manuscript.

Tanner, Frederick, 'Energy and Alliance Tensions: The Impact of Energy Vulnerability Upon the Conduct of Foreign Policy'. Unpublished Ph.D. Thesis. The Fletcher School of Law and Diplomacy, Tufts University (April 1984).

Turner, Louis, 'Energy, Technology and Vulnerability'. Unpublished draft manuscript (April 1985).

Warnecke, Steven J., 'Security Implications of Crude Oil Contract Patterns'. Unpublished issue paper prepared for the Atlantic Council of the United States.

Weinberger, Caspar, Statement of the Secretary of Defense Before the House Budget Committee. Washington, D.C. (20 March 1981). Department of Defense transcript.

V. Newspapers and Journals

The Economist
Financial Times
Guardian
International Herald Tribune
Journal of Commerce
New York Times
The Times
Washington Post

VI. Interviews

Interview with Dr Barry Blechman, Senior Fellow, Center for Strategic and International Studies, Georgetown University, Washington, D.C., 12 September 1984.

Interview with Dr Christopher Coker, London School of Economics and Political Science, London, 9 May 1986.

Interview with Dr Charles Ebinger, Director, Energy and Strategic Resources Program, Center for Strategic and International Studies, Georgetown University, Washington, D.C., 19 September 1984.

Interview with Dr Alton Frye, Carnegie Endowment for International Peace/Council on Foreign Relations. Washington, D.C., 14 September 1984.

Interview with Dr Geoffrey Kemp, Special Assistant to the President for National Security Affairs (NSC). Washington, D.C., 20 September 1984.

Interview with Ambassador Robert Komer, former Under-Secretary of Defense for Policy. RAND Corp., Washington, D.C., 17 September 1984 and 21 January 1986.

Interview with Hon. Winston Lord, President, Council on Foreign Relations. New York, 24 July 1984.

Interview with Joseph E. Muckerman, Deputy Director, Mobilization Concepts Development Center, National Defense University, Washington, D.C., 27 January 1986.

Interview with Hon. James R. Schlesinger, former Secretary of Defense and Energy, former Director, Central Intelligence Agency. Washington, D.C., 21 September 1984.

Interview with Ian Smart, consultant. Chatham House, London, 16 February 1982.

Interview with Professor J. A. A. Stockwin, St Anthony's College, Oxford, 1 May 1985.

Interview with Hon. Leonard Sullivan, Former Assistant Secretary of Defense, Washington, D.C., 13 September 1984.

Interview with Professor Robert Tucker, Johns Hopkins University, Washington, D.C., 17 September 1984.

Interview with Dr Harlan K. Ullman, Director, Political-Military Studies, Center for Strategic and International Studies, Georgetown University, Washington, D.C., 21 January 1986.

SECONDARY SOURCES

I. Books and Other Publications

Adie, W. A. C., *Oil, Politics and Sea Power: The Indian Ocean Vortex* (New York: National Strategy Information Center, 1974).

Adler-Karlson, Gunnar, *Western Economic Warfare: 1947–1967* (Stockholm: Almquist & Wiksell, 1968).

Albion, R. G., *Forests and Sea Power* (Cambridge, Mass.: Harvard University Press, 1926).

Albion, R. G., *Sea Lanes in Wartime* (New York: W. W. Norton, 1942).

Alden, John D., *The American Steel Navy* (Annapolis: Naval Institute Press, 1971).

Allen, H. R., *The Legacy of Lord Trenchard* (London: Cassell, 1972).

Anderson, Irvine H., *The Standard-Vacuum Oil Company and United States East Asian Policy 1933–1941* (Princeton: Princeton University Press, 1975).

Aron, Raymond, *Peace and War* (London: Weidenfeld & Nicolson, 1962).

Atlantic Council of the United States. Working Group on Security Affairs. *After Afghanistan—The Long Haul; Safeguarding Security and Independence in the Third World* (Washington: ACUS, 1980).

Aviel, Joann Fagot, *Resource Shortage and World Politics* (Washington: University Press of America, 1977).

Bamford, P. W., *Forests and French Sea Power, 1660–1789* (Toronto: University of Toronto Press, 1956).

Banse, Ewald, *Germany Prepare for War!* (London: Lovat Dickson, 1934).

Baylis, John and Segal, Gerald (eds), *Soviet Strategy* (London: Croom Helm, 1981).

Bertram, C. and Holst, J. J. (eds), *New Strategic Factors in the North Atlantic* (Oslo: Universiteitsforlagt, 1977).

Bissell, Richard E., 'The West in Concert: A Very Complex Score' in *Oil Diplomacy* (Philadelphia: Foreign Policy Research Institute, 1979).

Blechman, Barry M., *National Security and Strategic Minerals; An Analysis of U.S. Dependence on Foreign Sources of Cobalt* (Boulder: Westview, 1985).

Bloch, Jean de, *The Future of War in its Technical, Economic and Political Relations* (New York: Doubleday & McClure, 1899).

Bohi, Douglas and Quandt, William B., *Energy Security in the 1980's: Economic and Political Perspectives* (Washington: The Brookings Institution, 1984).

Braden, Samuel E., 'The Strategy of Raw Materials and Economic Policy' in Steiner, George (ed.) *Economic Problems of War* (New York: John Wiley & Sons, 1942).

Brodie, Bernard, 'Foreign Oil and American Security', Memorandum No. 23 (New Haven: Yale Institute for International Studies, 1947).

Brodie, Bernard, *Sea Power in the Machine Age* (Princeton: Princeton University Press, 1943).

Brooks, Benjamin T., *Peace, Plenty and Petroleum* (Lancaster: Jacques Cattell, 1944).

Brown, Anthony Cave, *Dropshot: The American Plan for World War III Against Russia in 1957* (New York: Dial, 1978).

Buckley, Wallace T., 'The Strategic Raw Materials' in Steiner, George A. (ed.) *Economic Problems of War* (New York: Wiley, 1942).

Burk, Kathleen, *Britain, America and the Sinews of War 1914–1918* (Boston: Allen & Unwin, 1985).

Butow, Robert J. C., *Tojo and the Coming of the War* (Princeton: Princeton University Press, 1961).

Byely, Col. B., *Marxism-Leninism on War and Army* (Moscow: Progress Publishers, 1972).

Carnegie Endowment, *Challenges for U.S. National Security* (Washington: The Carnegie Endowment, 1981).

Carroll, Berenice A., *Design for Total War; Arms and Economics in the Third Reich* (The Hague: Mouton, 1968).

Chambers, F. P., *The War Behind the War 1914–1918* (London: Faber & Faber, 1934).

Chubin, Shahram, 'Naval Competition and Security in Southwest Asia' in 'Power at Sea, III: Competition and Conflict', *Adelphi Paper* No. 124 (London: IISS, 1976).

Chubin, Shahram, 'Soviet Policy Towards Iran and the Persian Gulf', *Adelphi Paper* No. 157 (London: IISS).

Clarke, R. W. B., *The Economic Effort of War* (London: Allen & Unwin, 1940).

Cohen, Saul Bernard, *Geography and Politics in a Divided World* (London: Methuen, 1964).

Coker, Christopher, 'The Cape Route and the Persian Gulf: A Warsaw Pact Perspective', in RUSI/Brassey's *Defence Yearbook 1985* (London: Brassey's, 1985).

Coker, Christopher, 'Eastern Europe and the Middle East: The Forgotten Dimension of Soviet Policy' in Cassen, Robert (ed.) *Soviet Interests in the Third World* (London: Royal Institute for International Affairs, 1985).

Coker, Christopher, *NATO, the Warsaw Pact and Africa* (London: Macmillan, 1985).

Conant, Melvin A. and Gold, Fern Racine, *The Geopolitics of Energy* (Boulder: Westview, 1978).

Conant, Melvin A., 'Resources and Conflict: Oil—the Likely Contingencies' in 'Third World Conflict and International Security', *Adelphi Paper* No. 167 (London: IISS, 1981).

Consett, M. W. W. P., *The Triumph of Unarmed Forces 1914–1918* (London: Williams & Norgate, 1923).

Cooke, Ronald C. and Nesbit, Roy Conyers, *Target: Hitler's Oil; Allied Attacks on German Oil Supplies 1939–1945* (London: William Kimber, 1985).

Cottrel, Alvin J. and Burrell, R. M., *The Indian Ocean: Its Political, Economic and Military Importance* (New York: Praeger, 1974).

Davis, Shelby Cullom, *The French War Machine* (London: Allen & Unwin, 1937).

De la Tramerye, Pierre L'espagnol, *The World Struggle for Oil*, trans. by Leese, C. Leonard (London: Allen & Unwin, 1923).

De Weerd, Harvey A., 'Churchill, Lloyd George, Clemenceau: The Emergence of the Civilian' in Earle, E. M. (ed.) *Makers of Modern Strategy* (Princeton: Princeton University Press, 1943).

Deese, David and Nye, Joseph, *Energy and Security* (Cambridge: Ballinger, 1981).

Denny, Ludwell, *We Fight for Oil* (New York: Knopf, 1929).

Dorpalen, Andreas, *The World of General Haushofer; Geopolitics in Action* (New York: Farrar & Rhinehart, 1942).

Doughty, Martin, *Merchant Shipping and War* (London: Royal Historical Society, 1982).

Earle, E. M., 'The Economic Foundations of Military Power' in Earle (ed.) *Makers of Modern Strategy* (Princeton: Princeton University Press, 1943).

Earle, E. M., 'Hitler: The Nazi Concept of War' in Earle (ed.) *Makers of Modern Strategy* (Princeton: Princeton University Press, 1943).

Earle, E. M., 'Lenin, Trotsky, Stalin: Soviet Concepts of War' in Earle (ed.) *Makers of Modern Strategy* (Princeton: Princeton University Press, 1943).

Earle, E. M., *Turkey, The Great Powers and the Baghdad Railway* (New York: Macmillan, 1924).

Ebinger, Charles K. *et al.*, *The Critical Link: Energy and National Security in the 1980's* (Cambridge: Ballinger, 1982).

Einzig, Paul, *Economic Warfare* (London: Macmillan, 1940).

Ellis, C. H., *The Transcaspian Episode 1918–1919* (London: Hutchinson, 1963).

Emeny, Brooks, *The Strategy of Raw Materials; A Study of America in Peace and War* (New York: Macmillan, 1944).

Erickson, John, *The Soviet High Command 1918–1941; A Political-Military History* (London: Macmillan, 1962).

Erickson, John and Feuchtwanger, E. J. (eds), *Soviet Military Power and*

Performance (London: Macmillan, 1979).

Erickson, John, *The Road to Berlin* (Boulder: Westview, 1983).

Fanning, Leonard, M., *Foreign Oil and the Free World* (New York: McGraw-Hill, 1954).

Fayle, C. E., *Seaborne Trade* (London: Murray, 1920).

Feis, Herbert, *The Road to Pearl Harbor; The Coming of the War Between the United States and Japan* (Princeton: Princeton University Press, 1950).

Fischer, Fritz, *Germany's Aims in the First World War* (New York: Norton, 1961).

Fischer, Fritz, *War of Illusions: German Policies from 1911 to 1914* (London: Chatto & Windus, 1975).

Fischer, Fritz, *World Power or Decline* (New York: Norton, 1974).

Fisher, A. G. B., 'Economic Self-Sufficiency', *Oxford Pamphlets on World Affairs*, no. 4 (1939).

Gaddis, John Lewis, *Strategies of Containment* (New York: Oxford University Press, 1982).

Gallie, W. B., *Philosophers of Peace and War* (London: Cambridge University Press, 1978).

Gibson, Irving M., 'Maginot and Liddell Hart: The Doctrine of Defense' in Earle (ed.) *Makers of Modern Strategy* (Princeton: Princeton University Press, 1943).

Gilpin, Robert, 'Economic Interdependence and National Security in Historical Perspective' in Knorr, Klaus and Trager, Frank N. (eds) *Economic Issues and National Security* (Lawrence: Regents Press of Kansas, 1977).

Goldstein, Donald J. (ed.) *Energy and National Security; Proceedings of a Special Conference* (Washington: National Defense University, 1981).

Goralski, Robert and Freeburg, Russell W., *Oil and War* (New York: William Morow, 1987).

Gordon, David L. And Dangerfield, Roydon, *The Hidden Weapon; The Story of Economic Warfare* (New York: Harper, 1947).

Gorshkov, Sergei G., *The Sea Power of the State* (Oxford: Pergamon, 1979).

Graham, Gerald S., *Empire of the North Atlantic; the Maritime Struggle for North America* (Toronto: University of Toronto Press, 1958).

Graham, Gerald S., *Sea Power and British North America 1783–1820; A Study in British Colonial Policy* (Cambridge, Mass.: Harvard University Press, 1941).

Gray, Collin S., *The Geopolitics of the Nuclear Era: Heartlands, Rimlands and the Technological Revolution* (New York: Crane Russak, 1977).

Guerlac, Henry, 'Vauban: The Impact of Science on War' in Earle (ed.) *Makers of Modern Strategy* (Princeton: Princeton University Press, 1943).

Guichard, Louis, *The Naval Blockade 1914–1918* (London: Phillip Allan, 1930).

Gutteridge, William, *Mineral Resources and National Security* (London: Institute for the Study of Conflict, 1984).

Hackett, Sir John, 'Protecting Oil Supplies: The Military Requirements' in 'Third World Conflict and International Security, Part I', *Adelphi Paper* No. 166 (London: IISS, 1981).

Hagen, Paul, *Will Germany Crack?* (New York: Harper, 1942).

Hanks, Robert J., *The Cape Route: Imperiled Western Lifeline* (Cambridge:

Institute for Foreign Policy Analysis, 1981).

Hanks, Robert J., *The Unnoticed Challenge: Soviet Maritime Strategy and the Global Choke Points* (Cambridge: Institute for Foreign Policy Analysis, 1980).

Heckscher, E. F., *The Continental System: An Economic Interpretation* (Oxford: Oxford University Press, 1922).

Heckscher, Eli F., *Mercantilism* (London: Allen & Unwin, revised ed., 1955).

Henderson, H. D., 'Colonies and Raw Materials'. *Oxford Pamphlets on World Affairs*, no. 7 (1939).

Herrick, R. W., *Soviet Naval Strategy* (Annapolis: Naval Institute Press, 1968).

Hill-Norton, Peter, *World Shipping at Risk: The Looming Threat to the Lifelines* (London: Institute for the Study of Conflict, 1979).

Hirschman, Albert O., *National Power and the Structure of Foreign Trade* (Berkeley: University of California Press, 1945).

Hobson, John A., *Imperialism: A Study* (London: Allen & Unwin, 1948, first published 1902).

International Economic Studies Institute, *Raw Materials and Foreign Policy* (Washington: International Economic Studies Institute, 1976).

International Institute for Strategic Studies, *Strategic Survey* (London: IISS, yearly 1974–86).

Jack, D. T., *Studies in Economic Warfare* (London: P. S. King, 1940).

Johnson, U. Alexis *et al.*, *The Common Security Interests of Japan, the U.S. and NATO* (Cambridge: Ballinger, 1981).

Jukes, Geoffrey, 'The Indian Ocean in Soviet Naval Policy'. *Adelphi Paper* No. 87 (London: IISS, 1972).

Kaiser, Karl, 'The Energy Problem and Alliance Systems: Europe', *Adelphi Paper* No. 115 (London: IISS, 1978).

Kemp, Geoffrey and Maurer, John, 'The Logistics of *Pax Britannica*; Lessons for America' in Ra'anan, Uri (ed.) *Projection of Power; Perspectives, Perceptions and Problems* (Hamden: Archon, 1982).

Kemp, Geoffrey, 'Maritime Access and Maritime Power' in Cottrell, Alvin J., *Sea Power and Strategy in the Indian Ocean* (London: Sage, 1981).

Kemp, Geoffrey, 'Military Force and Middle East Oil' in Deese, David A. and Nye, Joseph S. (eds) *Energy and Security* (Cambridge: Ballinger, 1981).

Kennedy, Paul H. , *The Rise and Fall of British Naval Mastery* (London: Macmillan, 1983).

Kennedy, Paul H., *Strategy and Diplomacy 1870–1945* (London: Fontana, 1983).

Kent, Marion, *Oil and Empire; British Policy and Mesopotamian Oil 1900–1920* (New York: Harper & Row, 1976).

Klare, Michael T., *Beyond the Vietnam Syndrome: U.S. Interventionism in the 1980's* (Washington: Institute for Policy Studies, 1982).

Klein, Burton H., *Germany's Economic Preparations for War* (Cambridge, Mass.: Harvard University Press, 1959).

Knorr, Klaus and Trager, Frank N. (eds), *Economic Issues and National Security* (Lawrence: Regents Press of Kansas, 1977).

Knorr, Klaus, *Military Power and Potential* (Lexington: D. C. Heath, 1970).

Knorr, Klaus, *On the Uses of Military Power in the Nuclear Age* (Princeton: Princeton University Press, 1970).

Knorr, Klaus, *The Power of Nations; The Political Economy of International Relations* (New York: Basic Books, 1975).

Knorr, Klaus, *The War Potential of Nations* (Princeton: Princeton University Press, 1963).

Komer, Robert W., *Maritime Strategy or Coalition Defense?* (Cambridge: Abt Books, 1984).

Langer, William L., *The Diplomacy of Imperialism* (New York: Knopf, 1951).

Lauterbach, A. T., *Economics in Uniform* (Princeton: Princeton University Press, 1943).

Leach, Barry, *German Strategy Against Russia 1939–1941* (Oxford: Oxford University Press, 1973).

Leebaert, Derek (ed.), *Soviet Military Thinking* (London: Allen & Unwin, 1981).

Lefebvre, George, *Napoleon* (New York: Columbia University Press, 1965) two vols.

Leith, C. K. *et al.*, *World Minerals and World Peace* (Washington: Brookings, 1943).

Lenin, V. I., *Imperialism the Highest Stage of Capitalism* (London: Martin Lawrence, 1934, first published 1917).

Liddell Hart, B. H., *Defence of the West; Some Riddles of War and Peace* (London: Cassell, 1950).

Liddell Hart, B. H., *Europe in Arms* (London: Faber & Faber, 1937).

Lieber, Robert J., *The Oil Decade: Conflict and Cooperation in the West* (New York: Praeger, 1983).

Lieber, Robert J., *Oil and the Middle East War: Europe in the Energy Crisis* (Cambridge, Mass.: Harvard Center for International Affairs, 1976).

List, Friedrich, *The National System of Political Economy* (New York: A. M. Kelley, 1977, first published 1841).

Luttwak, Edward N., 'Intervention and Access to Natural Resources' in Bull, Hedley (ed.) *Intervention in World Politics* (Oxford: Clarendon Press, 1984).

Luttwak, Edward N., 'On the Meaning of Strategy for the U.S. in the 1980's' in Thompson, W. Scott (ed.) *National Security in the 1980's: From Weakness to Strength* (San Francisco: Institute for Contemporary Studies, 1980).

Luttwak, Edward N., *On the Meaning of Victory; Essays on Strategy* (New York: Simon & Schuster, 1986).

Luvaas, Jay, 'European Military Thought and Doctrine 1870–1914' in Howard, Michael (ed.) *The Theory and Practice of War* (London: Cassell, 1965).

Macartney, Maxwell H. and Cremona, Paul, *Italy's Foreign and Colonial Policy 1914–1937* (New York: Howard Fertig, 1972).

MacIsaac, David, *Strategic Bombing in World War II* (New York: Garland, 1976).

Mahan, Alfred Thayer, *The Influence of Sea Power Upon the French*

Revolution and Empire (London: 1892).

Mahan, Alfred Thayer, *The Influence of Sea Power Upon History 1660–1783* (Boston: Little Brown, 1943).

Marder, Arthur J., *British Naval Policy 1880–1905* (London: Putnam, 1940).

Marder, Arthur J., *Old Friends, New Enemies: The Royal Navy and the Imperial Japanese Navy; Strategic Illusions, 1936–1941* (Oxford: Clarendon Press, 1981).

Martin, L. W., *The Sea in Modern Strategy* (London: Chatto & Windus, 1967).

Marwick, Arthur, *Britain in the Century of Total War* (London: Bodley Head, 1968).

Mattern, Johannes, *Geopolitik; Doctrine of National Self-Sufficiency and Empire* (Baltimore: Johns Hopkins Press, 1942).

Maull, Hanns, *Raw Materials, Energy and Western Security* (London: Macmillan, 1984).

McCormick, Gordon H. and Bissell, Richard E. (eds), *Strategic Dimensions of Economic Behavior* (New York: Praeger, 1984).

McGruther, Kenneth R., *The Evolving Soviet Navy* (Newport: Naval War College, 1978).

MccGwire, Michael, 'Soviet Naval Doctrine and Strategy' in Leebaert, Derek (ed.) *Soviet Military Thinking* (London: Allen & Unwin, 1981).

MccGwire, Michael, *Soviet Naval Policy* (New York: Praeger, 1975).

Mendershausen, Horst, *The Economics of War* (New York: Prentice-Hall, 1941).

Millar, T. B., 'The Indian and Pacific Oceans: Some Strategic Considerations', *Adelphi Paper* No. 57 (London: IISS, 1969).

Miller, Aaron David, *Search for Security: Saudi Arabian Oil and American Foreign Policy 1939–1949* (Chapel Hill: University of North Carolina Press, 1980).

Milward, Alan S., *The German Economy at War* (London: Athlone, 1985).

Milward, Alan S., *War, Economy and Society 1939–1945* (London: Allen Lane, 1977).

Mohr, Anton, *The Oil War* (London: Martin Hopkinson, 1926).

Moineville, Hubert, 'Geopolitics and Naval Strategy in the Nuclear Era' in Zoppo, Ciro E. and Zorghibe, Charles (eds) *On Geopolitics; Classical and Nuclear* (Dordrecht: Martins Nijhoff, 1985).

Moodie, Michael, *Geopolitics and Maritime Power* (Beverly Hills: Sage, 1981).

Morgenstern, Oskar *et al.*, *Long Term Projections of Power* (Cambridge: Ballinger, 1973).

Murphy, Paul J. (ed.), *Naval Power in Soviet Policy* (Washington: US Air Force, 1978).

Neilson, Keith, *Strategy and Supply: The Anglo-Russian Alliance 1914–1917* (London: Allen & Unwin, 1984).

Nitze, Paul and Sullivan, Leonard, *Securing the Seas; Soviet Naval Challenge and Western Alliance Options* (Boulder: Westview, 1979).

Olson, Mancur, *The Economics of the Wartime Shortage* (Durham: Duke University Press, 1963).

O'Neill, Bard E., *Petroleum and Security: The Limits of Military Power in the*

Gulf (Washington: National Defense University, 1977).

Overy, R. J., *Goering: the 'Iron Man'* (London: Routledge & Kegan Paul, 1984).

Pakravan, Karim, *Oil Supply Disruptions in the 1980's: An Economic Analysis* (Stanford: Hoover Institution Press, 1984).

Perlman, Robert and Murray, Anthony, 'Resources and Conflict; Requirements and Vulnerabilities of the Industrialized World' in 'Third World Conflict and International Security, Part II', *Adelphi Paper* No. 167 (London: IISS, 1981).

Perry, Charles, *The West, Japan and Cape Route Imports: The Oil and Non-Fuel Mineral Trades* (Cambridge: Institute for Foreign Policy Analysis, 1982).

Pfaltzgraff, Robert L. and Hahn, W. F., *The Atlantic Community in Crisis* (New York: Pergamon, 1979).

Pfaltzgraff, Robert L., *Energy Issues and Alliance Relationships: The U.S., Western Europe and Japan* (Cambridge: Institute for Foreign Policy Analysis, 1980).

Pope, Samuel, 'Strategic Vulnerability' in *RUSI/Brassey's Defense Yearbook 1985* (London: Brassey's, 1985).

Possony, Stephen, *Tomorrow's War; Its Planning, Management and Cost* (London: William Hodge, 1938).

Pratt, Wallace E. and Good, Dorothy (eds), *World Geography of Petroleum* (Princeton: Princeton University Press, 1950).

Price, David Lynn, *Oil and Middle East Security* (Beverly Hills: Sage, 1976).

Ramazani, R. K., *The Persian Gulf and the Strait of Hormuz* (The Netherlands: Sythoff & Noordhoff, 1979).

Ranft, Bryan, *Technical Change and British Naval Policy, 1860–1939* (London: Hodder & Stoughton, 1977).

Ranft, Bryan and Till, Geoffrey, *The Sea in Soviet Strategy* (London: Macmillan, 1983).

Record, Jeffrey, *The Rapid Deployment Force and U.S. Military Intervention in the Persian Gulf* (Cambridge: Institute for Foreign Policy Analysis, 1981).

Richmond, Herbert W., *The Navy as an Instrument of Policy* (Cambridge: Cambridge University Press, 1953).

Richmond, Herbert W., *Statesmen and Sea Power* (Oxford: Clarendon Press, 1946).

Ritter, Gerhard, *The Sword and the Scepter; The Problem of Militarism in Germany* (Coral Gables: University of Miami Press, 1970).

Ropp, Theodore, 'Continental Doctrines of Sea Power' in E. M. Earle (ed.) *Makers of Modern Strategy* (Princeton: Princeton University Press, 1943).

Roskill, Stephen, *Naval Policy Between the Wars—Volume II—The Period of Reluctant Rearmament 1930–1939* (London: Collins, 1976).

Royal Institute of International Affairs, 'Occupied Europe; German Exploitation and its Post-War Consequences' (London: RIIA, 1944).

Royal Institute of International Affairs, 'Sanctions', *Information Department Papers*, no. 17 (London: RIIA, 1935).

Royal United Services Institute for Defence Studies, *The Cape Route; A Seminar Report* (London: RUSI, 1970).

Salmon, Patrick, 'British Plans for Economic Warfare Against Germany

1937–1939; the Problem of Swedish Iron Ore' in Laqueur, Walter (ed.) *The Second World War; Essays in Military and Political History* (London: Sage, 1982).

Schlesinger, James R., *The Political Economy of National Security* (New York: Praeger, 1960).

Schurman, D. N., *The Education of a Navy; The Development of British Naval Strategic Thought 1867–1914* (London: Cassell, 1965).

Shimkin, Dimitri B., *Minerals: A Key to Soviet Power* (Cambridge, Mass.: Harvard University Press, 1953).

Shotwell, James T., *What Germany Forgot* (New York: Macmillan, 1940).

Shwadran, Benjamin, *The Middle East, Oil and the Great Powers* (New York: Praeger, 1955).

Silberner, Edmund, *The Problem of War in Nineteenth Century Economic Thought*, trans. Krappe, Alexander H. (Princeton: Princeton University Press, 1946).

Skrine, Clarmont, *World War in Iran* (London: Constable, 1962).

Smith, Adam, *An Inquiry into the Nature and Causes of the Wealth of Nations* (London: G. Bell & Sons, 1908).

Sokolovsky, V. D., *Soviet Military Strategy*, edited by M. F. Scott (New York: Crane Russak, 1975, first published 1968).

Speier, Hans, 'Ludendorff: The German Concept of Total War' in Earle, *Makers of Modern Strategy* (Princeton: Princeton University Press, 1943).

Sprout, Margaret Tuttle, 'Mahan: Evangelist of Sea Power' in Earle, *Makers of Modern Strategy* (Princeton: Princeton University Press, 1943).

Spykman, Nicholas J., *America's Strategy in World Politics* (New York: Harcourt, Brace & World, 1942).

Sternberg, Fritz, *Germany and a Lightning War* (London: Faber & Faber, 1938).

Stockholm International Peace Research Institute, *Oil and Security* (Stockholm: Almqvist & Wiksell, 1974).

Stoff, Michael B., *Oil, War and American Security; the Search for a National Policy on Foreign Oil 1941–1947* (New Haven: Yale University Press, 1980).

Stone, Norman, *The Eastern Front 1914–1917* (London: Hodder & Stoughton, 1975).

Strategic Minerals: A Resource Crisis (Washington: Council on Economics and National Security, 1981).

Strausz-Hupe, R., *Geopolitics; The Struggle for Space and Power* (New York: Putnam, 1942).

Szylowicz, Joseph S., *Petropolitics and the Atlantic Alliance* (Washington: National Defense University, 1976).

Tanin, O. and Yohan, E., *When Japan Goes to War* (London: Lawrence & Wishart, 1936).

Thompson, W. Scott, *Power Projection: A Net Assessment of U.S. and Soviet Capabilities* (New York: National Strategy Information Center, 1978).

Thomson, George C., *Problems of Strategy in the Pacific and Indian Oceans* (New York: National Strategy Information Center, 1970).

Till, Geoffrey (ed.) *Maritime Strategy and the Nuclear Age* (New York: St. Martin's, 1982).

Toynbee, Arnold, *Mankind and Mother Earth* (Oxford: Oxford University Press, 1976).

Tucker, Robert W., *The Purposes of American Power* (New York: Praeger, 1981).

Van Creveld, Martin L., *Supplying War* (Cambridge: Cambridge University Press, 1977).

Vernon, Raymond, *Two Hungry Giants; The U.S. and Japan in the Quest for Oil and Ores* (Cambridge, Mass.: Harvard University Press, 1983).

Watt, D. C., *Too Serious a Business; European Armed Forces and the Approach to the Second World War* (London: Temple Smith, 1975).

Weigert, Hans W., *Generals and Geographers; the Twilight of Geopolitics* (New York: Oxford University Press, 1942).

Werth, Alexander, *Russia at War 1941–1945* (London: Barrie & Rockliff, 1964).

Weston, Rae, *Strategic Minerals—A World Survey* (London: Croom Helm, 1984).

Whittlesey, Derwent, 'Haushofer: The Geopoliticians' in Earle, *Makers of Modern Strategy* (Princeton: Princeton University Press, 1943).

Wohlstetter, Albert, 'Half-Wars and Half-Policies in the Persian Gulf' in Thompson, W. Scott (ed.) *National Security in the 1980's; From Weakness to Strength* (San Francisco: Institute for Contemporary Studies, 1980).

Wood, David, 'Conflict in the Twentieth Century', *Adelphi Paper* No. 48 (London: IISS, 1968).

Woodward, David, *The Russians at Sea* (London: William Kimber, 1965).

Wright, Quincy, *A Study of War* (Chicago: University of Chicago Press, 1942).

Wu, Yuan-li, *Economic Warfare* (New York: Prentice-Hall, 1952).

Wu, Yuan-li, *Japan's Search for Oil* (Stanford: Hoover Institution Press, 1977).

Wu, Yuan-li, *Raw Material Supply in a Multipolar World* (New York: Crane Russak, 1973).

Zoppo, Ciro E. and Zorghibe, Charles (eds), *On Geopolitics: Classical and Nuclear* (Dordrecht: Martinus Nijhoff, 1985).

II. Articles

Akins, James E., 'The Oil Crisis: This Time the Wolf is Here', *Foreign Affairs*, April 1973.

Baldwin, Hanson W., 'Strategy of the Middle East', *Foreign Affairs*, July 1957.

Barnett, H. J., 'The Changing Relationship of Natural Resources to National Security', *Economic Geography*, July 1958.

Bergstrom, Alan J., Letter to the Editor on 'Mineral Myths', *Foreign Policy*, no. 50, Spring 1983.

Bidwell, Percy W., 'Raw Materials and National Policy', *Foreign Affairs*, October 1958.

Brown, Lester, R., 'Depending on Others for Minerals', *New York Times*, 1 February 1971.

Brownfeld, Alan C., 'The Growing United States Dependency on Imported

Strategic Materials', *The Atlantic Community Quarterly*, Spring 1982.

Canby, Steven L., 'General Purpose Forces', *International Security Review*, Autumn 1980.

Cecil, Lamar J. R., 'Coal for the Fleet that Had to Die', *The American Historical Review*, vol. 69 (1964) no. 4.

Chubin, Shahram, 'Reflections on the Gulf War', *Survival*, July/August 1986.

Chubin, Shahram, 'Repercussions of the Crisis in Iran', *Survival*, May/June 1979.

Chubin, Shahram, 'U.S. Security Interests in the Persian Gulf in the 1980's', *Daedalus*, Autumn 1980.

Cooley, John K., 'The War over Water', *Foreign Policy*, Spring 1984.

Dafter, Ray, 'World Oil Production and Security of Supplies', *International Security*, Winter, 1979/80.

Deese, David A., 'Energy: Economics, Politics and Security', *International Security*, Winter 1979/80.

Deese, David A., 'Oil, War and Grand Strategy', *Orbis*, Autumn 1981.

Donnelly, Michael W., 'Japan's Search for Food Security', *Current History*, November 1978.

Durand, E. Dana, 'Economic and Political Effects of Governmental Interference with the Free International Movement of Raw Materials', *International Conciliation*, January 1927.

Earle, E. M., 'International Financial Control of Raw Materials', *International Conciliation*, January 1927.

Epstein, Joshua M., 'Soviet Vulnerabilities in Iran and the RDF Deterrent', *International Security*, Autumn 1981.

Erickson, Edward W., 'The Strategic-Military Importance of Oil', *Current History*, July/August 1978.

Feis, Herbert, 'Oil for Peace or War', *Foreign Affairs*, April 1954.

Feis, Herbert, 'Raw Materials and Foreign Policy', *Foreign Affairs*, July 1938.

Finlayson, Jock A. and Haglund, David E., 'Whatever Happened to the Resource War?', *Survival*, September/October 1987.

Frankel, P. H., 'Oil Supplies During the Suez Crisis', *Journal of Industrial Economics*, February 1958.

Fritz, Martin, 'Swedish Iron Ore and German Steel 1939–1940', *Scandinavian Economic History Review*, XXI, 1973.

Goldman, Marshall I., 'Will the Soviet Union be an Autarky in 1984?', *International Security*, Spring 1979.

Gray, Collin S., 'National Style in Strategy: The American Example', *International Security*, Autumn 1981.

Gustafson, Thane, 'Energy and the Soviet Bloc', *International Security*, Winter 1981/82.

Gwertzman, Bernard, 'CIA Revises Estimate, Sees Soviet as Oil Independent through 1980's', *New York Times*, 19 May 1981.

Hankee, William B. and King, Alwyn H., 'The Role of Security Assistance in Maintaining Access to Strategic Resources', *Parameters*, September 1978.

Hansen, Richard Earl, 'The Strait of Hormuz and Secure Oil Routes; A

Challenge to U.S. Strategy', *Conflict*, vol. 2 (1980) no. 2.

Harvey, Charles E., 'Politics and Pyrites during the Spanish Civil War', *Economic History Review*, XXXI, 1978.

Hoffmann, Stanley, 'The Crisis in the West', *New York Review of Books*, 17 July 1980.

Holland, Thomas H., 'Minerals and International Relations', *International Conciliation*, January 1931.

Hoskins, Halford L., 'Needed: A Strategy for Oil', *Foreign Affairs*, January 1951.

Howard, Michael, 'The Forgotten Dimensions of Strategy', *Foreign Affairs*, Summer 1979.

Jager, Jorg-Johannes, 'Sweden's Iron Ore Exports to Germany 1933–1944', *Scandinavian Economic History Review*, XV, 1967.

Janka, Les, 'Security Risks and Reactions', *AEI Foreign Policy and Defense Review*, vol. 2 (1980) nos. 3–4.

Jefferies, Chris L., 'NATO and Oil: Conflict and Capabilities', *Air University Review*, January/February 1980.

Jensen, W. G., 'The Importance of Energy in the First and Second World Wars', *The Historical Journal*, XI, 3, 1968.

Joesten, Joachim, 'The Scramble for Swedish Iron Ore', *Political Quarterly*, I, 1938.

Jones, Gareth C., 'The British Government and the Oil Companies, 1912–1924', *The Historical Journal*, vol. 20 (1977) no. 3.

Karlblom, Rolf, 'Sweden's Iron Ore Exports to Germany 1933–1944', *Scandinavian Economic History Review*, XIII, 1965.

Kemp, Geoffrey, 'Scarcity and Strategy', *Foreign Affairs*, January 1978.

Kidd, Isaac C., 'NATO's Double Dependence on the Atlantic', *NATO Review*, October 1978.

Kissinger, Henry, Interview in *Business Week*, 23 January 1975.

Klare, Michael T., 'Resource Wars', *Harper's Magazine*, January 1981.

Knorr, Klaus, 'The Limits of Economic and Military Power', *Daedalus*, Autumn 1975.

Kolkowicz, R., 'U.S. and Soviet Approaches to Military Strategy; Theory versus Experience', *Orbis*, Summer 1981.

Komer, Robert W., 'Bigger, Better and More Rapid Response', *Washington Post*, 4 March 1981.

Kroft, David J., 'The Geopolitics of Non-Energy Minerals', *Air Force Magazine*, June 1979.

Lamot, Denise, 'Soviet Threat Seen in Middle Eastern Oil', *Journal of Commerce*, 30 April 1980.

Lautenschlager, Karl, 'Technology and the Evolution of Naval Warfare', *International Security*, Autumn 1983.

Leifer, Michael, 'The Security of Sea Lanes in Southeast Asia', *Survival*, January/February 1983.

Lellouche, Pierre, 'Europe and Her Defense', *Foreign Affairs*, Spring 1981.

Lellouche, Pierre and Moisi, Dominique, 'French Policy in Africa: A Lonely Battle Against De-Stabilization', *International Security*, Spring 1979.

Levy, Walter J., 'Issues in International Oil Policy', *Foreign Affairs*, April 1957.

Levy, Walter J., 'Oil: An Agenda for the 1980's', *Foreign Affairs*, Summer 1981.

Levy, Walter J., 'Oil and the Decline of the West', *Foreign Affairs*, Summer 1980.

Levy, Walter J., 'Oil Power', *Foreign Affairs*, July 1971.

Lieber, Robert J., 'Energy, Economics and Security in Alliance Perspective', *International Security*, Spring 1980.

Mackinder, H. J., 'The Geographical Pivot of History', *Geographical Journal*, XXIII, 1904.

Mahan, A. T., 'Blockade in Relation to Naval Strategy', *USNI Proceedings*, November 1895.

Mansur, Abdul Kasim, 'The American Threat to Saudi Arabia', *Survival*, January 1981.

Maull, Hanns, 'Western Europe: A Fragmented Response to a Fragmenting Order', *Orbis*, Winter 1980.

MccGwire, Michael, 'Naval Power and Soviet Global Strategy', *International Security*, Spring 1979.

Meacham, James, 'The United States Navy: On the Crest of the Wave', *The Economist*, 19 April 1986.

Milward, Alan S., 'Could Sweden Have Stopped the Second World War?', *Scandinavian Economic History Review*, XV, 1967.

Mochizuki, Mike M., 'Japan's Search for Strategy', *International Security*, Winter 1983/84.

Moon, Parker T., 'Raw Materials and Imperialism', *International Conciliation*, January 1927.

Nitze, Paul, 'Strategy in the Decade of the 1980's', *Foreign Affairs*, Autumn 1980.

'Oil: Unmoved by Bombs', *The Economist*, 19 April 1986.

Okazaki, Hisahiko, 'Japanese Security Policy: A Time for Strategy', *International Security*, Autumn 1982.

Paarlberg, Robert L., 'Food, Oil and Coercive Resource Power', *International Security*, Autumn 1978.

Quandt, William B., 'The Middle East Crises', *Foreign Affairs (America and the World)* 1979.

Ramazani, R. K., 'Security in the Persian Gulf', *Foreign Affairs*, Spring 1979.

Richardson, Elliot, 'Power, Mobility and the Law of the Sea', *Foreign Affairs*, Spring 1980.

Rosenberg, David A., 'The U.S. Navy and the Problem of Oil in a Future War; The Outline of a Strategic Dilemma 1945–1950', *Naval War College Review*, Summer 1976.

Ross, Dennis, 'Considering Soviet Threats to the Persian Gulf', *International Security*, Autumn 1981.

Rothwell, V. H., 'Mesopotamia in British War Aims 1914–1918', *The Historical Journal*, XII, 2, 1970.

Russett, Bruce, 'Security and the Resources Scramble: Will 1984 be Like 1914?', *International Affairs*, vol. 58 (Winter 1981/82) no. 1.

Rustow, Dankwart A., 'Realignments in the Middle East', *Foreign Affairs (America and the World)* 1984.

Santini, James D., 'An Island Nation', *Sea Power*, January 1983.

Schlesinger, James R., 'The Geopolitics of Energy', *The Washington Quarterly*, Summer 1979.

Scroggs, William, 'Oil for Italy', *Foreign Affairs*, April 1936.

Shafer, Michael, 'Mineral Myths', *Foreign Policy*, Summer 1982.

Smith, George Otis, 'Theory and Practice of National Self-Sufficiency in Raw Materials', *International Conciliation*, January 1927.

Spero, Joan Edelman, 'Energy Self-Sufficiency and National Security', *Proceedings of the Academy of Political Science*, December 1973.

Spykman, Nicholas J., 'Geography and Foreign Policy', *The American Political Science Review* (two parts) February and April 1938.

Sterner, Michael, 'The Iran-Iraq War', *Foreign Affairs*, Autumn 1984.

'Strategic Petroleum Reserve', *The Economist*, 19 April 1986.

Summers, L. L., 'Economic Relations Between Raw Materials, Prices and Standards of Living: Their International Effect', *International Conciliation*, January 1927.

Thompson, W. Scott, 'The Persian Gulf and the Correlation of Forces', *International Security*, Summer 1982.

Toch, Thomas, 'Rapid Deployment, A Questionable Trump', *Parameters*, X, 3.

Tower, John, 'Challenges Facing the Atlantic Alliance', *RUSI Journal*, September 1981.

Tucker, Robert W., 'American Power and the Persian Gulf', *Commentary*, November 1980.

Tucker, Robert W., 'Oil: The Issue of American Intervention', *Commentary*, January 1975.

Tucker, Robert W., 'The Purposes of American Power', *Foreign Affairs*, Winter 1980/81.

Turner, Stansfield and Thibault, George, 'Preparing for the Unexpected: The Need for a New Military Strategy', *Foreign Affairs*, Autumn 1982.

Ullman, Richard H., 'Redefining Security', *International Security*, Summer 1983.

Van Hollen, Christopher, 'Don't Engulf the Gulf', *Foreign Affairs*, Summer 1981.

Vlahos, Michael, 'The Indian Ocean and Western Security', *Journal of Defense and Diplomacy*, April 1983.

Wegener, Edward, 'Theory of Naval Strategy in the Nuclear Age', *USNI Proceedings*, May 1972.

Werner, Roy A., 'Oil and U.S. Security Policies', *Orbis*, Autumn 1977.

Wright, Claudia, 'Implications of the Iran-Iraq War', *Foreign Affairs*, Winter 1980/81.

Young, Robert J., 'Spokesmen for Economic Warfare: The Industrial Intelligence Centre in the 1930's', *European Studies Review*, 6, 1976.

Zakheim, Dov S., 'Towards a Western Approach to the Indian Ocean', *Survival*, January/February 1980.

Zumwalt, Elmo R., 'Blockade and Geopolitics', *Comparative Strategy*, vol. 4 (1983) no. 2.

Index